Broderick Crawford
Starring in
Highway Patrol
By Gary Goltz and Ralph Schiller

**A CP Entertainment Books
First Edition
September 2019**

**Published by
CP Entertainment Books
e-mail: corriganvillepress@yahoo.com**

For a list of our books, please visit our web site at
www.cpentbooks.com

Copyright © 2019 by Gary Goltz and Ralph Schiller

ISBN 978-0-9993672-8-5 (softcover)

All rights reserved. No part of this book may be reproduced or transmitted in any form by any means, electronic, mechanical, photocopying, recording, or by any information source and retrieval system now known or to be invented, without prior written permission of the publisher, except for the quoting of brief passages in connection with a review of this book.

Some material herein, previously copyrighted, is in the Public Domain in the United States of America. Some quotes and images may be protected by copyright and are used in this reference/research work under the "Fair Use Doctrine" of the U. S. Copyright Law.

This book is dedicated to the Men (and now Women) whose training, skill, and courage have enforced and preserved our state laws, and to my wife Sharon for putting up with me, 10-4!

CHP Traffic Officier, Luis Bravo to the rescue after running out of gas following 10-4 Day 2017

Table of Contents

Credits and Acknowledgements	i
Forward	iii
Introductions	vi
Chapter One: History Of ZIV Television, INC.	1
Chapter Two: *Highway Patrol*, the Television Series	18
Chapter Three: *The Highway Patrol* Parodies	121
Chapter Four: After *Highway Patrol*	137
Chapter Five: Broderick Crawford's later career and life	151
Appendix A: Plot summary and original script pages for the pilot episode of *Highway Patrol*, "Prison Break"	163
Appendix B: Official ZIV Television Writer's Guide for the *Highway Patrol* series	178
Appendix C: The complete *Highway Patrol* episode guide	183
Appendix D: The *Highway Patrol/Star Trek* Connections	238
Appendix E: Complete *Motor Trend* magazine article	239
Appendix F: Complete *Zenith* magazine article	244
Appendix G: A Mystery From World War Two	245
Postscript 1: *ME-TV* article (10-03-2017)	247
Postscript 2: *Wall Street Journal* article (07-26-2016)	255
Postscript 3: The 13th Annual 2016 "10-4 Day" Parade 2016	271
Epilog: "The Star And The Car" Documentary	279
Index	283

Credits and Acknowledgements

I wish to thank and pay tribute to long list of friends I made along the road without whose help this book would never have been written. Bob Speed, Jr. of the Baltimore Police Department was the first one to reach out me in my quest to learn more about *Highway Patrol*. Bob had developed a relationship with CHP Advisor to the series Frank Runyon. He shared his letters from Frank, notes and photographs. He also sent me his collection of episodes on VHS tapes. His generosity led me to form friendships with Frank Runyon, Herb Strock, and eventually William Boyett, his lovely wife Joan, as well as the best voice in Hollywood, Art Gilmore. My obsession with collecting everything I could find related to the series including, scripts, ads, toys, and eventually even recreation of a 1955 Buick patrol unit became a passion. Then I met the soon to become Los Angeles City Councilmember, Tom LaBonge, (now retired) who got the Los Angeles Times to do a story on me. That led to CNN doing a 5-minute feature which catapulted my love of this series into the stratosphere. In addition to everyone mentioned above, I want to thank K-EARTH DJ's 'Shotgun' Tom Kelly, Les Randolph and his wife Margie, Glenn Davis, Jim Martinez, the cast of the *CHiPs* series, Erik Estrada and his wife Nannette, Larry Wilcox, Robert Pine, Paul Linke, and Lou Wagner, *Adam 12*'s, Kent McCord, the late Guy Daniels, the late Wayne Heffley, the late Jon Locke and his son Rusty Locke, the late Jim Ryan, Maisto's Charles Hepperle, California Highway Patrol Commissioner Spike Helmick and all the other top brass as well as traffic officers I've met, my friends at the CHP 11-99 Foundation, Kitty Gordillo of the Hollywood PAL, Mike Clark who produced the documentary on my car, and finally my friend, the late Kelly Crawford and his widow Jean for introducing us. Finally, thanks to Ralph Schiller who helped make my dream of writing this book come to fruition.

Gary Goltz, *10-4!*

Forward
By Jean Crawford

Thank you Gary and Ralph for telling Broderick Crawford's story. Broderick's son, Kelly Griffith Crawford, and I were married 25 wonderful years before he passed. He meant the world to me. He loved art, photography, the movie industry, his career and most of all his Dad. He had spent little time with him since his parent's divorce when he was seven years old. Much to the surprise of Kelly's mother, Katherine, he moved out of her house (on Coronado Island) the very day after he graduated from high school. With this new found freedom he and his Dad were able to connect and have a wonderful relationship. Kelly was with him the day he passed away in April of 1986.

His Dad became a huge influence in his life. He had fun working with him in the series *The Interns* on TV in the 70's. He would stand in for Brod between shots and also had a few little extra parts. Kelly would also run scripts with him. Kelly said his Dad had a photographic memory. One read through was all he needed. Then he would work on his style. Although they had fun working together, Brod told Kelly he should not become an actor. Instead he strongly suggested he get into post production in the film industry. Kelly did just that. He worked as a film editor and was well respected for many years.

Brod's parents also urged him not to become an actor. Helen Broderick and Lester Crawford were well known vaudeville stars. They would sing a little, dance a little then stop and make with the jokes. Lester: "Mind if I smoke?" – Helen: "I don't care if you burn!" And so on. Max Gordon included their act when the production toured Europe.

In an article dated August 2, 1951 (8 days after Kelly was born) Brod shared the highly critical advice from his parents and grandmother as well. In 1934 Helen didn't go unscathed either. Her mother was also in show business too. She was a well-known singer in her time which had to be in the late 1870's.

When Helen came backstage after many curtain calls in the Irving Berlin play As Thousands Cheer she found her mother there. After waiting what seemed an eternity of silence she asked her how she liked the show. Her mother responded, "You can't sing, hum nor whistle. Better save your money!" Then she promptly left! After Brod's successful run as Lenny on Broadway in the play Of Mice and Men his grandmother waited for him in his makeup room. She stated, "Son, you have a pretty good voice. Better get into radio."

Helen had missed eight of Brod's films. He arranged for a screening room at the studio so she could watch them. She went in at noon and came out at 7:30 that evening. Passing him in the hall on her way out, she gently said, "Son, why don't you stop all this nonsense and get yourself a job driving a truck." She always had a crafty way of turning a phrase.

This family was awash with talent. Both Helen and Brod stepped into the future of entertainment. First Helen was extremely discouraged when Vaudeville was no longer a crowd favorite. Without her husband, she decided to make the leap to film. Then decades later Brod made is leap from film to the early days of television.

Brod signed up in 1942 and served in the Air Corps for eighteen months during the Battle of the Bulge in World War II. He was the master of ceremonies with Glenn Miller's swing band entertaining troupes in the European Theater. While there he was thrilled to be able to take cooking classes in France. He loved to cook. The last meal we shared the night before Kelly passed was the favorite meal his Dad would make for him. Meat Pie.

Brod also loved art. The Arizona artist Ted DeGrasia was among his best friends. He would travel to Ted's studio in Tucson call the *Gallery In The Sun*. There they would spend days painting in the studio together. Kelly would often travel around the desert with the two of them in the 70's. These are stories best heard in person – if you get my drift.

Enjoy this wonderful book,
Jean Crawford

Below: Jean Crawford with her beloved husband Kelly Crawford at the 2005 'Ten-Four Day' parade in Los Angeles. (Photo Kelly Crawford collection).

Introduction

Like many baby boomers, watching *Highway Patrol* after school while eating a peanut butter sandwich, was a daily ritual for me. Which episode was going to be shown today? Would it be one with a helicopter? Or those big-finned '59 Dodges or one of the early ones with the '55 Buick's and their cool, front, fender portholes?

I actually remember watching several episodes in the late 50's when it was first run with my grandmother. One particular night they played the *'Narcotics'* episode. When the Skipper got hit over the head with the sugar shaker in his diner, my grandma shouted 'Oy veysimer!' in Yiddish! In the closing scene after Chief Dan Mathews fills the culprit with a bunch of lead from his trusty snub-nose .38, I heard my grandma breathe a sigh relief! To my grandmother and me, Dan Mathews and his police come to the rescue not a moment too soon—was like watching George Reeves' *Superman* fly in to save the day! This 1950's series thrived on the momentum that made police into superheroes, stopping those bad guys and restoring law and order! I'm sure my five-year-old mind concluded that I wanted to be just like him when I grow up; barking out orders, knowing the right thing to do and always saving the day. It was a simple formula for success as a leader. Throughout my kindergarten to third grade school years I was the head of my own, self-created *Highway Patrol Club*. These childhood memories faded to give way to college and a career in business as a manager, a vice-president, and a president for a growing national company before eventually starting several of my own.

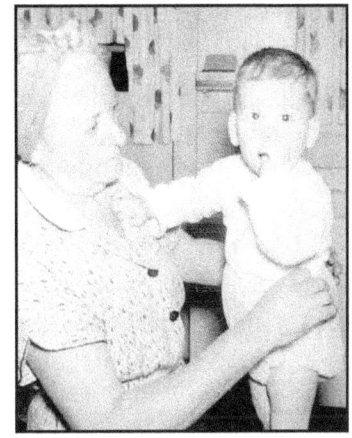

Grandma Tobias and Gary in 1954

Then one day in the early 1990's when video tapes were at their peak, I stumbled upon a mail order catalog which listed the pilot episode of *Highway Patrol* as available for purchase. Upon receiving the package and tearing off its cellophane cover, I pushed it into my VCR. A few seconds later there it was for the first time in several decades, that familiar opening of the Lincoln turning the corner of a California Freeway with that distinctive musical refrain and the words *'Broderick Crawford'*, *'Starring in'*, *'Highway Patrol'*. Soon the Buicks' which formed a roadblock gave way to preview scenes from the episode that followed. As I watched it, I first thought to myself that it was rather corny and couldn't believe that I had loved this show so much when I was a kid. Then I saw Broderick Crawford rip a bulletin off a teletype machine, read it to himself, and then hand it to the office secretary with an abrupt, politically incorrect, "Here! File this!" At that moment, my gut feeling told me I was watching my own brusque behavior as I've been described over the years.

Yes indeed, I had an epiphany of just how embedded the character that Broderick Crawford played on *Highway Patrol* would become my role model for success in leadership. Being the obsessive compulsive person that I am, I then made it my quest to collect every episode of the series I could find on video tape, plus many articles from *TV Guide*, toys, photos, and anything related to the series several years before eBay took off. My collection of memorabilia continued to grow. I even went to the University of Madison Wisconsin's Film Library where all the *ZIV-TV* shows are stored to view the episodes that I didn't have on video tape and secretly recorded them with my handheld VHS recorder. Over the next few years I began corresponding with other fans of the show who connected me with Frank Runyon, the California Highway Patrol's technical advisor for the entire run of the series.

Then in 1995, while perusing an *Old Car Trader* magazine at my local car wash, I came across an ad for a '55 Buick Special located at a dealership in Sacramento. A few weeks later while on a business trip to that area I stopped by the place and bought it. Upon delivery, I noticed that the gas cap was missing so I looked-up and found a place called *Classic Buick* in a nearby town that sold vintage auto parts. While paying the owner for the gas cap, I saw a picture on the wall of a '55 Buick CHP, souped-up into race car. The owner could tell I was more than intrigued, and I explained that *Highway Patrol* was my favorite show and was the reason why I had purchased the classic car. He shared with me that when people come to his shop for the very first time he always advises them to do what you really want to do with your new hobby toy. He then gave me the number for one of his best customers Les Randolph, a top mechanic and business owner with his own collection of classic cars that he had restored.

A few days later I was pulling up to meet Les for the first time, and there parked in his driveway was a genuine '55 Buick CHP unit exactly like the one Broderick Crawford drove on *Highway Patrol*. For me it was love at first sight and as expected by the end the evening I had made a new, best friend and decided to have my Buick turned into a replica like the one on the show. Six months later I drove my *Highway Patrol* Buick to its first car show near my house. It was a big hit and many more shows followed leading to an invitation from *The Automobile Club of California* to display my Buick at the 75th Anniversary of Griffith Park. That was the day I met Tom LaBonge, aka 'Mr. Los Angeles', who at the time was working for Mayor Reardon. We became best friends overnight and he arranged for an article to be written about me and my car in the *Los Angeles Times*. Once the article came out my phone was ringing off the hook. CNN did a five-minute piece based on the *LA Times* article. Then I was contacted by a fellow on the ever-rising Internet who wanted to make a *Highway Patrol TV Show* website using my vast collection of photos, letters, memorabilia, and articles as it base. Soon the guestbook for our website was a hotbed of discussion among friends of the show such as William Boyett's son, actor Kenneth Tobey who starred on *Whirlybirds,* and eventually the late Kelly Crawford's (Broderick Crawford's son) wife Jean Crawford. This resulted in my becoming good friends with Kelly and in 2001, we drove the *Highway Patrol* Buick coast-to-coast across the entire *Route 66*.

I met *Highway Patrol* co-star William Boyett, narrator Art Gilmore, and Herbert L. Strock who had directed the pilot episode of the series. These relationships turned into genuine friendships which I still cherish to this day. Over the next two decades many more television reports appeared along with magazine articles including most recently a large feature story in the *Wall Street Journal*. The list of celebrities I've got to know personally still blows my mind.

I also befriended the leaders of the California Highway Patrol and the Los Angeles Police Department and have been proud to help their police benevolent foundation's fundraising efforts. I've learned a great deal about the entertainment industry and even created an annual police parade event called *'10-4 Day',* for Tom LaBonge when he was the city councilmember representing Hollywood. As I proudly drove my '55 Buick Broderick Crawford *Highway Patrol* car down Hollywood Boulevard during our '10-4 Day' or the 'Hollywood Christmas Parade', this thought goes through my head: never in my wildest dreams did I anticipate that my affection for *Highway Patrol* would become a lifetime obsession resulting in so many encounters and adventures!

I hope you enjoy this book co-authored by my good friend Ralph Schiller who previously wrote the book *The Complete Films Of Broderick Crawford*, and had the painstaking task of compelling my recollections.

I thank and pay tribute to long list of friends I made along the road in the credits and acknowledgements.

Many Happy Highway Patrols!

10-4,

Gary Goltz

Below: Gary and his Buick (Patrick Ecclesine, Photo)

Ralph Schiller (with co-author Gary Goltz at Broderick Crawford's Movie Star, 10-4 Day 2016, photo Goltz Collection).

Preface

My first memory of Hollywood movie great Broderick Crawford was as a child watching the *Highway Patrol* series on television. This powerhouse actor with a commanding voice and unforgettable screen presence made an impression on me that remained for the rest of my life. Soon I started to recognize that my favorite TV cop starred in one film after another as either the 'bad guy' carrying a gun or 'good guy' carrying a badge and a gun! It really didn't matter because Broderick Crawford was great in anything he did. I came to love watching movies on television and on the big screen and avidly read anything I could find on the history of Hollywood and its great film stars. To my dismay, even though Broderick Crawford had a long career spanning five decades, and had won an Academy Award Oscar for 'Best Actor In A Starring Role', and starred in a smash hit television series, there was not a single book on his life and career. For that reason, I wrote the book *The Complete Films Of Broderick Crawford* which detailed all of his 95 films and his television career. Walking through his movies, I discovered an actor of even greater range and depth than I could have ever imagined who had left behind a body of work representing an incredible rogue's gallery of characters and performances. When I interviewed many of his co-stars, they all raved about his great talent as an actor and his great kindness as a generous person. I soon met the world's number one *Highway Patrol* fan and the only person trying to honor Broderick Crawford, Gary Goltz. When publishers gave me a hard time about text and photo rights, it was my friend Gary who put me in contact with the right publisher which made the book a reality. It was Gary who also connected me with Broderick Crawford's gallant son Kelly Crawford and his wife Jean who supported the book tremendously. Besides his *Highway Patrol* car, Gary Goltz is the 'unofficial curator' of the only museum in the world dedicated to everything about a television series that hit the airwaves the way a three-mast schooner cuts through the waves like a juggernaut. Gary's collection is not just complete but staggering in size and detail, and a historical archive treasure of the *Highway Patrol* TV series! Gary had the vision to preserve the series and its history into the book you are now reading. He accurately pointed out to me that the *Highway Patrol* television series was instrumental in restoring public confidence not only for the California Highway Patrol but to all state highway patrols, and state police forces everywhere. Like many other Hollywood movie stars in the 1950's, Broderick Crawford's film career was slipping and it was the *Highway Patrol* television series that put him back on top again (and made him quite wealthy)!

Gary Goltz was right in that a book on the *Highway Patrol* series is needed to preserve its history and should have been written thirty-five years ago. By riding in Gary's 'Broderick Crawford Special' HP car, I could see firsthand the public's universal joy and good will manifested towards the *Highway Patrol* series and Broderick Crawford's memory! We invite the readers to join us in that mythical *Highway Patrol* car on our journey to a great television series and the people who made it extraordinary. Also as a bonus, read the true life mystery of World War Two involving Broderick Crawford that is exclusive to this book only!

Ralph Schiller

Chapter One
History of ZIV Television, Inc.

Highway Patrol was produced and created by Frederick W. Ziv. He was born in 1905 in Cincinnati, Ohio of immigrant Jewish parents from Lithuania. According to a dissertation on ZIV Television written by Morleen Getz Rouse in 1976 for the University Of Cincinnati's ZIV School of Broadcasting, young Frederick Ziv wrote for on the Hughes High School Yearbook (Class Of 1923), "This early writing apparently had a profound and lasting effect, for from that time Ziv considered himself a writer and always found time to practice his craft." Young Ziv graduated with a law degree from the University of Michigan where he was the editor of the campus humor-literary magazine *The Gargoyle*. He returned to Cincinnati to open his own advertising agency and met businessman John Sinn in 1937. Ziv wanted his clients to receive major radio air time but the big networks had no mechanism for targeting advertisement to a specific market region. So Ziv and Sinn became partners and founded the Frederick W. Ziv Company. After experiencing many obstacles in trying to buy radio advertising for nationally broadcasted radio programs, Ziv would successfully produce his own pre-recorded shows for local markets which in fact gave birth to syndication.

Frederick W. Ziv became the father of first-run television syndication in 1948 when he moved into the exciting new medium. He and Sinn created the subsidiary ZIV Television Programs, Inc., which produced and syndicated low-budget, pre-filmed television shows for local, independent TV stations across America. The ZIV television shows were cheaply produced and rapidly shot. Frequently two episodes were filmed back-to-back each week while Frederick Ziv held the budgets down from a slick $12 thousand to $25 thousand per episode. His first ZIV-TV series was *Boston Blackie* (1951-1953) starring Kent Taylor and it was also the first mystery series on television. Herbert L. Strock, who directed countless episodes of many ZIV TV shows, said that Mr. Ziv regularly rotated directors, writers, producers, and actors to prevent them from becoming indispensable to a single series and then demanding higher salaries. Strock said "When making television shows, many studios combined the director and producer functions intentionally rather than by default. At ZIV this was the rule, not the exception. Making the director responsible for the production forced him or her to keep budgetary considerations in the foreground at all times." In 1951 Strock produced the pilot episode for the *Dragnet* television series starring Jack Webb, and later he produced and directed the pilot episode of *Highway Patrol* in April 1955.

ZIV's first big hit was the popular western series *The Cisco Kid* (1949-1955) starring Duncan Renaldo in the title role with movie character actor Leo Carrillo as his comical sidekick Pancho. Although the first color television sets were not even available, ZIV cheaply shot all 156 episodes in 16MM color. The series brought in $11 million in its first ten years and ran in syndication for decades. ZIV would later splice two episodes together and then release them overseas as *Cisco Kid* color feature films! In 1954 ZIV Television purchased a Hollywood film studio (the former *Educational Pictures/Grand National Pictures/Producer's Releasing Corp./Eagle-Lion* studio lot on Santa Monica Blvd) and turned it into a television factory. Mr. Ziv also rented out his film studio to independent producers. The last two seasons of *The Adventures of Superman* (1955-1957) starring George Reeves, were shot on the ZIV lot.

The ZIV studio was just around the corner from the nearby famed Charles Chaplin studios and the Samuel Goldwyn studios. In fact, as a courtesy to Quinn Martin Productions on the Goldwyn lot (producer Martin began his career at ZIV as an audio supervisor for *Highway Patrol*), a scene from the opening credits of the unforgettable, ABC blockbuster series *The Fugitive,* which showed David Janssen wearing broken handcuffs running from a train wreck, was shot at ZIV studios as late as 1963.

Cast and crew from all three studios lots frequented Hollywood's landmark *Formosa Café* nearby on Santa Monica Boulevard at Formosa Avenue. The popular watering hole began in 1925 out of an abandoned Los Angeles trolley car (and later expanded with a dining room, kitchen and bar added on). Among the famous *Formosa Café* customers was the infamous Elizabeth Short, better known as the *'Black Dahlia'*. Her bizarre and gruesome 1947 murder remains unsolved and a source of endless speculation. A memorable scene in the 1997 thriller *L.A. Confidential* involving Lana Turner at the *Formosa Café* was actually filmed there. The *Formosa Café* is also famed for being haunted.

To run day-to-day operations at the new studio Sinn contacted his old college pal Maurice 'Babe' Unger, who owned a mattress factory in Ohio. Sinn begged him to sell his company and move to Hollywood to run his studio operations. At first Unger declined claiming he knew nothing about making films. However, Sinn insisted it was no different that manufacturing mattresses and even insisted that a TV pilot film was like making a sample mattress! Unger sold his mattress factory, moved to Beverly Hills and became Vice-President in charge of production for ZIV television. Unger was astonished when he realized that early television was so hungry for product to fill the airways that everything sold immediately! After his retirement, 'Babe' Unger kept book bound copies of the scripts for every single TV episode produced by ZIV-TV.

Babe Unger's book-bound library of scripts for every ZIV-TV show (Photo from Goltz Collection).

Frederick Ziv believed that TV syndication was the best way to advertise local clients. His sales and marketing program consisted of basic, simple ad campaigns that were brilliantly effective.

The ZIV studio lot circa 1935 during its heyday as Grand National Studio (Photo Goltz Collection).

Aerial shot of the same location today after the studio lot was demolished (Photo Goltz Collection).

Script for pilot of *The Fugitive* 1963 TV series, *Fear in a Desert City* by Quinn Martin productions at the Samuel Goldwyn studio which was across the street from ZIV Studios (Photo Goltz Collection).

ZIV produced over two dozen television series during the 1950's. His best shows included *Your Favorite Story* (1953-1955) an anthology series hosted by Adolphe Menjou, *I led Three Lives* (1953-1956) based on a true story of the 'McCarthy Red Scare' era with Richard Carlson, *Science Fiction Theater* (1955-1957), *The Lock Up* (1959-1961) with Macdonald Carey, and the western series *Tombstone Territory* (1957-1960). One of ZIV's most popular television shows was the underwater adventure series *Sea Hunt* (1958-1961) starring Lloyd Bridges which ran for 155 episodes. When Britain's Labor government passed legislation prohibiting Hollywood film studios from taking profits earned in the British Isles out of country, Frederick Ziv tapped his 'frozen funds' by filming two television series in the United Kingdom. *The New Adventures of Martin Kane* (1958) with William Gargan, and *Dial 999* (1959, the London police emergency phone number) which played on both sides of the Atlantic. By far ZIV Television's biggest and longest lasting hit series was *Highway Patrol* (1955-1959, for 156 episodes one more than *Sea Hunt*).

**Industry Ballyhoo for syndicated ZIV television series
(Photo Goltz Collection).**

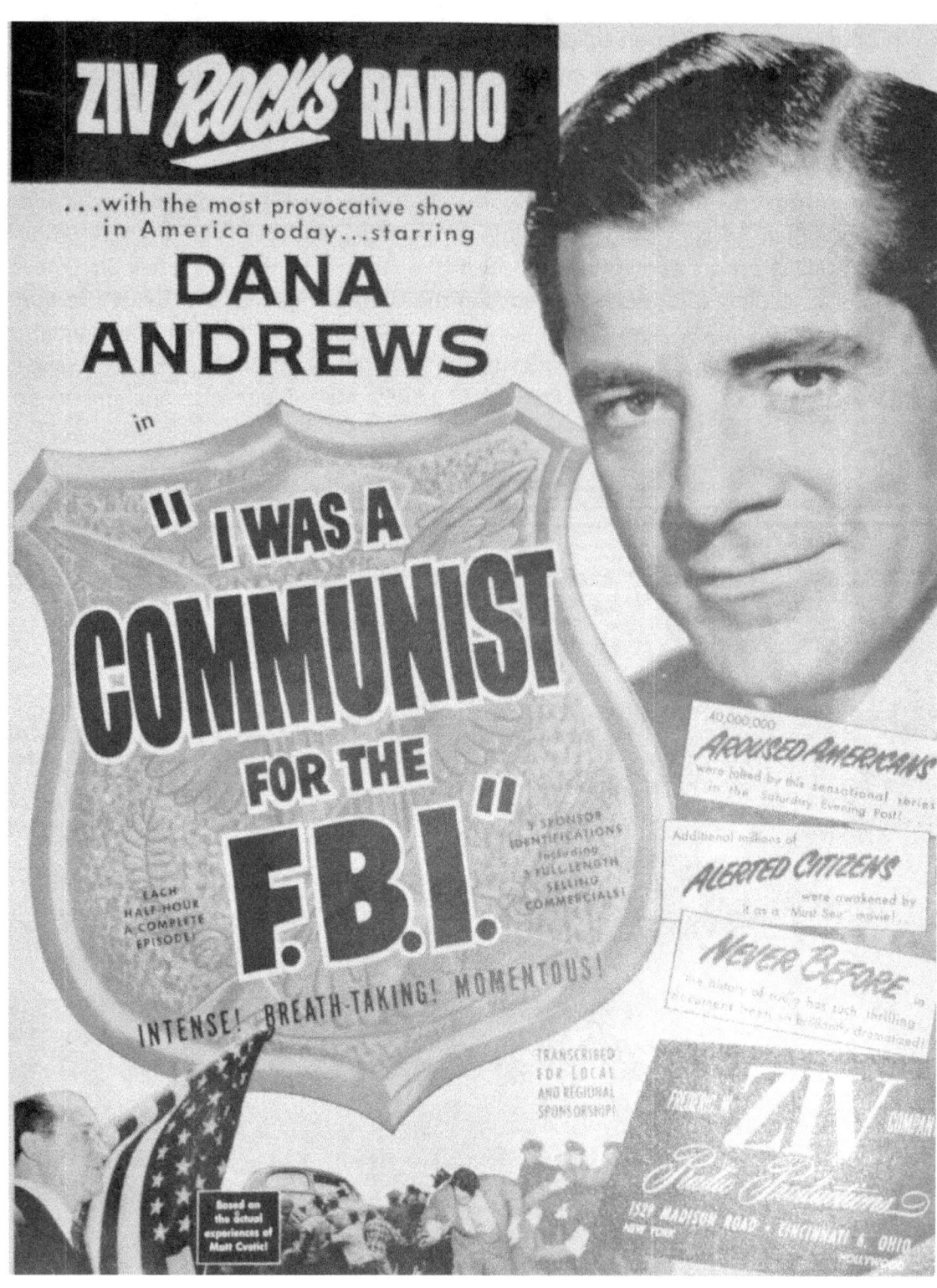

Promotion ad for the ZIV radio series with Dana Andrews, *I Was a Communist for the FBI*. (Photo Goltz Collection).

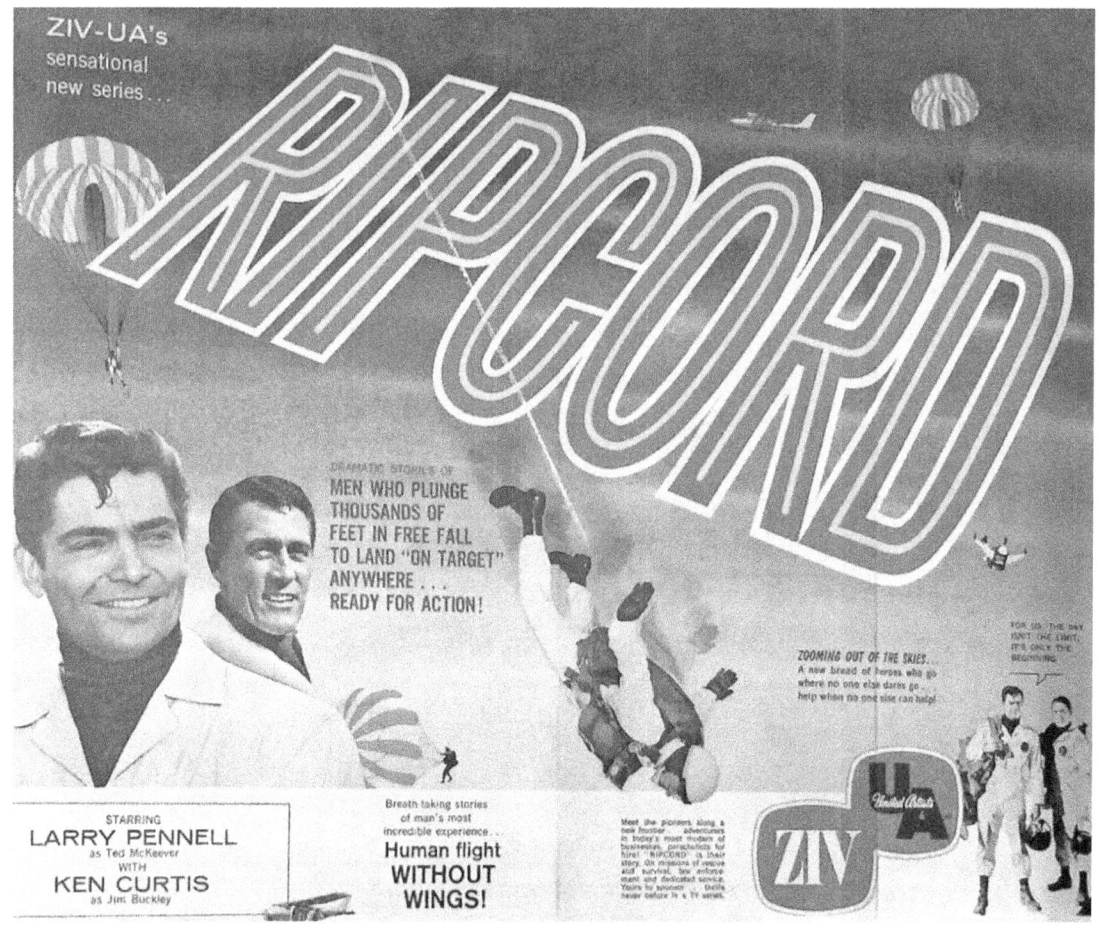

Poster for ZIV-TV 1961 series *Ripcord* (Photo Goltz Collection).

Typical ZIV-TV 16MM film canister containing a *Highway Patrol* episode as shipped to local TV stations for broadcast (Photo Goltz Collection).

ZIV-TV press books for the series, *The Man and The Challenge, The Cisco Kid, Highway Patrol (aka Ten-4*), Sea Hunt,* and *Men into Space*. (Photo Goltz Collection).

From Rick Jason's autobiography *Scrapbooks of My Mind,* **2000**

On *Sea Hunt*

"They (ZIV) made a bunch of junk, but it all sold. Television was like a vacuum cleaner on a polished marble floor: it sucked up anything it could get hold of. Most of the shows ZIV did only lasted a year, until a producer named Ivan Tors, who knew what he was doing, went to the studio with a show called *Sea Hunt.* The actor they hired was an up-and-coming young fellow with a great build who could swim. Lloyd Bridges, originally from Broadway, had been working his way up in the business to second leads and was signed at twelve hundred dollars a segment against ten percent of the gross after the break. It cost twelve thousand dollars to make a half-hour show in 1954. Paul Stader, a great water stunt man and second unit director, was sent with a crew to Silver Springs, Florida, where the water is clear as glass, to shoot all the underwater action footage with a double for Bridges. He shot tens of thousands of feet of film. By the time "Bud" Bridges finished making *Sea Hunt,* his salary was two thousand a segment and there was so much underwater footage that they were shooting one segment a day, five a week. Bridges walked away from the show with better than six million dollars. He'd become a household name and a big star in television, which by then had gained some notice, but not much respect, in the feature film business. *Sea Hunt* continued in syndication for years after he finished shooting it, and ten cents of every dollar that came in went into Bridge's pocket."

In a 1999 interview Frederick Ziv said "Most of my shows were about the chase... the chase is a wonderful attention-getter. You have suspense, action, we had the chase on horseback, the chase on the highway, the chase underwater and the chase in the air (and in space) …. The chase provides a minimum of dialogue and a maximum of tension." However, Ziv believed that action only worked with a good script which was the hallmark of any successful program. In a 1998 interview he said "It all begins with the paper – a good script." Ziv frequently hammered out the first draft for his own shows with his two-finger typing skills. Herbert Strock once said about his boss "He was a nice enough guy with little or no motion picture knowledge but he would listen to you and make a decision, right or wrong. He was more of a business executive." Frederick Ziv wisely ran his studio like a successful business. By the late 1950's the syndication television market had changed. The three big networks were now offering local stations repeats of their former prime-time TV shows. Network re-runs were a cash bonanza for the networks and soon first-run syndicated shows were pushed right out of the market. ZIV Television produced several series for the networks but only *Bat Masterson* (1958-1961) starring Gene Barry became a hit with 108 episodes. In 1960 Frederick Ziv sold his television studio to United Artists which was eager to get into TV production. It was renamed ZIV-UA Television and later simply United Artists Television with Babe Unger as President. The new company had very few hit series except *The Patty Duke Show* (1963-1966) and *The Outer Limits* (1963-1965). United Artists sold off the old three and a half acre ZIV-TV lot to a real estate developer who then demolished it. The former haunt of James Cagney, Bela Lugosi, Hedy Lamarr, and Abbott &

Costello is now a shopping center. In an internet article by Christopher Anderson, Ziv said "I sold my business because I recognized the networks were taking command of everything and were permitting independent producers no room at all... The networks demanded a percentage of your profits... they demanded script approval and cast approval... You practically were no longer an independent producer. You were just doing whatever the networks asked you to do... I didn't care to become an employee of the networks." Frederick Ziv retired from Hollywood and returned home to Cincinnati. For twenty-two years, he taught at the University of Cincinnati – College Conservatory of Music which still presents an annual award for broadcasting achievement which bears his name. Frederick W. Ziv, a genuine pioneer of television, died in 2001 at the age of 96. United Artists, which owns the ZIV-TV film library, donated copies of every single ZIV series to the Wisconsin Center For Film and Theater Research at the University Of Wisconsin-Madison.

Below:
University of Wisconsin-Madison (Photos Goltz Collection).

Facing Page:
The extensive ZIV film library at the Wisconsin Center for Film and Television research including film cans containing *Highway Patrol* episodes.

Other ZIV television shows:

Acapulco (1961, 8 episodes) Ralph Taeger, James Coburn, Telly Savalas
The Aquanauts (1960-1961, 32 episodes) Ron Ely
Bat Masterson (1958-1961, 108 episodes) Gene Barry
Bold Venture (1959-1960, 39 episodes) Dane Clark, Joan Marshall
Boston Blackie (1951-1953, 58 episodes) Kent Taylor
Case of The Dangerous Robin (1960-1961, 38 episodes) Rick Jason
Cisco Kid (1950-1956, 156 episodes) Duncan Renaldo, Leo Carrillo
Dial 999 (1958, 39 episodes British filmed)
Dr. Christian (1956-1957, 39 episodes) Macdonald Carey, Jean Hersholt
Eddie Cantor Comedy Theatre (1955-1956, 39 episodes) Eddie Cantor
Everglades (1961-1962, 38 episodes) Ron Hayes
Harbor Command (1957-1958, 39 episodes) Wendell Corey
Harbor Master (1957-1958, 26 episodes) Barry Sullivan, Paul Burke
Home Run Derby (1959-1960, 26 episodes) sports show hosted by Mark Scott, Art Passarella
I Led 3 Lives (1953-1956, 117 episodes) Richard Carlson
Keyhole (1961-1962, 38 episodes) Jack Douglas
King of Diamonds (1961-1962, 38 episodes) Broderick Crawford
Klondike (1960-1961, 18 episodes) Ralph Taeger, Mari Blanchard, James Coburn
Lock Up (1959-1961, 78 episodes) Macdonald Carey
Mackenzie's Raiders (1958-1959, 39 episodes) Richard Carlson
Man and The Challenge (1959-1960, 36 episodes) George Nader
Man Called X (1956-1957, 39 episodes) Barry Sullivan
Meet Corliss Archer (1954-1955) Ann Baker
Men Into Space (1959-1960, 39 episodes) William Lundigan
Men of Annapolis (1957-1958, 39 episodes) anthology series about the U.S. Naval Academy
Miami Undercover (1961-1962, 38 episodes) Lee Bowman
Mr. District Attorney (1954, 78 episodes) David Brian
New Adventures of Martin Kane (1958-1959, 39 episodes British filmed) William Gargan
Ripcord (1961-1963, 76 episodes) Larry Pennell
Rough Riders (1958-1959, 39 episodes) Kent Taylor, Jan Merlin, Peter Whitney
Science Fiction Theatre (1955-1957, 78 episodes) anthology series hosted by Truman Bradley
Sea Hunt (1958-1961, 155 episodes) Lloyd Bridges
Target (1958-1959, 39 episodes) mystery anthology series hosted by Adolphe Menjou
This Man Dawson (1959-1960, 39 episodes) Keith Andes
Tombstone Territory (1957-1960, 91 episodes) Pat Conway
Troubleshooters (1959-1960, 26 episodes) Keenan Wynn, Bob Mathias
The Unexpected (1952-1953, 39 episodes) mystery-anthology series hosted by Herbert Marshall
Waterfront (1954-1956, 78 episodes) Preston Foster
West Point (1957-1958, 39 episodes) anthology series on the U.S. Military Academy
World of Giants (1959, 13 episodes) Arthur Franz
Your Favorite Story (1953-1955, 78 episodes) literary anthology series hosted by Adolphe Menjou

The golden days of the ZIV Studios lot with every studio employee posing with their chief, Frederick W. Ziv (center front in sport jacket) (Photo Goltz Collection).

ZIV Television, Inc. business stationary (Photo Goltz Collection).

ZIV Television, Inc. screen logo (Photo Goltz Collection).

FREDERIC W. ZIV
COMPANY
Radio Productions
1529 MADISON ROAD
CINCINNATI 6, OHIO

1954 Letterhead for FWZ Radio (Photo Goltz Collection).

Next Page: Professional Business Portrait Of Maurice 'Babe' Unger used in the *Highway Patrol* episode *"Escort"* and his card (Photo Goltz Collection).

PRODUCTIONS, INC.

AREA CODE 213 273-4961

MAURICE UNGER
PRESIDENT

9229 SUNSET BOULEVARD
LOS ANGELES, CALIFORNIA 90069

TV legend George Reeves filming *The Adventures of Superman* **at ZIV Studios in 1956 (Photo R. Schiller).**

Chapter Two

Highway Patrol (1955-1959)

The Blockbuster Seminal Television Series

Highway Patrol was a nationally syndicated half-hour television series that ran for four seasons (1955-1959) and 156 episodes. It was produced in black and white by ZIV Television Programs Inc. The producer was Frederick W. Ziv. The theme music and score was composed by David Rose. Art Gilmore was the narrator.

Originally Guy Daniels, the public civilian spokesman for the California Highway Patrol (later uniformed CHP officers were designated spokespersons), was dispatched by the CHP Commissioner Bernard Caldwell himself to Hollywood in hope of persuading Jack Webb, producer of the TV hit *Dragnet* (about the Los Angeles Police Department) to build a new series about their law enforcement organization. Webb committed himself to producing the new series until Warner Brothers signed him up as producer, director and star in a major film based on his old radio series *Pete Kelly's Blues.* The outstanding, hit 1955 film co-starred Janet Leigh, Edmond O'Brien, Lee Marvin, and singer Peggy Lee (her performance was nominated for a *Best Supporting Actress Oscar*). Webb, known throughout the industry for keeping his word, reluctantly broke his promise in favor of his dream project. Frederick Ziv made the most of this opening and produced the series himself. For the record, Jack Webb also produced a 1959 television series of *Pete Kelly's Blues* that lasted for 13 episodes.

That same year Frederick Ziv enjoyed Broderick Crawford's riveting performance as a dedicated FBI agent in the classic thriller *Down Three Dark Streets* (1954). Crawford's G-Man is on the trail of a killer who murdered his partner Special Agent (played by Kenneth Tobey, star of the popular *Whirlybirds* television series). The film was based on the novel *Case File FBI* by Gordon and Mildred Gordon and co-starred Ruth Roman, Martha Hyer, Marisa Pavan, and Claude Akins. Broderick Crawford's FBI Special Agent sports a classic fedora hat that quickly became his trademark on *Highway Patrol.* His character also barks into his undercover car's microphone during the film's exciting climax. After seeing Broderick Crawford play a good guy carrying a badge, Ziv was determined to build a police show around the powerhouse actor.

Young Broderick Crawford (with full head of hair) in his second of 95 films *Start Cheering* (1938) with co-stars Raymond Walburn (left) Joan Perry (center), cowboy star Charles Starrett (right) and Larry Fine (partially hidden on the left) (Photo R. Schiller).

Broderick Crawford stars as the hero in Universal's 1940 mystery classic *The Black Cat* **(Photo R. Schiller).**

At 1950 Academy Awards both Olivia de Havilland and Broderick Crawford bask in their Oscar wins for 'Best Actress' for *The Heiress* and 'Best Actor' for *All The King's Men* (Photo R. Schiller).

Robert Rossen (the film's director and producer) joins his star after winning the 'Best Picture' (Photo R. Schiller).

Below:

Photos from the 1950 Friar's Frolics Hollywood charity event. Broderick Crawford and Red Skelton in drag (Photos Goltz Collection).

WEEK ENDING MAY 5th, 1950

CREDIT: PHOTO BY NAT DALLINGER

COPYRIGHT, KING FEATURES SYNDICATE, INC.

FRIAR'S FROLIC OF 1950

Red Skelton, left, and Broderick Crawford, two of Hollywood's top screen stars, were among the leading men who donned feminine makeup and attire for their roles in the Floradora Sextet number, a highlight of the charity event which annually raises funds for needy charities. Except for the hair on his chest, Skelton was hilariously convincing with his clowning. Brod, also a tremendous hit with the spectators, is Filmdom's newest Academy Award-winning actor. He won the golden Oscar for "Best actor of 1949."

Below: Errol Flynn, Harpo Marx and Van Johnson clown with Broderick Crawford at the Friar's Frolics (Photo Goltz Collection).

Hollywood movie star Broderick Crawford in a 1950 Chesterfield Cigarettes magazine advertisement (Photo Goltz Collection).

Below: Broderick Crawford as a police detective saves his fiancée Betty Buehler in the rugged crime film *The Mob* (1951) (Photo Goltz Collection).

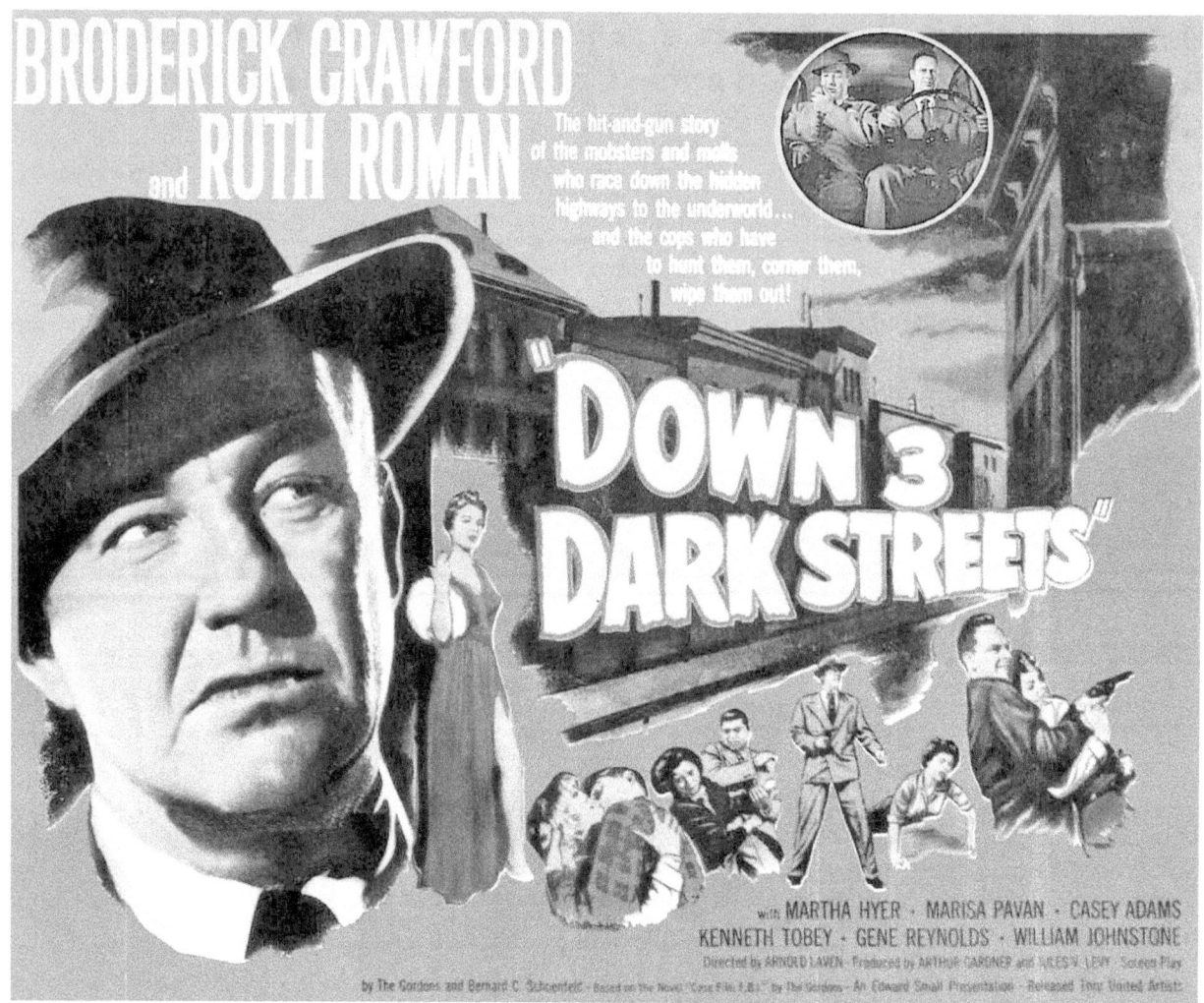

Lobby card for the exciting United Artists hit film *Down Three Dark Streets* (1954) starring Broderick Crawford as an FBI agent, with Ruth Roman, Marisa Pavan, and Claude Akins. Note insert of Brod with mic, a year prior to *Highway Patrol* (Photo Goltz Collection).

G-Man FBI Agent Broderick Crawford saves Ruth Roman's life in *Down Three Dark Streets* (1954 photo Goltz Collection).

Hard-boiled Broderick Crawford wears his trademark trench coat and fedora for the 1947 'film noir' gem *The Flame* at Republic Pictures (Photo Goltz Collection).

By 1954 Columbia Pictures had dropped Broderick Crawford's contract. The magic was fading fast from his 1949 Oscar win and he was slipping into villain and character roles. In fact, his career had declined to the point where his most recent film (shot overseas in Rome, Italy, *The Swindle* directed by Federico Fellini) wasn't even released in the USA until 1962! In 1954 Broderick Crawford starred in and produced a television pilot *U.S. Secret Service Agent* with the full cooperation of the U.S. Treasury Department. Unfortunately this potentially good idea for a weekly television series on the U.S. Secret Service was squandered by a drab, colorless, pilot film that was never picked up by the networks. U.S. Treasury officials ran roughshod over the entire production and squeezed every bit of excitement and action out of it. With no other offers on the table, Broderick Crawford, along with a wife and two little boys to support, and needing a regular paycheck, accepted a starring role in an off-network television series with 10% equity in the series. John Sinn remembered going to lunch with Herbert Strock and Broderick Crawford to discuss the screenplay of the pilot and noticed that the Oscar-winning star ordered only cottage cheese! In fact, Crawford looks very fit during the first season before putting on weight during the run of the series.

According to Guy Daniels in a 1995 interview with author (Goltz) "Bernard Caldwell was not happy that Broderick Crawford was chosen for the show and would have preferred someone less known, I wasn't happy about it either. Broderick Crawford was a movie star who had just come off an Academy Award winning performance in *All The King's Men*. And Brod had his own ideas about playing his *Highway Patrol* character with a very tough, brusque, performance and plenty of action which Bernard Caldwell didn't want at all. Broderick Crawford was the first Academy Award winning actor to star in a television show and did things his way. Because of his age we decided not to have him in uniform and made him the chief of *Highway Patrol* so he wore civilian clothes. Unfortunately, Brod was getting divorced from his first wife Kay after many years of marriage and it upset him very much. He lost his two boys and it broke his heart." Guy Daniels was a highly decorated World War Two, U.S. Navy combat veteran who served in the South Pacific. He died in 2006.

Highway Patrol was cheaply-produced with a fast shooting schedule. The producers considered the series a throw away but nearly overnight this 'sleeper' in syndication became a runaway hit coast to coast. Although an off-network syndicated show, *Highway Patrol* in some markets regularly beat the top-rated network shows including *I Love Lucy*! In 1937 when Broderick Crawford first arrived in Hollywood, he dated and was briefly engaged to a very young, beautiful, blonde-haired Lucille Ball. However, Brod Crawford's television success nearly two decades after their split annoyed Lucille Ball who never asked him to do a guest shot on *I Love Lucy* which would have boosted both series. *Highway Patrol* instantly made Broderick Crawford a national television star with his great American face seen in every household of the USA. Even today over a half-century later, he is remembered more for *Highway Patrol* than for any of his films.

Broderick Crawford with fiancée Lucille Ball in 1937 Hollywood (Photo R. Schiller).

Below: Universal Studios post-war 1946 portrait of contract player Broderick Crawford (photo Goltz Collection).

**ZIV Studio portrait of Broderick Crawford circa 1958
(photo Goltz Collection).**

Beyond the shadow of a doubt *Highway Patrol* was the biggest smash hit in the ZIV stable of television series. It came at the right time, and in the right place. It was enormously successful for three major reasons: David Rose's riveting theme music, Art Gilmore's crisp narration, and most of all Broderick Crawford's powerhouse performance as Dan Mathews, chief of Highway Patrol. Frederick Ziv said it best in Morleen Getz Rouse's dissertation, "Somehow a script that seems only fair, catches fire with a star. The star's sudden burst of power rubs off on all round him. There's a chemistry that suddenly ignites the stage, whether Broadway or Hollywood sound stages. A fusion of unpredictable elements that a single sparkle like from a diamond that suddenly causes all facets to sparkle as they never did before. A hit show results… It is exciting to be on a Hollywood lot when the rumor spreads that something exciting is happening on Stage 8… There's a buzz on the lot."

The series had a budget of $20,000 per episode (rising to $30,000 if a helicopter was used). Interiors were filmed at ZIV Studios, but outdoor scenes were shot on state roads in what was then the still undeveloped rural San Fernando Valley and Simi Valley. Other locations included both Griffith Park and Bronson Canyon just above Hollywood. Although *Highway Patrol* was dedicated to state police organizations across America, it was based on the California Highway Patrol which gave its full support and cooperation to ZIV Television. CHP Officer Frank Runyon (badge number 475) was assigned as technical advisor to the series because according to Guy Daniels in an interview with author (Goltz), "Frank Runyon was chosen because he did a lot of public relations for the California Highway Patrol. He had visited many schools and did public appearances in uniform that presented an authentic and professional image of the force. " The CHP even provided several actual enforcement units including a '54 Oldsmobile, and a '55 Buick Century with the *Highway Patrol* emblem on the car doors pasted (sometimes double-taped) over the actual CHP emblem star. When asked by author (Goltz) why the generic *Highway Patrol* name was chosen for the emblem, Guy Daniels said "We tried different names like State Patrol, State Police before settling on that because the *Highway Patrol* logo was designed to appeal nationwide and not just the California Highway Patrol, and it worked! Before this ZIV's biggest hit was *The Cisco Kid* with Leo Carrillo and Duncan Renaldo. I knew *Highway Patrol* was going to be a big hit when it sold very early."

When the CHP dropped its support for the series, ZIV switched to making their own patrol cars from non-police models but outfitted like the CHP squad cars without roof lights but with a red, driver-side spotlight in front (named the 'Ruby') and a yellow-flashing light in the rear window. ZIV also ran a different acknowledgement thanking the CHP for their cooperation for a dozen or so episodes. On the road Guy Daniels recalled to author (Goltz), "We shot a lot of outdoor scenes in the West Valley near the Ventura County Line. There were a lot of rural country roads out there that you could block off for an hour of filming!" In an interview with the author (Goltz), Frank Runyon recalled the friendly rivalry between the Los Angeles Police Department (LAPD) and the California Highway Patrol (CHP). During the shooting of an episode of *Highway Patrol*, LAPD assigned an enforcement vehicle with two uniformed officers to control traffic. While the somewhat bored police officers sat in their vehicle, Runyon stealthily crept up and slapped a *Highway Patrol* logo over the LAPD logo painted on the door. After calling it a day, the LAPD officers, who never got out of their vehicle, drove off with the generic HP sticker on the front door! Runyon recalled "I got the job as technical advisor after the civilian representative of CHP didn't work out. He had a bad relationship with Broderick Crawford. ZIV preferred a uniformed officer with five to ten years of experience on the force. Caldwell had told Brod and Herb Strock that 'Whatever this man says is good and has the final word.' And I did! There was one CHP officer assigned to the show who had a SAG (Screen Actors Guild Union) card and I remember he gave me a hard time when back I was a rookie. I asked Brod not to use him again and he was gone." On the shooting schedule Runyon said "ZIV worked two days on location and day at the studio. I wasn't impressed at first and thought *Highway Patrol* was going to lay an egg but the writing got better! One thing I did was on the first episode was I noticed the police siren sounded odd. Right away I made them change it to a real police siren which made the show more exciting! CHP came back then and said that they owned the emblem on the door so ZIV changed it to *Highway Patrol*! " Frank Runyon disagreed with Guy Daniels' contention that Broderick Crawford wore civilian clothes rather than a uniform due to his age saying "He didn't wear a uniform so he would stand out as Dan Mathews, chief of *Highway Patrol*!" In an interview with Morleen Get Rouse for his dissertation, Ziv said, "It was a dynamic program ... because the man with the badge proved its appeal. Not the man in the uniform. You put a man in uniform and you downgrade him. So, Dan Mathews, our head of our highway patrol, was not in uniform – he was the head of the patrol. And the part was played by Broderick Crawford who dynamism to the role. He spoke so fast and moved so fast that we edited our film accordingly. Today we hear about quick cuts, but the quick cutting technique really was put into television film in *Highway Patrol* ... It started a whole new trend." Like his counterpart, LAPD Sgt. Joe Friday of *Dragnet*, *Highway Patrol* Chief Dan Mathews became a first-rate plainclothes detective on the force. As chief he was one of them but also separate at the same time with higher rank and responsibility. On top of that the uniformed patrol officers of *Highway Patrol* did not wear blue uniforms like regular city police. Instead they wore military-style khaki uniforms which made these state police stand out above the rest.

During the run of the series, the cast and crew at ZIV studios always remarked that the most stunning woman on the lot was Babe Unger's attractive secretary Lois whose beauty outshined the many lovely actresses appearing on the show!

Broderick Crawford and his lifelong pal California Highway Patrol technical advisor Frank Runyon enjoy a laugh on the set (Photo Goltz Collection).

The series' popularity spawned copycat shows like Universal's *State Trooper* (with a bigger budget than *Highway Patrol*) starring former cowboy star Rod Cameron. Although popular enough to last for 104 episodes, it never surpassed the *Highway Patrol* juggernaut. ZIV-TV got into the act with their new series *Harbor Command* (1957-1958) which was really a waterlogged version of *Highway Patrol* for a season of thirty-nine episodes starring movie character actor Wendell Corey. According to Herbert Strock, Corey was not nearly as popular with the cast and crew as Broderick Crawford was.

On the night of October 3, 1955, America tuned-in for the premiere episode of *Highway Patrol, "Prison Break"*. The theme music commences with an aerial helicopter shot of a white convertible Lincoln Capri approaching a police roadblock (driven by Babe Unger with Guy Daniels in the passenger seat). The camera soars over the squad cars and the screen is filled with large, block letters spelling out "BRODERICK CRAWFORD" with smaller letters underneath "STARRING IN". The letters fade away but are replaced by equally large block letters "HIGHWAY PATROL". Frederick Ziv put Herbert L. Strock in charge of creating the pilot episode who also directed it (he would direct 17 episodes of the series in total). Strock also created the exciting opening credits of the series that became its trademark with the helicopter shot of Babe Unger and Guy Daniels in the Lincoln Capri on a collision course with the police roadblock. Except for the pilot (see the screenplay for *"Prison Break"*), every episode began with Art Gilmore's commanding narration, "Whenever the laws of any state are broken, a duly authorized organization swings into action. It may be called the State Police, the State Troopers, Militia, the Rangers, or the Highway Patrol. These are the stories of the men whose training, skill, and courage have enforced and preserved our state laws."

Next Two Pages: Two standard pre-written, personal ZIV-TV press release letters signed by Broderick Crawford promoting *Highway Patrol* (Goltz Collection).

BRODERICK CRAWFORD
HOLLYWOOD, CALIFORNIA

Mr. Howard Scripps, Publisher
Metropolis Daily News
Metropolis, U.S.A.

Dear Mr. Scripps:

As publisher of a major newspaper in your city, you will be gratified to know that a great public service has been undertaken by a firm doing business in your locality.

The Smith Company is going to sponsor HIGHWAY PATROL, a new TV drama series soon to appear on Station WZIV-TV on Channel 7. In sponsoring HIGHWAY PATROL, the Smith Company has committed itself to promoting safety and safe driving on the roads leading in and out of your city.

Your city's TV viewers will see, in exciting true-to-life adventures, how their State Highway Police work for them...preventing accidents, safeguarding homes, factories and farms along the way, inspecting and regulating school transportation, investigating accidents and crimes on the road.

HIGHWAY PATROL is filmed on the highway, at the scenes of real mishaps and investigations. The series is authentic, supervised by qualified officials of a State Highway Police Department.

When I played the Academy Award-winning role of "Willie Stark", in "All The King's Men", some years ago, I portrayed a high public official who was corrupted by power. At that time, I determined that, sooner or later, I would play an important role depicting a public servant of an entirely opposite kind...one who unselfishly and devotedly fulfills the responsibilities of public trust.

The opportunity to do this came when ZIV TELEVISION PROGRAMS, INC., offered me the role of head of a State Highway force, in HIGHWAY PATROL. Of all of the many assignments I've had on stage, screen, and TV, this is the most important I've ever had. This is the story of a leader who leads...a man up from the ranks who has devotion to duty as his Creed...and the highway officers under him, whose daily assignment is heroism.

ZIV-TV, producers of SCIENCE FICTION THEATRE, I LED 3 LIVES, MR. D.A. and other popular programs, are spending $45,000 per film to bring the very best entertainment and most thoroughly researched information to your city. Safety councils, auto clubs and chambers of commerce throughout the country are cooperating with us and with the local sponsor to enlarge the effect of the "safety story" of this series. Naturally, as a leading newspaper in your city, you will be doing a great and important public service in bringing HIGHWAY PATROL to the attention of your readers, week after week.

I trust that I will have the pleasure of entertaining you, in your home, when The Smith Company brings this vital program to your city.

Sincerely,

BRODERICK CRAWFORD

BRODERICK CRAWFORD
HOLLYWOOD, CALIFORNIA

TV Editor
Metropolis Daily News
Metropolis, U.S.A.

Dear Mr. Editor:

Station WZIV-TV has no doubt informed you that the powerful ZIV-TV production, HIGHWAY PATROL, is about to appear on Channel 7 at 10:30 P.M. every Friday, sponsored by The Smith Company.

In this series of half-hour dramatic adventures, I have the pleasure of portraying the role of head of a state highway patrol force. I consider this the most important role of my long career on stage, screen and TV...and that includes my work in "All The King's Men", for which I was awarded the "Oscar" as Best Actor of the Year. As I portray a man up from the ranks whose Creed is devotion to duty...a leader who leads...commanding at the scene of action. As guardian of public safety, it is a great and exciting role in a great and exciting series of stories, each of which is a complete half-hour adventure.

The producer, ZIV TELEVISION PROGRAMS, INC., is spending over $45,000 per program to bring the best entertainment and most completely researched information to the TV fans who read your columns. The Ziv production crews have gone out on the highways, into homes, farms and factories along the way, into real Highway Police headquarters...to scenes of real mishaps and investigations...to give your readers a true picture of how and where State Patrols operate.

HIGHWAY PATROL is based upon the vital every day experiences of Highway Police and State Troopers throughout the country. It is dedicated to men whose daily assignment is heroism.

You will agree that it is important that your readers get the kind of information about safety and safe driving on the highways leading in and out of your city that this series gives them. At the same time, your readers will thrill to the excitement, drama and suspense that makes this the greatest TV entertainment offered them to date. They will certainly appreciate being kept posted on forthcoming HIGHWAY PATROL programs.

Sincerely,

BRODERICK CRAWFORD

Broderick Crawford calls for back-up in the riveting pilot episode *'Prison Break'*. The Oscar-winning actor kept his weight down during filming (Photo Goltz Collection).

A publicity shot of eternal movie tough guy Broderick Crawford enjoying a smoking break while filming *Highway Patrol* in the late 1950's (Photo Goltz Collection).

Publicity still from the first episode *'Prison Break'* showing Broderick Crawford as Dan Mathews setting up highway roadblocks with fellow officers Paul Hahn and Frank Hanley. (Photo Goltz Collection).

Next Page: From *'Prison Break'* of Broderick Crawford as an angry Dan Mathews finds wounded officer's uniform on the school bus that he used to pass through police lines. Note: In the episode itself, Mathews did not use the snub nose .38 but the police special shown here (Photo Goltz Collection).

Above: Publicity still of Broderick Crawford from the pilot episode *'Prison Break'*. Note: the seal on the police car says 'State Patrol' instead of *Highway Patrol* (Photo Goltz Collection).

Below: May 1955, ZIV studio film editors Asa Clark, Erwin Dumbrille, and Leete Browne work on the pilot episode *'Prison Break"*. Note: In an interview with author Goltz, Erwin said the pilot came in at five reels long but had to be cut down to three (Photos Goltz Collection).

Broderick Crawford (and unknown actor) enjoy a break and leans on a police *Highway Patrol* motorcycle (Photo Goltz Collection).

Broderick Crawford as Chief Dan Mathews brandishes his snub nose .38 revolver! (Photo Goltz Collection).

Dan Mathews inspects fender damage of a car involved in an accident in the episode *'Hit and Run'* (Goltz Collection).

On the *Highway Patrol* set at ZIV studio, Broderick Crawford proudly watches his son Kelly tinker with a movie camera! According to Jean Crawford this was Kelly Crawford's favorite photo with his Dad. (Photo Courtesy Jean Goltz).

Below: Trade ad for 1957 TV toy fair (Photo Goltz Collection).

**Next Page:
Broderick Crawford and son Kelly Crawford in 1956 play cops and robbers with the *Highway Patrol* toy set (Photos Goltz Collection).**

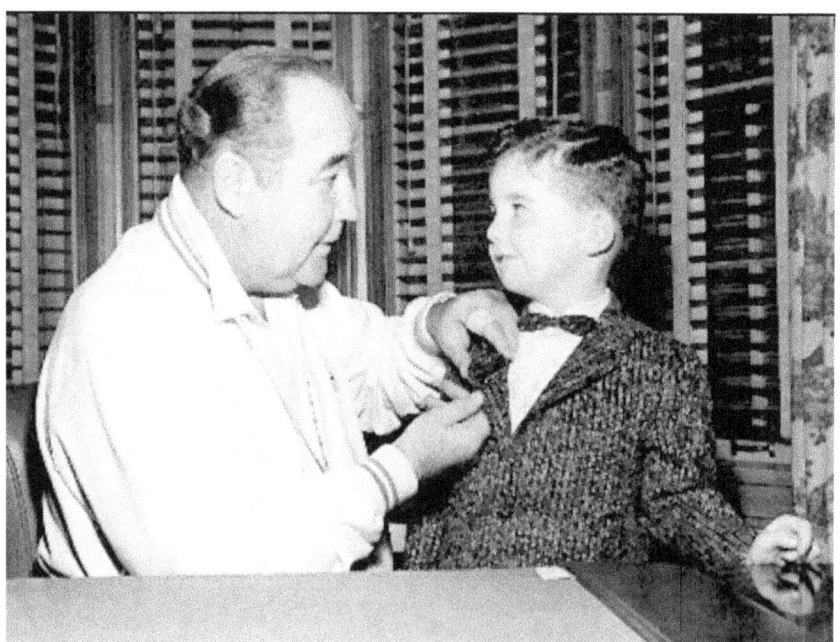

    To insure the series' success, the opening episode was an exciting, audience-grabbing show that hit one out of the park! Herbert Strock made sure to begin the episode's action with the very first scene of convict Ralph Neal heartlessly betraying his wounded fellow convict to the law in order to aid his escape. Although the series was on its way, a few details needed to be ironed out before the second episode. The police cars or enforcement units in this first episode were adorned with the logo 'State Patrol' while the patrol officers' uniforms sported shoulder patches that say *'Highway Patrol'*.

Original *Highway Patrol* badge for the series (Photo Goltz Collection).

Note the badge Larry Thor as Officer Ed Wylie (with Cecie Zito playing his wife Linda) considers ending his police career in the 2nd season episode *'Officer's Wife'* (Photo Goltz Collection).

Gold, *Highway Patrol* Dan Mathews & Ken Williams badges Florida Insignia (Photos Goltz Collection).

Season Four *Highway Patrol* Badges (Photos Goltz Collection).

Toy Badges (Photos Goltz Collection.)

Custom-made replica hat made for co-author Gary Goltz (Photos Goltz Collecton).

Above: Tie-clasp, cufflinks, and lapel pin with the *Highway Patrol* shield, custom-made by Florida Insignia (Photos Goltz Collection).

Photos of the badges, shoulder uniform patches, and uniform officer cap shields used in seasons 1–3, and the generic revised versions for season 4 (Photo Goltz Collection).

The seal from the pilot episode on the left and at right, the final generic seal for the series (Photos Goltz Collection).

(Photo Goltz Collection).

Broderick Crawford portrayed the head of *Highway Patrol* (sometimes referred to as chief) Dan Mathews as brave, strong, and incorruptible. He is dedicated to protecting the public, and relentless in his pursuit of criminals. In the epilog before the closing credits, Broderick Crawford, sitting at his desk in headquarters, says with a smile "How do you do ladies and gentlemen, I'm Broderick Crawford. I hope you enjoyed the program we brought to you and you'll be with us next week at this time." In later episodes after asking viewers to return for next week's unusual episode, Broderick Crawford often delivered traffic safety tips including:

"The Laws of your community are enforced for your protection, obey them!"

"Leave your blood at the Red Cross, or your community blood bank, not on the highway!"

"The careless driver isn't driving his car, he's aiming it!"

"Try to be as good a driver as you think you are!"

 "It isn't the car that kills, it's the driver!"

"Reckless driving doesn't determine who's right, only who's left!"

"If you care to drive, drive with care!"

"It isn't what you drive, but how you drive that counts!"

"No matter how new, the safest device in your car is you!"

"The clowns at the circus, they're real funny, but on the highway they're murder!"

"Remember, when you drive, use a car! Ten-4!" (safety message from the 1976 *Saturday Night Live* parody sketch on *Highway Patrol*!)

When Ballantine Beer sponsored *Highway Patrol* in certain television markets, special promo bumpers were filmed including the safety tip: "This is Broderick Crawford, I hope you enjoyed tonight's show brought to you by Ballantine Beer. Next week's *Highway Patrol* story is a very unusual one. I hope you will be with us then. In the meantime be sure and make the three-ring sign [gestures with his right hand] and ask the man for Ballantine Beer and Ballantine Ale. One more thing, the laws of your community are enforced for your protection. Obey them!"
Note:
    A safety message outtake shows Broderick Crawford at his desk before saying "Be sure and drive carefully or you may be in a *&!#% accident!"

With his film career at stake, Broderick Crawford knew that this was the role of a lifetime and gave a brilliant, powerhouse performance. He was already famous for his machine-gun delivery of lines but on *Highway Patrol* his dialogue is at lightning speed dazzling audiences from coast-to-coast. During the series' four-year run Broderick Crawford's performance never wavered but as he got older (and heavier) the producers added a regular cast member Bill Boyett to pick-up some of his lines to help him carry the workload.

One of Guy Daniels's duties, after being assigned by the California Highway Patrol to this fast-shot series where time was money, was to keep an eye on the star Broderick Crawford, often to his annoyance. While shooting the Season 1, Episode 14 *"Resort"*, Mathews enters the vacation lodge and is asked by the desk clerk for his name. The script said to use Mathews, but Broderick Crawford correctly stated that an undercover officer using an unmarked patrol car would never give his own name while in disguise. When told to come up with a name, Broderick Crawford gave Guy a dirty look and barked "Daniels!" into the microphone!

One time a former CHP officer showed up at ZIV studios and tried to hand Guy Daniels several unsolicited scripts which he had written for a *Highway Patrol* episode. In a 1995 interview with the author (Goltz), Daniels said "We had gotten sued for $900,000 in a plagiarism suit during our first year of production. The suit named Frederick Ziv, Broderick Crawford, Herbert Strock and myself! I got the brunt of it because he had left the scripts with me. All of our authorized scripts came through ZIV and the producers so as soon as he left I had my secretary package them up and mail it back to him without even looking at them. I had gone to journalism school and knew how to handle the situation with witnesses signing that the scripts were never read. Of course it was obvious that he had set up the whole thing with a lawyer. We were annoyed that the California Attorney-General refused to back us. He didn't want the state of California to publicly admit how many public servants were assigned to making this television series but that was our job, public relations for the California Highway Patrol!"

1957 Court documents of the dubious plagiarism lawsuit against ZIV Television (Photo Goltz Collection).

Ironically the series gave Broderick Crawford greater fame and recognition as a national television star than his Oscar-winning performance in *All the King's Men* (1949). At the height of the show's popularity he made extensive personal appearances. Author Lou Koza discovered a UPI wire story dated February 12, 1958 of a charity event at North Hollywood's *Sportsman's Lodge*, where Broderick Crawford, Walter Brennan of *The Real McCoy's*, Andy Devine of *Wild Bill Hickok*, Clint Walker of *Cheyenne*, Pat Conway of *Tombstone Territory,* and George Reeves of *The Adventures of Superman* fished Chinook Salman from a water tank! Broderick Crawford's famous likeness was prominently displayed on many *Highway Patrol* merchandise products, including a toy *Highway Patrol* friction car with Dan firing his moving revolver out the window at criminals!

Below: Near the series end in Season 4, Broderick Crawford and Bill Boyett enjoy a smoke break while shooting episode 143 (Photo Goltz Collection).

Pages from the Spanish-language comic book of *Highway Patrol* (Photo Goltz Collection).

Below: Photos of Bell's jigsaw puzzle for the *Highway Patrol* TV series from 1958 (Photos Goltz Collection).

Below and Facing Page: Photos of Shuco's popular *Highway Patrol* Squad Car Road Set from 1956 (Photos Goltz Collection).

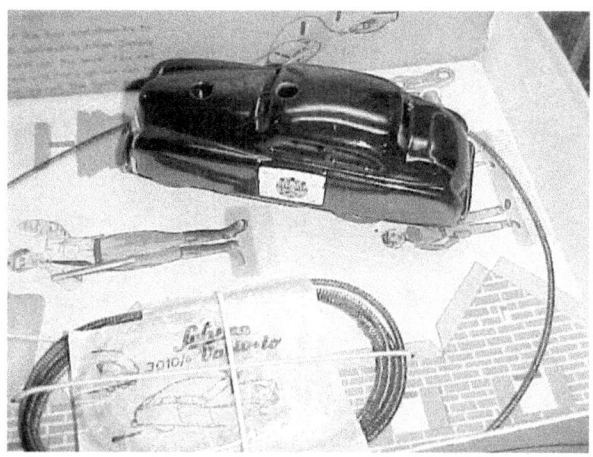

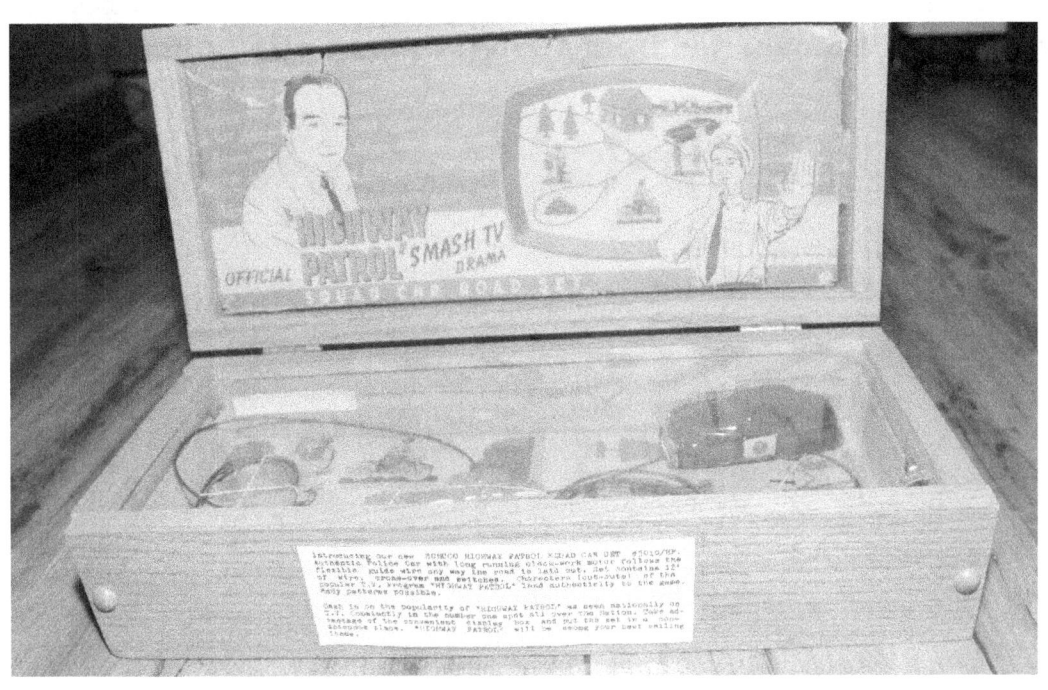

Below and Facing Page: Photos of Bell's *Highway Patrol* board game and accessories from 1958 (Photos Goltz Collection)

Below: Made In China *Maisto* model of 1955 Buick of California Highway Patrol (CHP) (Photo Goltz Collection).

Below and Facing Page: Handsome, well-crafted *Highway Patrol* car from Argentina (Photos Goltz Collection).

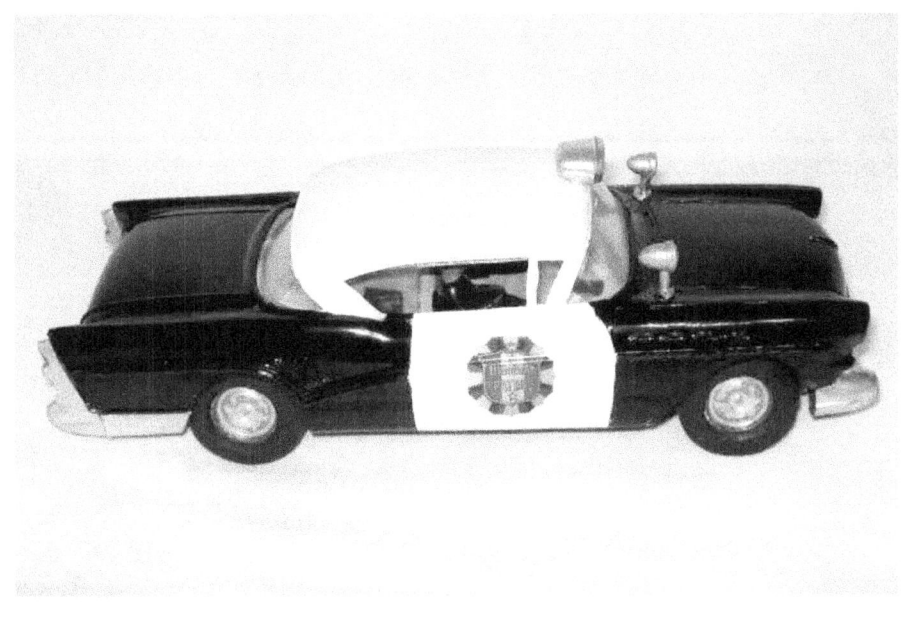

Below: From Oxford in Great Britain, a 1955 Buick Century Model California Highway Patrol (CHP) Car (Photos Goltz Collection).

Below and Next Page: Various models of popular Japanese-made toy *Highway Patrol* friction cars from 1957, made with Broderick Crawford's likeness! (Photos Goltz Collection).

Below and Facing Page: *Highway Patrol* toy car and box from Argentina. Note: The Spanish-speaking world uses '2050' instead of '2150' (Photos Goltz Collection).

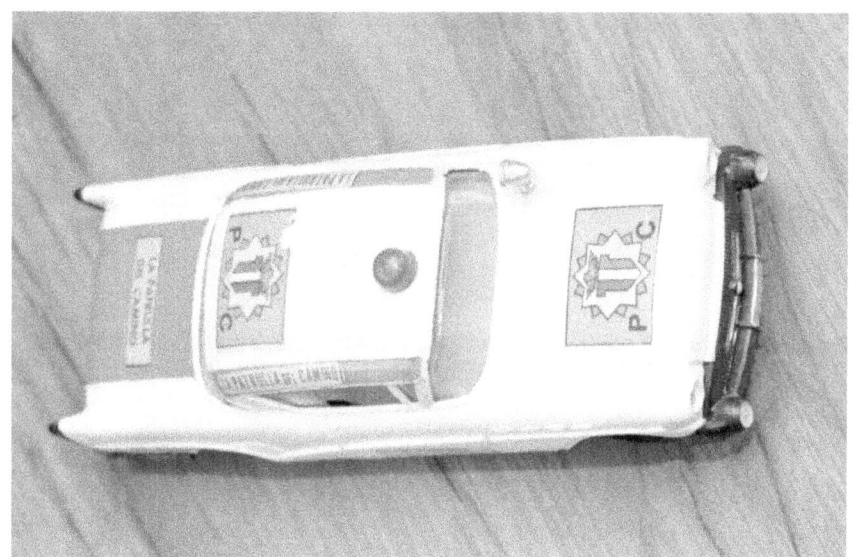

Below and Facing Page: *Highway Patrol* siren toy car and box from Britain (Photos Goltz Collection).

Below and Next Page: Popular toy *Highway Patrol* helicopter complete with Broderick Crawford as Dan Mathews wearing his trademark fedora hat in the passenger seat. (Photos Goltz Collection).

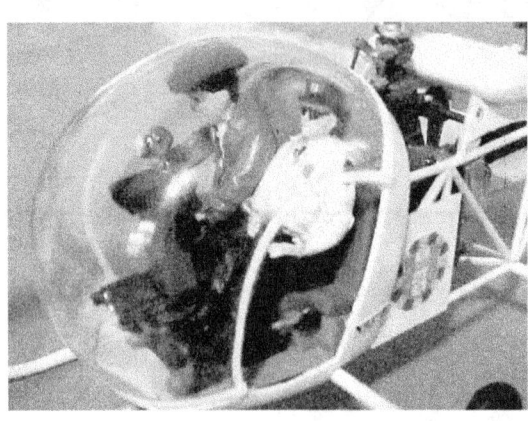

Below: *Highway Patrol* **hand toys, with Broderick Crawford and Bill Boyett prominently displayed, produced in Argentina. (Photos Goltz Collection).**

**Dimestore toy *Highway Patrol* siren from 1958
(Photo Goltz Collection).**

**Ballantine Beer giveaway badge (for children?) circa 1957
(Photo Goltz Collection).**

Below and Next Two Pages: Best-selling *Highway Patrol* toy holster and gun set with dummy bullets and siren, including original ads (Photos Goltz Collection).

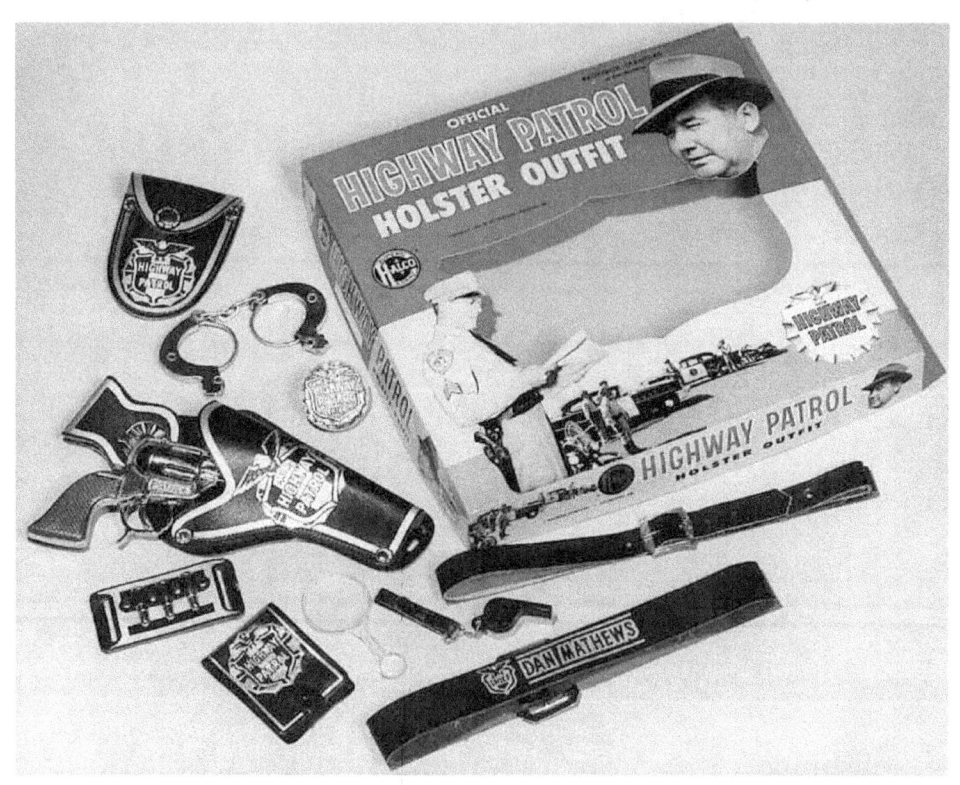

BILLY SAYS, "SHOW YOUR TOYS TO ME"

OFFICIAL HIGHWAY PATROL SET
(5 to 10 years)
A super outfit just like the patrolmen wear on TV's "Highway Patrol!" Swivel pocket holster, repeating pistol, wide belt, shoulder belt, handcuffs with case, magnifying glass, more! **4.98**

By J. Halpern.

Another *Highway Patrol* toy gun and badge toy (Photo Goltz Collection).

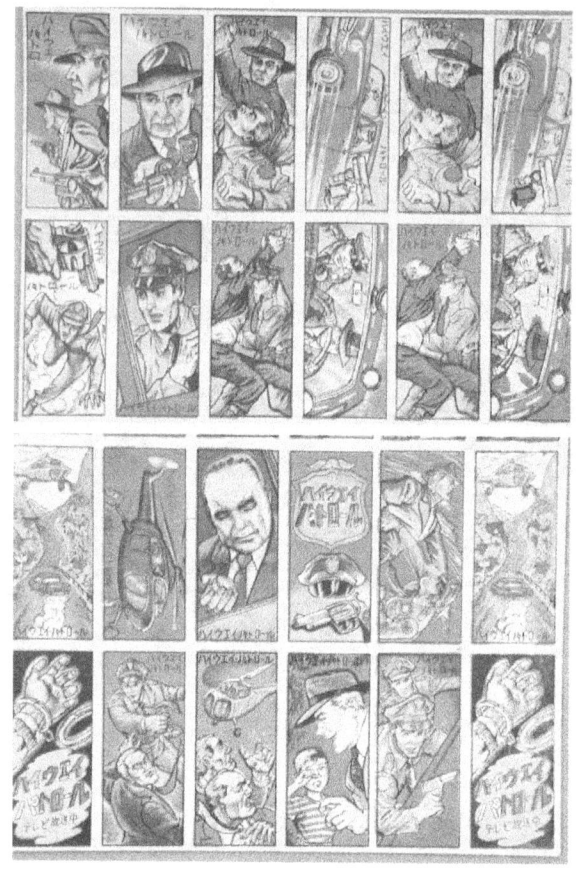

Highway Patrol **action-packed card of stamps from Japan where the series is eternally popular (Photo Goltz Collection).**

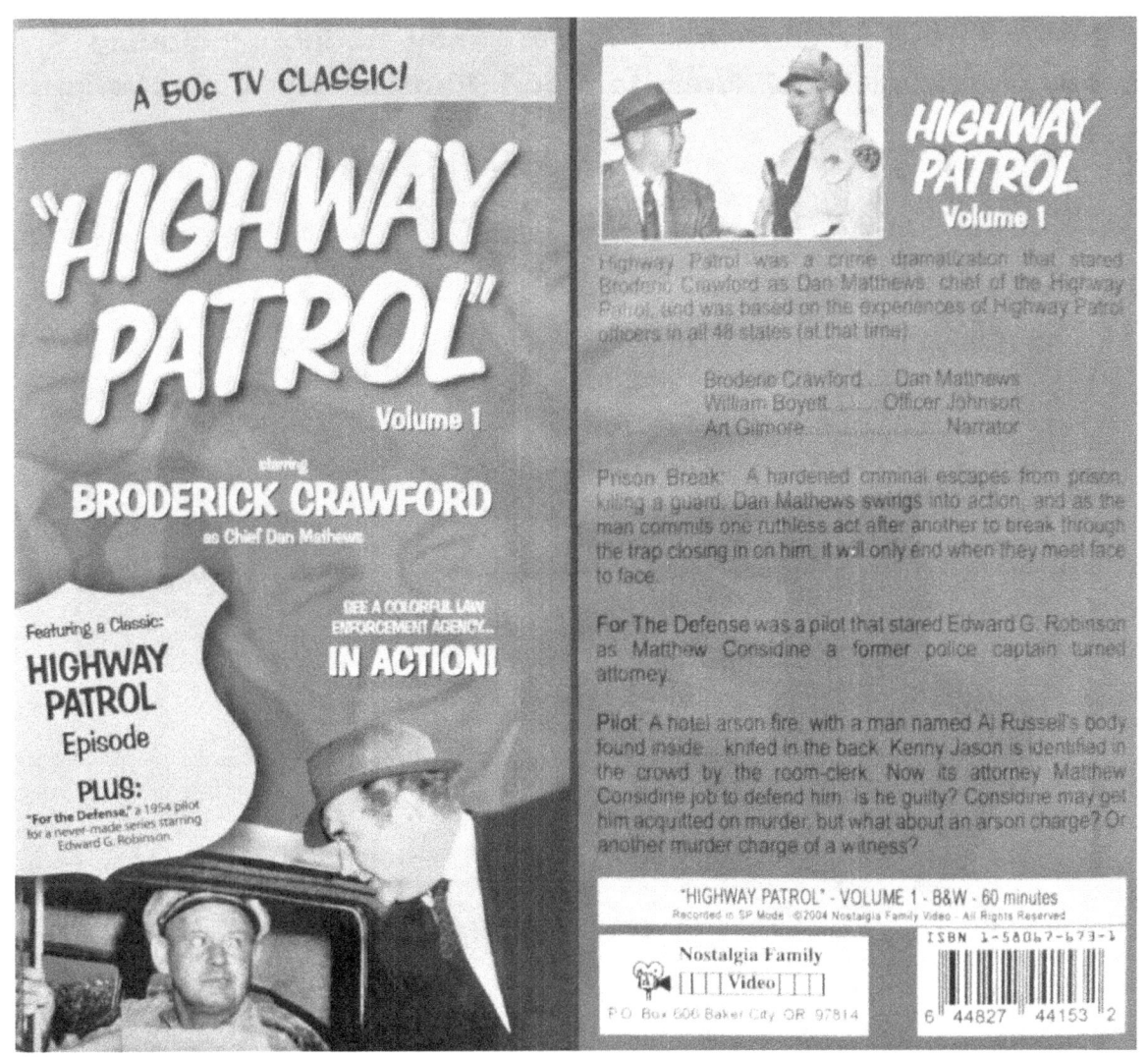

Box cover for *Highway Patrol* on VHS cassette from 2004 (Photo Goltz Collection).

Below: British-made *Highway Patrol* candy products including candy cigarettes for children, ten-four! (Photos Goltz Collection).

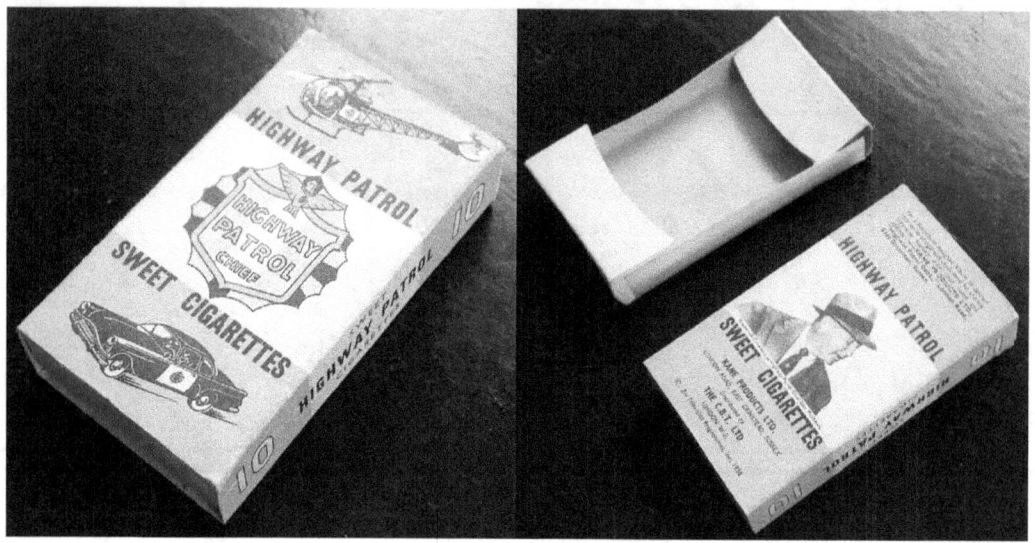

ZIV-TV cast sheet and shooting schedule for 'Hostage Copter', with Barbara Eden in her first acting role (Photos Goltz Collection).

```
                                            January 2, 1957

                        CAST SHEET
                        HIGHWAY PATROL 72B
                        (Revised 1/3/57)

    DAN MATHEWS         BRODERICK CRAWFORD        HO 4-7171

    ED CAIN             BRAD TRUMBULL             CR 5-1023
                        Wilson       CR 4-5915

    TED ELLIS           RAY QUINN                 ST 7-4395
                        Seabury      CR 4-2210

    OFFICER WALTERS     STUART WHITMAN            GR 9-2631
                        Lance        CR 6-6014

    RALPH OWENS         GLEN DIXON                CR 6-6452
                        Shaw         BR 2-1011

    KATHY OWENS         BARBARA EDEN              HO 5-3166
                        Shurr        CR 4-8111

    WORKER              GUY PRESCOTT              OL 4-0642
                        Donaldson    OL 2-0355

    DRIVER              YVONNE WHITE              HO 5-8211
                        Winters      CR 4-6301

    OFFICER WICKS       JOE PATRIDGE              SY 3-8171
                        No Agent

    PILOT               ROY BOURGOIS

    PRODUCER            VERNON CLARK
    DIRECTOR            JACK HERZBERG
    1st ASSISTANT       EDDIE STEIN
    2nd ASSISTANT       DON SCHIFF

    so
```

PRODUCER: ZIV TELEVISION PROGRAMS, INC.
DIRECTOR: JACK HERZBERG
ASST.DIR: ED STEIN

B R E A K D O W N

HIGHWAY PATROL #72B

1ST DAY - THURS., JAN. 3, 1957 - LOCATION - LEAVING 7 AM

    Vicinity Mulholland 16500 block - phone Fire Station #2 - Stanley 7-1428

2ND DAY - FRI., JAN. 4, 1957 - LOCATION - LEAVING 7 AM

    12040 Riverside Dr. - P.O. 3-9021 - Then return to Mulholland Dr.

3RD DAY - MONDAY, JAN. 7, 1957 - LOCATION - LEAVING 7 AM

    Vicinity Mulholland 16500 block - Phone Fire Station #2 - Stanley 7-1428

1ST DAY - THURS., 1/3/57 - LOCATION

    EXT. HIGHWAY - COPTER LANDS NEAR SEDAN - TAG - DAY - 11 scs. - 1-1/2 pg.   22

    Scs: 165, 166, 167, 168, 169, 170, 171, 172, 173, 174, 175
    Convertible comes to halt - Ellis out over wheel - copter lands and Mathews and Walters run in to the convertible - Cain tries to take a pot shot but the officers are too quick and get him first - officers look at the two bodies and then they move back to their copter - copter takes off for the FADE OUT.

CAST	VEHICLES
Pilot	A sedan
Cain	Helicopter
Ellis	
Dan	
Walters	

1ST DAY - THURS., 1/3/57 - LOCATION

    INT. COPTER - DAY - 20 scs. - 2-1/2 pgs.   12

    Scs: 47, 51, 53, 55 - Walters, Mathews and pilot in flight - Walters talks on mike to hq. and then to Wicks in HP sedan below.

                                    (CONTINUED)

Ever-lovely screen star Ruta Lee appeared in the 1957 episode of *Highway Patrol*, "Armored Car". In an interview with the author (Schiller) she said, "I'm always asked about either my first acting job as a teenager on *Superman* with handsome George Reeves or *Highway Patrol* with Broderick Crawford. He was such a kind, dear, sweet man to work with. He liked to play the tough guy all the time but he really was a sweet pussycat! I remember doing that show with Brod and being up in a helicopter for the first time in my life!" Ms. Lee also co-starred with Broderick Crawford in a 1964 episode of *Burke's Law*.

Gorgeous movie starlet Helene Stanton, who starred in the 'B' films, *Jungle Moon Men* (1955) with Johnny Weissmuller, and the seminal monster epic *The Phantom From 10,000 Leagues* (1955), decorated a cracker-jack, first season episode of *Highway Patrol*, 'Blast Area Copter'. Ms. Stanton is the mother of television's Dr. Drew Pinsky, who starred on the popular television series *Dr. Drew Live*.

Below: Helene Stanton's contract with ZIV-TV (Photo Goltz Collection).

Many wonderful actors appeared on *Highway Patrol,* including the late Jeanne Cooper, a forty-year veteran of the CBS daytime serial *The Young And The Restless.* The glamorous actress had the title role in a 1956 episode, *"Girl Bandit".* She enjoyed a long career playing hard-boiled, tough dames on the screen and was the mother of actor Corbin Bernsen. In an interview with the author (Schiller), Jeanne Cooper said, "Oh my God! I remember making that show with Broderick Crawford. He was a wonderful actor and great star. I just loved working with that man!" She died in 2013.

Future film and television star Barbara Eden made her screen debut in the title role of a 1957 episode of *Highway Patrol*, *"Hostage Copter"* In an interview with the author (Schiller), the enchanting Barbara Eden said, "That was my first job as an actress! It was such an honor to work with a great actor like Broderick Crawford, so I stayed very quiet and watched him all the time. He was a very nice man."

Robert Dix is excellent in a 1957 episode, *"Careless Cop"* as a police officer trying to clear himself of a false criminal accusation. In an interview with the author (Schiller), he said "I remember that episode. Broderick Crawford was great to work with, a complete professional. I learned a lot from him!" Robert Dix and Broderick Crawford also co-starred in a cheapjack motorcycle 'Drive-In' epic, *Hell's Bloody Devils* (1970) directed by Al Adamson (who was mysteriously murdered in 1995).

Paul Burke, who later starred on the hit series *Naked City* (1960-1963), played Officer Halsey in *"Prison Break".* Burke also co-starred with Broderick Crawford in the strange, little seen Philippine film production *Maharlika* (1969). Prolific TV western actor Joe Patridge appeared as a *Highway Patrol* officer in nine episodes. In an interview with author Gary Goltz, Patridge said "Broderick Crawford was razor sharp on learning his lines, a real pro and a great guy!"

In an interview with his friend and colleague (co-author Gary Goltz) veteran movie stuntman and Judo champion Gene LeBell said that he recalled doing occasional stunts for Broderick Crawford on *Highway Patrol* and "Brod was always real nice guy to work with. He was a pro!" Broderick Crawford and Gene LeBell worked together again in the under-rated, made-for-TV movie *The Challenge* (1970).

Film and television star Brett Halsey appeared in two episodes of *Highway Patrol*, 'Temptation' (1957), and 'Breath of A Child' (1958). In an e-mail to the author (Schiller) Brett Halsey wrote, "I was always envious of actors like Broderick Crawford who with their photographic memory, could give a glance at his script and have it letter perfect. In 1976 we were both guest stars on the TV series *City of Angels*. I couldn't help watching Crawford as he sat quietly observing. I had the impression that I was watching a large cat, silently poised to pounce on its victim. He had been sitting conserving his energy for when it was important. It wasn't as though he stole the scene from the stars – it was more like he buried them with his massive talent!"

Film star and director Clint Eastwood appeared in a 1956 episode, 'Motorcycle A', as a biker youth threatened by a shotgun-wielding owner of a diner. He won the role because he could ride a motorcycle which saved the budget-minded ZIV the cost of a stunt double! In an interview with the author Guy Daniels said "Clint Eastwood always spoke fondly of working with Broderick Crawford on *Highway Patrol*." Eastwood and Broderick Crawford would work together again for an unforgettable two-part episode of *Rawhide* (1964).

Broderick Crawford listens as motorcycle pals John Compton and Clint Eastwood report a crime in the 1956 episode *"Motorcycle A"*.

Below: Clint Eastwood's ZIV-TV contract. Since he knew how to ride a motorcycle, he also saved ZIV-TV the expensive cost of a stuntman for episode *'Motorcycle A'*. Followed by a page from the screenplay (Photos Goltz Collection).

```
                    ZIV TELEVISION PROGRAMS, INC.
                 7324 SANTA MONICA BOULEVARD, HOLLYWOOD, CALIF.

                            STANDARD CONTRACT

Date of Agreement        Name                      COMPENSATION AND ADVANCES
  2/3/55                   CLINT EASTWOOD
Date Employment Starts   Address                   Daily Picture Rate  $ 80.00
                           4020 Arch Dr. N. Hwyd.  Single Picture
Weather Condition        Phone No.                  —3 Days
                           SU 2-2473               Weekly
Time on Set              Part                      Advance for
                           JOE KEELEY              Television
Wardrobe or Make-up Call Production                Re-runs             $
                         No. HP 28B
                         Title                     Advance for
                           HIGHWAY PATROL          Theatrical Use      $

                                                   Total              $ 80.00
```

This agreement covers the employment of the above named Player by

ZIV TELEVISION PROGRAMS, INC. in the production and at the rate of compensation set forth above and is subject to and shall include, for the benefit of the Player and the Producer, all of the applicable provisions and conditions contained or provided for in the Producer-Screen Actors Guild Codified Basic Agreement of 1952 and the Television Supplement thereto; and the Player warrants and agrees that the Player is now a member in good standing of Screen Actors Guild, Inc., and will remain so for the duration of this employment.

The Player hereby grants to ZIV TELEVISION PROGRAMS, INC., its successors and assigns forever, all rights of every kind and character whatsoever, without limitation, throughout the world in and to all results and proceeds of the Player's services rendered hereunder, including but not limited to, the rights to reproduce, use, perform, exhibit, broadcast and dispose of, in any manner or through any means or medium whatsoever, whether now known or hereafter devised, any pictures, likenesses or reproductions of the Player, his poses, acts, plays, performances and appearances, and any recordation or reproductions of the Player's voice, and of all instrumental, musical or other sound effects produced by the Player, together with the right to display and use the foregoing and the Player's name and likeness for commercial and advertising purposes.

Producer shall have the unlimited right to re-run the film on television or release the film theatrically. If the film is re-run on television in the United States or exhibited theatrically in the United States or Canada, the Player will receive therefor the minimum additional compensation prescribed by the Television Supplement above mentioned; and amounts, if any, appearing as advances in the appropriate blanks above and paid to the Player during his employment shall be credited against such minimum additional compensation.

                                           ZIV TELEVISION PROGRAMS, INC.

     Clint Eastwood   By   Nina Vine
         Player   Casting Director

Release No. 10274
Production No. 28B

HIGHWAY PATROL - "Motorcycle" by Don Brinkley

CAST:

Dan Mathews	Broderick Crawford
Joe Wesley	Clint Eastwood
Nick Keeley	John Compton
Bernie Sills	Jack Edwards
Mrs. Sills	Paula Houston
Ralph Hogan	Steve Masino
Dorsey	Jay Douglas
Officer #1	Sandy Sanders
Narrator	Art Gilmore

CREW:

Cameraman	Curt Fetters	Set Dec.	-	Bruce MacDonald
Production Supervisor	Vernon Clark	Property	-	Max Pittman
Director	Lambert Hillyer	Script	-	Larry Lund
Assistant Director	Willard Kirkham			
Sound Mixer	Garry Harris			
Sound Editor	Monroe Martin			
Film Editor	John B. Woelz			

SYNOPSIS:

Eight months ago, the tiny town of Sunland Park was raided and ransacked by a renegade motorcycle club. Property damage was high, and BERNIE SILLS' wife was crippled. The town, and Bernie, still simmer in their bitterness when JOE WESLEY and NICK KEELEY -- members of an accredited AMA cycle club -- stop there for something to eat. Bernie orders them out at gunpoint; a fight ensues. When a Highway Patrol officer gives chase, he is killed in the resultant accident, caused by a TRUCK DRIVER failing to stop at an intersection. Bernie and his wife testify to MATHEWS that Keeley and West caused all the trouble, and are therefore responsible for the death of the officer. Sills even tries to turn Keeley's and Wesley's own cycle club against them. Mathews sends two HP Officers into Sunland Park, dressed as motorcycle bums. The bitter scene is repeated as Bernie again tries to run them out at gunpoint. This time, though, Mathews is a witness to the truth.

SHOOTING TIME:

Start Photography 12/7/55
Finish Photography 12/8/55

Movie serial king Kirk Allyn, who was the screen's first *Superman* in two serials (in 1948 and 1950), and also starred in the title role for the serial based on comic book hero *Blackhawk* (1952), appeared as a patrol officer and sergeant in two episodes (his police uniform barely contains his still-muscular *Superman* physique).

Striking beauty Diane Brewster who played second-grade teacher Miss Canfield on *Leave It To Beaver* (1957-1963) and for the comeback series the *New Leave It To Beaver* (1983-1986), also appeared in the pilot episode of *Highway Patrol*, 'Prison Break' as a dispatcher. Brewster is remembered for playing the iconic role of Helen Kimble, Dr. Richard Kimble's (David Janssen) star-crossed wife on the hit TV series *The Fugitive* (1963-1967) including the spectacular finale episode. Pat Conway, who later starred in ZIV-TV's rugged Western hit series *Tombstone Territory* (1957-1960) for 91 episodes, also appeared in the first season episode of *Highway Patrol*, 'Radioactive'.

William 'Bill' Boyett co-starred with Broderick Crawford in *Highway Patrol* (1955-1959) for sixty-five episodes first as Officer Johnson and later as Sergeant Ken Williams. The producers of *Highway Patrol* actually broke their no major co-stars rule by giving Broderick Crawford a regular co-star to help carry the heavy load for this fast-shot television series. In an interview with the author (Goltz), Guy Daniels stated that Paul Burke was also asked to be a regular on *Highway Patrol* during the first season but had turned it down. This would definitely have been inconsistent with ZIV-TV's policy of having no regulars until the last season. In an interview with the author (Goltz) Bill Boyett said that they were considering Stuart Whitman (excellent as Sergeant Walters) but Boyett said "I told them, 'Hey what about me?' and they agreed on the spot!" Boyett, who previously played Officer Johnson, was promoted to Sergeant Ken Williams. It was a lucky break for both of them since Stuart Whitman signed a contract with Twentieth Century Fox and became a film star. In an interview with the author (Goltz), Guy Daniels said "I can barely remember Clint Eastwood on the series but I vividly recall Stuart Whitman who was an excellent actor. He did I think at least six episodes on the show and a tremendous asset." For the record Stuart Whitman appeared in thirteen episodes of *Highway Patrol*, and later co-starred with Broderick Crawford in the films *The Decks Ran Red* (1958) and *Convicts 4* (1962). Whitman also made sure to have his old friend Brod Crawford on his own Western series *Cimarron Strip* for a great 1968 episode entitled *'The Blue Moon Train'*. Ironically Broderick Crawford's final performance on film before bad health ended his 45 year film career, was again with Stuart Whitman was on the hit series *Simon & Simon* in a 1982 season 2, episode 6 entitled 'Rough Rider Rides Again'. Bill Boyett had served in the U.S. Navy in the South Pacific during World War Two. Afterward he attended the University of Southern California and pursued acting. With his broad shoulders, tall physique, square jaw, and commanding voice, Boyett was a natural playing one police officer after another. Jack Webb cast him as a cop in both the original and revival series of *Dragnet* and Boyett also co-starred as Sergeant MacDonald on *Adam-12* (1968-1975). Bill Boyett also starred in several, grisly, traffic safety films as a fictional state trooper for the National Transportation Safety Board in the 1960's. While filming the last season of *Highway Patrol*, Broderick Crawford gifted William Boyett with a Rolex watch that was engraved, "To Bill, Ten-4, Brod Crawford". He treasured the watch his entire life. William Boyett retired after a long career and died in 2004. His *Adam-12* co-star Kent McCord attended the funeral. The author (Goltz) recalled riding with Bill Boyett in the '10-4 Day Parade' in his authentic 1955 Buick, Highway Patrol squad car. Boyett donned the soft uniform cap from the series and was cheered by crowds all along the way! In an interview with the author (Goltz), CHP Technical Advisor Frank Runyon said "Bill Boyett was a hell of an actor and really knew how to play a policeman!"

Bill Boyett, in full *Highway Patrol* uniform as Sgt. Kenneth Williams relaxes on the set between takes (Photo Goltz Collection).

Bill Boyett's badge with a personally inscribed publicity photo with Broderick Crawford (Photo Goltz Collection).

Scene from 1959 episode *'Expose'* with Broderick Crawford, future comic TV star Ted Knight playing it straight, and Bill Boyett (Photo Goltz Collection).

Below: Professional portrait of Broderick Crawford personally inscribed to his pal Bill Boyett (Photo Courtesy Jean Boyett).

**Autographed late professional photo of William Boyett
(Photo Goltz Collection).**

Character actor Terry Frost co-starred on *Highway Patrol* for twenty episodes (1955-1957) as Mathews' uniformed sergeant. Frost acted on nearly all the ZIV television series including *I Led Three Lives*, *Bat Masterson*, and *Science Fiction Theatre*. In a sparkling 1991 interview for *Film Fax* magazine with author Jan Alan Henderson, *"Riding the Range with A B-Western Bad Man"* Frost said, "Broderick Crawford was a great guy. Brod and I used to rehearse our scenes together, and you know with him he never gave you a cue. In the theater, you learned to handle that, you anticipate the other actor. For me, it was no problem. You could tell with Broderick just by watching him, the way he walked and moved when he'd finish his lines, so we worked well together. Now the studio ZIV gave him a chauffeur to drive him. There was a cast and crew bus that ran us in and out from the various locations by his apartment in the *Sunset Towers* on the Sunset Strip, so before quitting time, he'd send the chauffeur to go pick up cold cuts and caviar. I'd drive my car to his apartment and then ride up with him in the limo. We'd come back on the studio bus and be dropped off at his place, go up and have drinks and hors d'oeuvres! This aggravated my wife [laughs] because she'd be waiting dinner. Brod really knew how to lay out a spread!" Terry Frost and Broderick Crawford also decorate the box cover for the *Highway Patrol* Halco toy holster outfit. Terry Frost, who died in 1993, left the industry to become a successful travel agent. Besides circling the globe several times, Frost wrote several popular travel books.

Actress (and future daytime serial television producer) Judy Lewis starred in a last season 1959 *Highway Patrol* episode 'Narcotics Racket'. Officially Judy was the legally adopted daughter of film star Loretta Young. However in fact she was actually Loretta Young's biological daughter with Clark Gable, the result of a love affair during the making of *Call of The Wild* (1935). Broderick Crawford, who had co-starred with Judy Lewis' mother Loretta Young in the hit comedy *Eternally Yours* (1939) and with her father Clark Gable in the robust Western classic *Lone Star* (1952), was delighted to work with the rookie actress who acquitted herself well on *Highway Patrol*. The delicate subject of Judy's parentage was common knowledge in Hollywood but Loretta Young closely guarded her daughter from the truth for another twenty years after the *Highway Patrol* episode. Broderick Crawford knew the secret but discreetly kept it from the pretty young actress whom he liked. Judy Lewis, who later became a psychologist, died in 2011.

Frank Miller (billed as Frank Warren) played Officer Simpson on *Highway Patrol* in the third and fourth seasons. Miller became close friends with Broderick Crawford and loved him so much that he named his son Broderick. Prior to becoming an actor, Frank Miller was a rugged Longshoreman. While filming *Highway Patrol*, Miller and the rough and tumble Broderick Crawford often preferred the blue-collar camaraderie of a local Longshoreman's bar over the regular Hollywood saloons! The Oscar-winning Crawford even gave Frank Miller one of the fedora hats he wore on the series. The author (Goltz) offered an absurdly high price for the battered fedora but Frank Miller refused to part with his memento of beloved dear friend Broderick Crawford for any amount.

Herbert L. Strock was the genius and creative force behind *Highway Patrol* and was determined to make the series the blockbuster success it became. It was Strock who gave the series its trademark documentary look, with plenty of fast-moving action. It was also Strock who directed the best episodes of *Highway Patrol* including the thrilling pilot episode *"Prison Break"*. Herbert Strock was a big proponent of adding helicopters which pushed up costs but gave the series its most riveting and exciting episodes. National Helicopter provided ZIV-TV with the flying machines (Bell 47's), and the licensed pilots (Strock also directed the 1955 Korean War film *Battle Taxi* for Ivan Tors-United Artists starring Sterling Hayden that featured the military version helicopter Bell 47 used in *Highway Patrol* or H-13 Sioux used in the popular *M.A.S.H.* television series.) In the episode *'Hostage Family Copter'* Wayne Heffley, who played Officer Dennis, was afraid of going up in a flimsy helicopter with no doors! In an interview with the author (Goltz), Heffley said "Broderick Crawford took one look at me and said with a smile, 'Don't worry if it falls the company (ZIV) will give you a great funeral!'" On another occasion Heffley was grief-stricken over the recent death of his father and showed-up at ZIV studios slightly hung-over. Heffley said that the producers nearly dismissed him without pay and he never forgot that Broderick Crawford stepped forward to say "If he goes home then I'm going home too!" Frank Runyon told author (Goltz), "Broderick Crawford did all of his own stunts on the show and he always went up in the helicopter. He once tried to get me to go up in one and I told him to go to hell! [laughs] Actually CHP never used aircraft to identify units on the ground. They were used mainly for rescues and the pilot was an armed uniformed officer." He also said "One time Herb Strock, Brod and I were out on location and with the second trio of choppers it was hot as hell out there. Between shots Brod took off his jacket and forgot to put it back on again when the cameras rolled. It wouldn't match the scene and [laughs] Herb was afraid to tell Brod so he asked me to do it! I told Brod that he needed to put it on the jacket but he didn't like it!" Runyon also said that the star often lost patience with Herbert Strock's artsy directing, "Brod never liked how Herb used all these gadgets for artistic shots like shooting through a tire! He was a real D.W. Griffith type and Brod preferred a simple plain picture without delays! He was annoyed at Brock because he wanted to get it done and leave early." According to Guy Daniels in an interview with author (Goltz), "Herb Strock was considered a very artsy director by Bernard Caldwell who would have preferred a less exciting but more-by-the-book police show." Ironically it was Herbert Strock's ambitious, professional direction and motion-picture camera shots with quick-cutting editing that made *Highway Patrol* a cut above routine police shows and another reason why the series still seems so fresh today.

Classic *Highway Patrol* helicopter shot with Broderick Crawford. Note: Herbert Strock realized that aircraft would add excitement and thrills to the series (Photo Goltz Collection).

Sales brochure of Bell Helicopters, the supplier of helicopters for the *Highway Patrol* series (Photo Goltz Collection).

Herbert Strock directs Broderick Crawford and pilot Roy Bourgois in a scene with the Bell 47 helicopter (Photo Goltz Collection).

Exciting helicopter shot of Chief Dan Mathews flying to the rescue, in a photo autographed by Broderick Crawford to pal Verne Clark (Photo Goltz Collection.)

Herbert Strock told the author (Goltz) the he always locked horns with the budget-minded John Sinn over getting more professional and expensive equipment to film the series. Strock advised National Helicopter pilot Roy Bourgeois to apply for a Screen Actors Guild (SAG) union card since he had a few lines in the episode. This resulted in another battle with the ZIV money-man Mr. Sinn, who now had to pay the pilot a higher salary! At ZIV-TV Herb Strock did everything including directing, producing, and screenwriting many of the studio's television series. He began working as a director of Fox newsreels until World War Two began. Then he served in the U.S. Army's Ordinance Motion Picture Division. In the 1950's Herbert L. Strock began directing television including the first episode of the original *Dragnet* series without official credit (taken by Jack Webb whom Strock did not enjoy working for). Strock recalled to the author (Goltz) that Jack Webb was such a fastidious, knit-picker that he ordered the lettering painted on the doors of the police station sets re-painted because they were not exactly like the lettering script at LAPD headquarters! Daniels admitted "I didn't save a lot of stuff from *Highway Patrol* because it just wasn't the happiest period of my life. Now I really enjoyed shooting film for the show *You Asked For It* for ten years!" Herbert Strock and Broderick Crawford became close friends. In an interview with the author (Goltz) Strock recalled an incident in the Formosa Café when a tall Stetson-wearing Texan in cowboy hat and a big belt buckle challenged the Oscar-winning actor to a fight. Without saying a word, Crawford suddenly hit the cowboy in the gut and knocked him unconscious flat. He also badly cut his fist on the cowboy's fancy belt buckle!

Strock eventually directed twelve feature films, primarily low-budget science-fiction and horror movies, including several for American-International Pictures, *Blood of Dracula* (1957), *I Was a Teenage Frankenstein* (1957), and *How to Make a Monster* (1958). Herbert Strock is best known today for directing the low-budget, United Artists science-fiction color film *Gog* (1954), which has since become a cult movie classic! In the early 1960's Strock was a house director for Warner Brothers Television and directed episodes of their series including *Maverick, Cheyenne, 77 Sunset Strip*. Strock's reputation as a producer/director was of being a meticulous professional. After a long career Herbert Strock retired in 1980. In 2000 he published the highly-regarded book *Picture Perfect* that became a how-to guide on filmmaking for many film school students. Herbert L. Strock died in 2005 but is remembered by several generations of fans of schlocky horror films and for *Highway Patrol*.

David Rose (under the pseudonym Ray Llewellyn) composed the superb, unforgettable theme music of *Highway Patrol*. It is Rose's riveting music that grabs the audience's attention in the show's opening credits with jarring, warning notes. The music then changes into a courageous march dedicated to the men and women who protect the nation's highways. It was so commanding that if you heard it in another part of the house, you'd run to the living room to catch the show! Rose scored background music for the episodes, including musical bridges for commercial breaks. In Great Britain, the *Highway Patrol* theme became a hit 45-RPM as recorded by Cyril Stapleton and his Orchestra. Earle Hagen, proving that imitation is the sincerest form of flattery, composed a theme mimicking *Highway Patrol* for Don Knott's Deputy Barney Fife character on the *Andy Griffith Show*. Rose's musical talent and genius put him in great demand with Hollywood stars. Rose also married and divorced two of them, Martha Raye and Judy Garland. For twenty years David Rose was the musical director for the beloved *Red Skelton Show* (1951-1971). He also composed the comedian's trademark theme music *Holiday for Strings* that became a big hit for Spike Jones and his City Slickers Orchestra. Ironically Rose's biggest career hit was *The Stripper*, which was actually just a filler or B-Side of a 7" vinyl with *Ebb Tide* on the A-Side. *The Stripper* hit number 1 on the Billboard chart and earned a gold record in sales for David Rose! He later composed theme music for the hit series *High Chaparral* (1967-1971) and *Bonanza* (1959-1972 for which he won an Emmy Award for his score). For Michael Landon, Rose wrote the theme music and scored *Little House On the Prairie* (1974-1984 for which he won two more Emmy Awards) and *Highway to Heaven* (1984-1989). David Rose died in 1990.

London Records' hit 45 RPM recording of Ray Llewellyn's (David Rose) *Highway Patrol Theme* music by Cyril Stapleton and his Orchestra (Photo Goltz Collection).

Art Gilmore's clear, sober voice narrates all 156 episodes of *Highway Patrol,* adding a documentary touch to the series. Gilmore told the author (Goltz) that he only ran into Broderick Crawford one time in the men's room at ZIV Studios even though they were both the only ones with roles in all 156 episodes! Gilmore, a graduate of Washington State University, was originally a successful radio staff announcer in Hollywood, California. He was also under contract to the Warner Brothers studio where his golden voice was used on and off camera in films to great effect (including several dozen of the studio's popular *Joe McDoakes* comedy shorts series starring George O'Hanlon). He also narrated Jack Webb's *Dragnet* series (both the original hit from the 1950's and the popular revival in the late 1960's) and played an occasional role on the series as a police captain. Art Gilmore narrated many theatrical trailers (previews) for countless Hollywood films and was the staff announcer on the *Red Skelton Show* for 17 years. He was also the staff announcer for Garner Ted Armstrong's conservative syndicated religious television series *The World Tomorrow*. Art Gilmore died in 2010. At his funeral services the author (Goltz) recited Art Gilmore's famed, iconic *Highway Patrol* introduction to the delight of all the family and friends in attendance. Art Gilmore was also the founding President of the Pacific Pioneer Broadcasters (PPB) professional organization. At their Annual Luncheon, the PPB presents to a broadcasting legend the Art Gilmore Career Achievement Award! On top of that Washington State University also presents the Annual Art Gilmore Broadcasting Award in his honor!

By the fourth and last season of *Highway Patrol*, the series was practically a regular cop show with Dan Mathews and his HP officers solving crime cases that normally fall under the jurisdiction of municipal and county law enforcement agencies. The new California Highway Commissioner Bradford Crittenden had no love for the ZIV-TV series and withdrew CHP support. The producers stopped using badges, uniform shoulder patches and officer cap shields like the CHP (the same patch with the words 'California' and 'Eureka' the state motto removed while retaining the California seal and bear from the state flag) in favor of plain generic badges that simply said *Highway Patrol*. In all fairness, *Highway Patrol* would never have become a television success if the series confined itself to authentic traffic cases.

In 1959, *Highway Patrol* ended its four-season run with the episode "*Bank Messenger*". ZIV had wanted a fifth season in color and had even planned a *Highway Patrol* motion picture. Frank Runyon told the author (Goltz) "The show was never cancelled. Brod just got tired of it after 156 episodes in four years! He said that he had it! It could have gone on a few more years. I was tired of it too! I had never quit my job with CHP. Instead I used all my vacation time, sick leave, and personal time to work on the show. Still, I was sad when Brod ended the show but it had to happen sometime!" Broderick Crawford, who was also afraid of typecasting, declined season 5 and instead returned to motion pictures. He accepted financially lucrative film offers in Italy and Yugoslavia (for independent producers who knew his star status guaranteed an American release). During the run of the series Crawford starred in villain roles for three major films, *Between Heaven and Hell* (1956) for 20th Century Fox, and two for MGM *Fastest Gun Alive* (1956), and *The Decks Ran Red* (1958).

1956 Airport photo for press release of Broderick Crawford arriving at New York's Idlewild (now JFK) airport, being greeted by flight attendant Mary Rae Keefe. (Photo Goltz Collection).

Broderick Crawford's enduring fame from *Highway Patrol* was documented in an article for the June 1997 *Motor Trend* magazine, entitled *"55 Highway Patrol Buick: Recreating the Most Famous Cop Car in Television History"* by John Pearley Huffman. It showcases California healthcare industry executive/Black Belt judo instructor and co-author Gary Goltz's restored vintage 1955 Buick Century that was customized into a replica of the *Highway Patrol* squad car. It's authentic down to the last detail, including a working siren and a stereo sound system that plays the theme music. Dan Mathews' radio call numbers 21-50 are on the license plates. Goltz maintains the patrol car in absolutely pristine condition, and drives it in parades, car shows, and California Highway Patrol retiree days. Until 2012 Broderick Crawford's late son Kelly was an honored passenger. Goltz, Kelly Crawford, and the *Highway Patrol* car were mobbed by cheering spectators who remember the series and Broderick Crawford with great affection. Goltz, a lifelong fan of the series, used his own extensive background material to build a website dedicated to *Highway Patrol* and Broderick Crawford; www.highwaypatroltv.com. It contains hundreds of photos, sound bites, memorabilia and unseen film clips from *Highway Patrol* plus Broderick Crawford's many film/TV appearances. In the site's 'Guest Book', hundreds of police officers have posted their love for the series that inspired them to pursue a career in law enforcement. In the *Motor Trend* article, California Highway Patrol Adviser Officer Frank Runyon (CHP Badge #475 and called 'Pappy' with great affection by everyone on the series and the CHP) said of Broderick Crawford's death in 1986, "I sure liked working with Brod. He was a straight-shooting guy. I called up Ed Gomez, the district supervisor and a good friend of mine, and fifteen motorcycle cops showed up. Boy, they were spit and polished. That man put highway patrol on the map. He did nothing but good for us."

Frank Runyon was a distinguished police officer with CHP and was the first officer to carry teddy bears in the police cars to comfort children in need (now standard). Runyon was first an officer with the Los Angeles Police Force from 1938 until 1942 when he joined the California Highway Patrol. In an interview with the author (Goltz) Runyon said "I always wanted to be a policeman from the time I can remember, my whole life!" During the filming of the first episode, Runyon saw that the actors playing officers had incorrectly handcuffed the suspects with their hands front in a clear-cut violation of all police safety procedures. From then on he insisted that criminals always be handcuffed with their hands behind their back! Runyon said "Most of the CHP officers watched *Highway Patrol* and thought it was great! That the way it was back then to be a cop! Today after losing too many good officers we have strict felony procedures and regulations. California Highway Patrol really just does traffic control and safety with very few criminal cases but back then that was what the public wanted to see on television!" Runyon said "I was paid a salary for the show because Bernard Caldwell said I was getting too much overtime. ZIV wanted me to stay and I named a high figure and they accepted it! [laughs] I wished I had asked for more! Back then I was getting $75.00 a day which was only half of what the LAPD technical advisor got, $150.00 a day over at *Dragnet*!" Runyon was also the pioneering founder of the *'Asphalt Arabs',* the original and unofficial fraternal organization for members of the CHP and their families. During the run of the series Frank Runyon and Broderick Crawford became close drinking pals and loved to frequent taverns and restaurants in Long Beach. Runyon laughed as he recalled to the author (Goltz) that his wife didn't approve of him spending so much time with his buddy Broderick Crawford! One story he told to author (Goltz) regarding the episode *"Human Bomb"*, "Brod was holding in his hand the dead man's switch and his line was 'What shall I tell the people?' I whispered a vulgar comment in Brod's ear and he actually said it for the line! That broke up the set with laughter!" Runyon said "I usually rode out to the location in my CHP car with Brod. Now one time I turned on the siren and lights and pulled over a driver. Suddenly Broderick Crawford hops out and reads the riot act to the driver, chewed him out great... The driver was silent but you could see it register on his face that he recognized Brod who never admitted whom he was! [laughs]" Runyon, always grateful to his friend, said "A couple of hungry CHP sergeants were jealous of my job as technical advisor, and tried to blackmail ZIV studio. They threatened to shut down production over the uniforms used by the officers on the show (then blue). I told Brod and he said to change our uniforms to grey and they would have nothing to say which is what ZIV did! Later they tried to cut me from the show but Brod Crawford was loyal and told ZIV to 'keep Runyon on, he's doing a great job for us!' Brod could look at a script, memorize all of it and then do more with just one page than any ham actor star could with the whole script! I really loved that guy and I sure miss him!" Frank S. Runyon died in 2005. At the funeral service both Gary Goltz and Ed Gomez gave eulogies. Afterward Gary Goltz pulled his '2150' Buick squad car from *Highway Patrol* to the front to lead the procession and in honor of Frank Runyon played the series trademark theme song through its massive speaker system.

During the third season of *Highway Patrol*, the California Highway Patrol Commissioner Bernard Caldwell was replaced by Bradford Crittenden. In 1958 Crittenden officially sanctioned the television subsidiary of Universal Pictures, Revue-TV to produce a pilot episode, *Roadblock* starring Michael 'Touch' Connors' as a genuine California Highway Patrol motorcycle officer. The show was a hybrid with elements of *Dragnet, Highway Patrol,* and the future hit series *CHiPs*. Although well-produced, the networks declined to green light the new series. Instead *Highway Patrol* continued its successful run for another season. Mike Connors would later star in his own series *Tightrope* (1959-1960) and his long-running hit CBS series *Mannix* (1967-1975). In a 1995 interview with the author (Goltz) Guy Daniels revealed "It was my job to go to Universal studios or MCA and offer the full cooperation, support, equipment and assistance of the California Highway Patrol in the making of a new series because Bernard Caldwell wanted it to be authentic. We shot two pilots at Universal. The first was an hour-long show with Jimmy Brown (James Brown) who starred as Lieutenant Rip Masters on *The Adventures Of Rin-Tin-Tin*. After that failed we shot the half-hour pilot with Mike Connors. In both shows Jimmy Brown and Mike Connors were playing uniformed members of the California Highway Patrol." Although *Roadblock* is widely available for viewing on *YouTube*, there is virtually no information on the first hour-long TV pilot which is buried somewhere in Universal's extensive film vaults.

Television talk show host David Letterman is also a big fan of Broderick Crawford and *Highway Patrol*. When actor Matthew Broderick appeared on the late-night *David Letterman Show*, the talk show host confused the names Dan Mathews and Broderick Crawford assuming the actor guest was related. Paul Shaffer's house band musician played the *Highway Patrol* theme music as a perplexed Matthew Broderick walked on stage to David Letterman shouting "Ten-4!" Matthew Broderick is actually the son of fine character actor James Broderick! *Highway Patrol* also enjoyed a large following in the black community. Popular comedian, game show host, and talk show host Steve Harvey was named by his parents Broderick Stephen Harvey in honor of their favorite film and TV star Broderick Crawford!

MGM-UA, which owns the *Highway Patrol* series, put the complete first season on DVD. Seasons two, three, and four were authorized by MGM-UA for release on DVD by TGG Direct, LLC. All four seasons of 156 episodes are pristine and beautiful to look at. The DVD boxes for seasons 2, 3, and 4 shows a facsimile of co-author Gary Goltz' car on the cover (an unauthorized DVD case actually had Goltz in his HP 1955 Buick instead of Broderick Crawford!)

Kelly Crawford established a legacy donation to *'California Highway Patrol 11-99 Foundation'*, a non-profit organization providing emergency benefits to California Highway Patrol employees and family members (11-99 is radio code for "Officer needs assistance."). The bequest is named *'The Broderick Crawford Benefits Program'*. The *California Highway Patrol 11-99 Foundation* actually used a clip from the third season *Highway Patrol* episode, *"Female Hitchhiker"* where Dan Mathews asks a citizen to call into his office and tell them '11-99'!

KELLY CRAWFORD
1951-2012

Kelly Crawford and his wife, Jean have been longtime friends of the 11-99 Foundation. Kelly was the son of Broderick Crawford, who played Chief Dan Mathews on the hit 1950s show "Highway Patrol." We admired Kelly and he will be greatly missed. We extend our condolences to Jean.

Kelly Crawford tribute in the *11-99 Foundation* newsletter (Photo Goltz Collection).

In 2003 at the annual *11-99 Foundation Banquet,* author Gary Goltz was approached by the Academy Award 'Best Actor' Oscar winner Jon Voight who introduced himself. He asked to meet Kelly Crawford because he spent his entire life as an actor admiring the distinguished stage and screen work fellow Oscar-winning actor Broderick Crawford. For Kelly Crawford it was a happy and proud memory. At the same banquet the master of ceremony Tom LaBonge asked his dollar-a-year-man, author Gary Goltz to come up and take a bow as Chief Dan Mathews! Wearing his trench-coat and fedora hat, Goltz began spouting his "10-Four" jargon when he was joined at the podium film and TV star Dan Aykroyd who recreated his dead-on-the money impersonation of Jack Webb's Sergeant Joe Friday from his 1987 *Dragnet* film! The pair bantered police jargon to thunderous laughter and applause from the audience on that golden evening.

Below: Photocopy of John Hart's contract with ZIV-TV. Hart previously replaced Clayton Moore as *The Lone Ranger* (1950-1953) for 52 episodes. (Photo Goltz Collection).

Date of Agreement October 1955	Name GUY WILLIAMS	COMPENSATION AND ADVANCES
Date Employment Starts	Address 1330 HARPER AVE., LA 46	Daily Picture Rate $80.00 Single Picture —3 Days
Weather Condition	Phone No. OL 4-1731	Weekly
Time on Set	Part DORSEY	Advance for Television
Wardrobe or Make-up Call	Production No. HP 18B	Re-runs $
	Title HIGHWAY PATROL	Advance for Theatrical Use $
		Total $80.00

This agreement covers the employment of the above named Player by ZIV TELEVISION PROGRAMS, INC. in the production and at the rate of compensation set forth above and is subject to and shall include, for the benefit of the Player and the Producer, all of the applicable provisions and conditions contained or provided for in the Producer-Screen Actors Guild Codified Basic Agreement of 1952 and the Television Supplement thereto; and the Player warrants and agrees that the Player is now a member in good standing of Screen Actors Guild, Inc., and will remain so for the duration of this employment.

The Player hereby grants to ZIV TELEVISION PROGRAMS, INC., its successors and assigns forever, all rights of every kind and character whatsoever, without limitation, throughout the world in and to all results and proceeds of the Player's services rendered hereunder, including but not limited to, the rights to reproduce, use, perform, exhibit, broadcast and dispose of, in any manner or through any means or medium whatsoever, whether now known or hereafter devised, any pictures, likenesses or reproductions of the Player, his poses, acts, plays, performances and appearances, and any recordation or reproductions of the Player's voice, and of all instrumental, musical or other sound effects produced by the Player, together with the right to display and use the foregoing and the Player's name and likeness for commercial and advertising purposes.

Producer shall have the unlimited right to re-run the film on television or release the film theatrically. If the film is re-run on television in the United States or exhibited theatrically in the United States or Canada, the Player will receive therefor the minimum additional compensation prescribed by the Television Supplement above mentioned; and amounts, if any, appearing as advances in the appropriate blanks above and paid to the Player during his employment shall be credited against such minimum additional compensation.

Photocopy of dashing Guy William's contract with ZIV-TV, who played an officer in four episodes of *Highway Patrol* (1956-1957), and appeared in four episodes of *Men of Annapolis* (1957-1958). Guy Williams was Walt Disney's choice to play the swashbuckling *Zorro* (1957-1961) for 82 episodes and two films (see photo below) He also starred as Professor Robinson in *Lost in Space* (1965-1968) for 84 episodes! (Photos Goltz Collection).

Below and Following Pages: ZIV-TV production location sheets for an episode of *Highway Patrol* (1957) (Photos Goltz Collection).

```
                                                February 20th, 1956

                          C A S T     S H E E T
                          HIGHWAY   PATROL
                               No.  34B


    DAN MATHEWS                  BRODERICK CRAWFORD........HO 4-7171

    MARGE WILLIS                 /HELENE STANTON...........SU 3-1934
                                   Barskin CR 6-6950

    JIM BARNABY                  /PAUL RICHARDS............OL 4-4301
                                   Salkow CR 5-4505

    FRED LESSER                  /TYLER MC VEY.............SU 3-4909
                                   Winters HO 2-1149

    SGT. COREY                   /MORGAN JONES.............OL 4-1253
                                   Weil  OL 2-2872

    COPTER PILOT                 /ROY BOURGOIS.............ST 6-9741
                                   No Agent

    NARRATOR                     ART GILMORE..............ST 4-0655


              *       *       *       *       *       *

              PRODUCER:                VERNON CLARK
              DIRECTOR:                LEW LANDERS
              FIRST ASSISTANT DIRECTOR: WILLARD KIRKHAM
              SECOND ASSISTANT DIRECTOR: BRUCE BILSON


    mr
```

PRODUCER: ZIV TV PROGRAMS, INC.
DIRECTOR: Lou Landers
ASS'T. DIR: Willard Kirkham

BREAKDOWN
Highway Patrol #34

1ST DAY - MONDAY, FEB. 20, 1956 - LOCATIONS:

Company will leave at 7:30 AM

1. Bronson Canyon, near tunnel area.
2. Al Kothe residence, 6001 Beachwood Dr., HO 9-3232

2ND DAY - TUESDAY, FEB. 21, 1956 - LOCATIONS:

1. Jim Woolvin - Richfield Station
2. Bronson Canyon Areas

3RD DAY - WEDNESDAY, FEB. 22, 1956 - LOCATIONS:

1. Al Kothe residence, 6001 Beachwood Dr., HO 9-3232

1ST DAY - MON., 2/20/56 - LOCATION

INT. COPTER IN FLIGHT (DIALOGUE) - DAY - 1 sc. - 3/4 pg.- 6

Sc. 27 - Dialogue about easy to clear roads.

CAST   CARS
Pilot (Roy)   Helicopter
Lesser
Mathews
(Corey's Voice)

1ST DAY - MON., 2/20/56 - LOCATION

INT. COPTER IN FLIGHT (DIALOGUE) - DAY - 7 sc. - 1/2 pg.- 11

Sc. 54 - C.U. on Mathews and Roy as Dan radios.

Sc. 59 - C.U. Dan on radio.

Sc. 71 - C.U. Dan with binoculars and checking his watch.

Sc. 73 - Dan scans area with binoculars. (V.O.)

Sc. 83 - Dan checks watch and grabs radio.

Sc. 85 - Dan looking down becomes curious, grabs binoculars.

(CONTINUED)

3/6/57

PRODUCER: ZIV TELEVISION PROGRAMS, INC.
DIRECTOR: JACK HERZBERG
ASST.DIR: ED STEIN

B R E A K D O W N

HIGHWAY PATROL - CHAP. #76B

1ST DAY - <u>THURS., MARCH 7, 1957</u> - LOCATION - Leaving 7:00 AM
(FOR CHATSWORTH)

Location progression:
1 - INT. & EXT. REST., 21824 Devonshire - DIA. 8-2335
    Mr. Berg
2 - STREET & GROCERY STORE - This vicinity
3 - INT. & EXT. RANCH - Mrs. Muellenbach,
    22231 Devonshire - DIA. 8-1945
4 - CHATSWORTH R.R. STATION
5 - HIGHWAY LOCATIONS - This vicinity

2ND DAY - <u>FRI., MARCH 8, 1957</u> - LOCATION - Leaving 7:00 AM
(FOR MULHOLLAND DRIVE -
VICINITY FIREHOUSE #2)

Locations: Streets and Highways between Beverly Glenn
and Firehouse #2 on Mulholland Drive

1ST DAY - THURS., MARCH 7, 1957 - STAGE

INT. RESTAURANT - DAY - 6 sc. 4 3/4 pg.   7

Sc. 39, 40 - Tony enters as Shirley and Wanda talk -
Shirley is getting off and Tony moves up to her and
tells her they are going on a picnic, etc., the girls
talk and then Shirley leaves with Tony.

Sc. 46, 47 - Killer enters cafe and asks for Shirley;
he talks to Wanda and quizzes her, then leaves.

Sc. 65, 66 - Dan enters to Wanda and introduces
himself - he asks questions about Tony and how he
was dressed etc. She tells him Shirley and Wanda
went on a picnic - Dan exits cafe.

<u>CAST</u>   <u>EXTRAS</u>
Tony   Customers
Shirley
Wanda
Killer
Dan (sc. 65)
  (3 pgs. later)

ZIV-TV production sheet for *Highway Patrol* cast commercial for Phiffer Beer (Photo Goltz Collection.)

Photo gallery of the entire fleet of *Highway Patrol* police cars, helicopters and motorcycles (Photo Goltz Collection).

Ziv Television Programs, Inc.
PRODUCTION DIRECT OPERATION REPORT

Series: Highway Patrol Prod. # 121 B Title: The Trap
Producer: Jack Herzberg Director: Bill Conrad
Starting date: 10/2/58 Estimated Shooting days: 2
Interior (which days): 10/3
Exterior (which days): 10/2
Film: [X] Plus-X [ ] Tri-X [ ] Other (specify)
Stock shots: [X] Yes [ ] No
Estimated travel time: _____ Make-Ready & shooting time: 6:30 am lvg.

CREW	NAME	No. Days	CREW	NAME	No. Days
1st Asst. Dir.	Bob Agnew	2	Electricians	Not set yet	2nd day
2nd Asst. Dir	Bill Poole	2		" " "	" "
1st Cameraman	Dick Rawlings	2		" " "	" "
2nd Cameraman	Ed Nugent	2			
1st Asst. Cam.	Jim Bell	2			
2nd Asst. Cam.	Harry May	1st day	Const. chief	Archie Hall	
Still Photog.	Jack Albin	" "	Set labor	Not set yet	2
Sound Mixer	Garry Harris	2	Greensman		
Recorder	Lloyd Hanks	2	Process proj.		
Boom man	John Erlinger	2	Animal trainers		
Cableman	Al Overton, Jr.	2nd day			
1st Co. Grip	Carl Miksch	2	Wranglers		
2nd Co. Grip	Earl Mussey	2			
3rd Grip	Not set yet	2nd day	Drivers	Ray Stoddard	1st day
Prop master	James Harris	2		Jess Hamilton	" "
Asst. Prop man	Martin Hershey	2		Larry Budman	" "
Dresser	Bruce MacDonald	2		Jerry Weinman	" "
Designer	Bob Kinoshita			Harry Dahlstrom	" "
Special effects				Jack Osborn	" "
Make-up man					
Wardrobe man	Jack Muhs	2			

ZIV-TV production sheet for the episode 'The Trap' (1959) of Highway Patrol directed by actor William Conrad. Ten years later Conrad and Broderick Crawford co-starred in a 1969 episode of The Name of The Game (Photo Goltz Collection).

1998 poster for the *Highway Patrol* Festival in Sierra Madre, California. In attendance were Herbert L. Strock, William Boyett, Frank Runyon, and Frank Miller (Photo Goltz Collection).

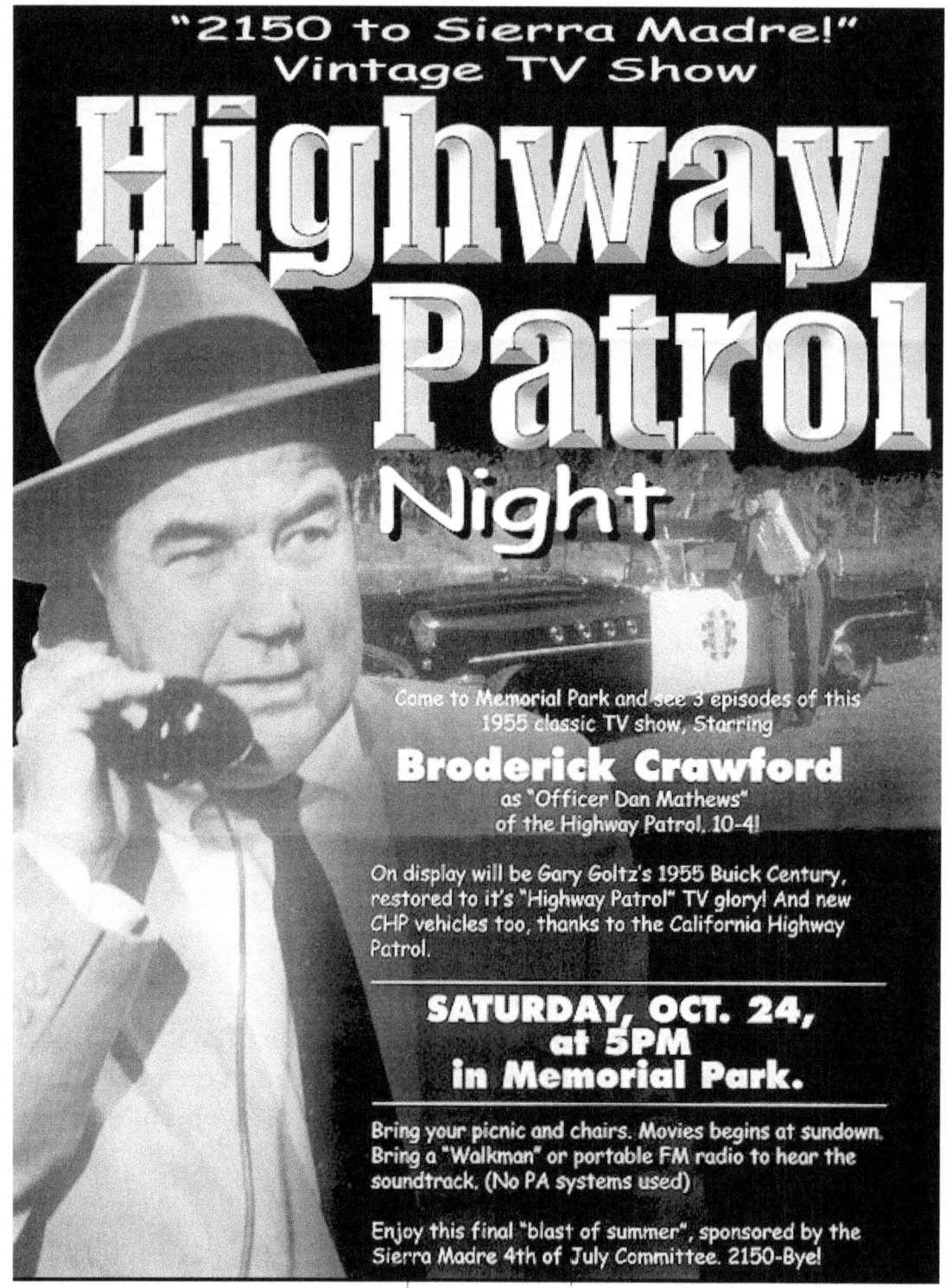

Below and Next Page: Typical publicity below with photocopy of article and cover from *The Pittsburg Press TV Graphic* Sunday magazine insert for July 28, 1957 (Photos Goltz Collection).

TV Graphic Cover

21-50 To Headquarters, 10-4

*Balding Broderick Crawford
And His 'Highway Patrol' Are Making
Police Code Part Of Our Language*

CALLING HEADQUARTERS. Crawford uses two-way radio on helicopter which he flies in on many episodes in series.

TELEVISION'S most looked-at actor is middle-aged, burly and balding Broderick Crawford in his role of a state highway police official.

Not Steven Allen nor Perry Como nor Ed Sullivan nor any star of a heavily-budgeted network show is seen on as many stations as Broderick Crawford's syndicated film series, "Highway Patrol." Currently the series is seen on 185 stations around the country, more, probably, than any other TV vehicle.

It comes into the Pittsburgh area on three district stations—Channel 2 on Wednesdays (9:00 p. m.); Channel 9 on Thursdays (8:00 p. m.); Channel 6 on Fridays (9:30 p. m.). It is what is known in TV circles as a bread and butter property.

The success of shows like "Highway Patrol" and "Dragnet" suggest that people prefer programs dealing with authentic police methods to the nine-dollar bill fictions of private eyes.

Like its progenitor, "Dragnet," "Highway Patrol" heavily employs police jargon. The terse "10-4" with which Crawford in his role of Dan Mathews of the "Highway Patrol" terminates conversations, is fast becoming a part of the language.

Also like "Dragnet," whose dum-da-dum-dum theme swept the country, the "Highway Patrol" signature music has achieved wide popularity. (It's on the London label, recorded with full orchestra treatment by Cyril Stapleton).

The melody is a compelling sort of theme, suggesting the inexorable sweep of the forces of right and order across the highways of the land.

Brod, as everyone is prone to call Crawford after knowing him five minutes, is in his second year of starring in "Highway Patrol."

"It was a sort of schizophrenic-type switch to be a lawmaker rather than a lawbreaker," he grins. "I had done so many movies in which I played a gangster or other type of shady character, it was rough for me to adapt for the first few shows. But I had one jump on some of my fellow actors: I know how to handle a gun!"

Actually, faithful viewers of "Highway Patrol" will note that Crawford rarely resorts to violence himself. He solves his crimes, true, in the stipulated 26 or 27 minutes, but the executives at Ziv TV Programs, producers of the series, feel that gunplay or violence for its own sake doesn't belong on home screens where it can be seen by impressionable youngsters.

"Naturally, if a gun battle is essential to the story line we're not going to water it down and be Pollyanna-ish about the thing," Brod points out, "but we don't go out of our way to show gore or violence."

Production recently was halted on "Highway Patrol" when Crawford suffered a freak accident, which fortunately was less serious than first believed. What exactly happened?

"It was a very hot day—as they always seem to be when we go on location. And I was resting in the back of a truck waiting for the next scene to be set up. Our producer, Vernon Clark, called that they were ready for me. I stood up, ready to jump off the truck, and the heel of my shoe caught in the cam. This was one time I literally fell right on my face." Brod laughs in retrospect. "It wasn't funny at the time, though I did get a couple of weeks' rest out of it."

A fractured wrist and painful bruises were the injuries, but Brod is back at work now, after his two weeks' "vacation."

Brod does not subscribe to the theory that an actor can wear out his welcome by appearing on TV, and that people won't pay to see him henceforth.

"I figure if you turn in the best performances of which you are capable, and if you select your stories carefully, people will want to see you either at home or at the corner movie house."

The actual stories, Brod explains, if taken from the files of the California Highway Patrol, are so changed around that no innocent person can be injured by the filming.

"We have the sanction of the Highway Patrol and a technical adviser on the set with us at all times. We try to make certain that everything on the show is factually correct, even to the way I get in and out of the car, draw a gun, or talk into the hand microphone in our car or helicopter."

About the helicopter, which figures in so many episodes, Brod jokes, "I figure I'm airborne more than I'm in a car, we do so much flying around in it. But again, that's the documentary flavor of the show. The regular Highway Patrol is using helicopters more and more, so we do too.

"I told Vernon Clark, our producer, that maybe one of these days we should change the name of the show to 'Airway Patrol.' But that was one suggestion that he regarded very dimly," laughed Crawford.

AUTHENTIC PRODUCTION. Brod Crawford says "Highway Patrol" producers "try to make certain that everything on the show is factually correct."

TV Page 6—The Pittsburgh Press, Sunday, July 28, 1957

Below: ZIV-TV's *Highway Patrol* exhibit at the Auto Show in 1957 complete with the '56 Dodge patrol car (Photo Goltz Collection).

Broderick Crawford's signature (Photo Goltz Collection).

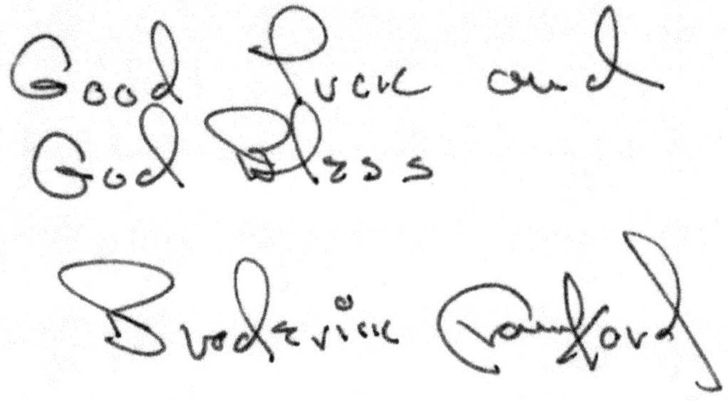

Good Luck and God Bless

Broderick Crawford

Chapter Three
The *Highway Patrol* Parodies!

Caricature of Broderick Crawford as Dan Mathews on Highway Patrol circa 1957 artist unknown (Photo Goltz Collection).

At the peak of *Highway Patrol's* popularity Broderick Crawford was in great demand to appear on prime-time television shows as guest star. Frederick Ziv whole heartedly approved of free national television publicity for any of his shows even parodies.

"He's been hooked on Cinemax ever since we stumbled on a great old Broderick Crawford movie."

New Yorker Magazine cartoon (Photo Goltz Collection).

Steve Allen Show (1957)

On NBC's live, comedy-variety series *The Steve Allen Show* (1957) telecast in on October 6, 1957 Broderick Crawford did a funny cameo playing Dan Mathews of *Highway Patrol*. Steve Allen was conducting a *'Man on The Street'* interview about space travel with cast regulars Tom Poston, Louis Nye, and Don Knotts. Broderick Crawford, wearing his trademark trench coat and fedora, appears as Dan Mathews of *Highway Patrol* to great cheers from the studio audience. Host Allen tells him that one day the Martians may invade Earth. Dan Mathews disagrees saying "Take it from me Steve, as a man on the street with *Highway Patrol*, the Martians will never be able to invade!" Allen asks "Why not?" Mathews barks "No parking!"

I've Got A Secret (1957)

A few weeks later on October 30, 1957 Broderick Crawford (wearing his trademark fedora) was a special guest on the live, prime-time CBS game show *I've Got A Secret* (1952-1967) hosted by Henry Morgan who was substituting for an ailing Garry Moore. The panel, Jayne Meadows, Carl Reiner, Bill Cullen, and Faye Emerson was blindfolded as they tried to guess Broderick Crawford's secret. A television was brought on stage, turned on but with the volume off. Crawford was secretly watching *Highway Patrol* on another channel during the broadcast. As he left the stage to great applause Broderick Crawford told Henry Morgan, "Tell Garry I hope he feels better." The episode is preserved on kinescope and is available on youtube.com.

Smokey The Bear:
National Radio Public Service Advertisements for the U.S. Forest Service (1960)

In the 1950's and 1960's the U.S. Forest Service and the Ad Council produced an effective public service advertisement campaign to prevent forest fires. The PSA's starred the U.S. Forest Service's beloved mascot, Smokey the Bear (wearing his ranger hat), the famed Western singing group the *Sons of The Pioneers* and famous guest stars. In this one the PSA begins with the golden harmonic tones of the *Sons of The Pioneers* singing the *Smokey the Bear* theme song. Smokey announces that we are on our way to a forest road where the *Highway Patrol* says that Broderick Crawford will meet us. Listeners hear a wailing siren as a *Highway Patrol* car suddenly brakes and Broderick Crawford hops out. The Oscar-winning actor stamps out a small brush fire caused by a still-lit, cigarette butt that a careless motorist tossed out onto the road. He reminds listeners and Smokey that the driving public must be careful in our national forests to prevent the needless destruction of the forests, the watershed and the native wildlife. Smokey says "Thanks a lot Chief! Err, I mean Mr. Crawford!" He asks everyone to relax as the *Sons of The Pioneers* sing a campfire song *"Silent Trails"*. The PSA lasts nearly five minutes.

MAD Magazine (1960)

A film or television series is not truly a cultural hit or a national sensation unless it receives the full-parody treatment from satirical *MAD Magazine*. To Broderick Crawford's dismay *Highway Patrol* was so honored with the October 1960 issue of *MAD*. It contains a drop-dead, hilarious, take-off of the series entitled *Highway Squad* that was superbly drawn by the great Mort Drucker, and written by comic genius Larry Siegel. Dan Mathews was re-named Dan Mildew! *MAD* was known for being unmerciful in their parodies but this entire four-page spread (see below) is a loving, wonderful tribute to this legendary television series. Even Broderick Crawford's image is drawn in a deeply flattering style. No doubt the Oscar-winning actor and his two boys Kelly Crawford, and Kim Crawford read this issue of *MAD* together for some big belly laughs!

Following Four Pages: The Complete 4-page *Mad Magazine* parody of *Highway Patrol* from October 1960 (Reprinted with permission of *Mad Magazine*).

Morris And Mitch's *Highway Patrol* parody on a 45RPM record from 1958 and album jacket (Photos Goltz Collection)

Leave It To Beaver (1960)

There was even a funny reference to *Highway Patrol* on the incredibly popular *Leave It To Beaver* series in season four, episode eight that was telecast November 19, 1960 entitled *"Eddie's Double-Cross"*. Series trouble-maker Eddie Haskell (brilliantly played Ken Osmond) tells his pals Wally Cleaver (Tony Dow) and Beaver Cleaver (Jerry Mathers) that he now has a girlfriend named Caroline Shuster. A dubious Wally looks up her photo in the high school yearbook and says "Boy Eddie, that Caroline's a very pretty girl! This wouldn't be another one of your stories, would it? The last time you said that you saw Broderick Crawford riding a bus!" Later Eddie and Wally go to the malt shop and sit on stools. Eddie recognizes Caroline sitting in a booth with her girlfriends. Wally asks, "Hey Eddie if she's supposed to be your girl, then why are you sitting here and she's sitting way over there?" An indignant Eddie protests, "Hey, in the Rock Hudson-Doris Day movies does Rock Hudson run right over to Doris Day or does he first let his charm ooze across the room!" Incredibly Ken Osmond, after a hitch in the U.S. Army, joined the Los Angeles Police Department and became a dedicated career officer. He was three-times wounded in the line-of-duty and has retired from the force with honors.

An Unknown Audio Recording (Circa 1960)

A professionally produced audio recording parody of *Highway Patrol* made the rounds of radio stations across the country and probably surfaced on a vinyl record somewhere. It even includes Cyril Stapleton and his orchestra's outstanding 1960 hit single of the *Highway Patrol* theme in the score. Unfortunately, the first-rate ensemble cast of this recording is unknown but their work is flawless especially the actor mimicking Broderick Crawford as *Highway Patrol* chief Dan Mathews.

CBS Television Special "The Zany Adventures of Xavier Cugat In Madrid" (1965)

This was a sixty-minute filmed black & white television special for the CBS network. Popular orchestra leader Xavier Cugat hosted this charming travelogue about his native city Madrid to sell tourism in sunny Spain. It was telecast only once. Several Hollywood stars shooting films in Spain did guest shots for the special including Arlene Dahl, Phil Silvers, Robert Taylor, and Marc Lawrence. Cugat, in white helmet and uniform, plays a police officer in the center of Madrid's famed traffic circle. A car pulls up and Broderick Crawford (who was making three Westerns back-to-back in Spain) asks Officer Cugat for directions. Cugat says "Sir your face is very common. [pause] No sir, your face is very famous! Aren't you..." The camera pulls back to reveal the sedan is actually an American *Highway Patrol* squad car. Broderick Crawford laughs "Yeah, I'm Dick Tracy! [looks at the driver] Let's go!" The squad car takes off with its siren wailing leaving a stunned Xavier Cugat behind.

Get Smart (1970)

Broderick Crawford was 'Guest Star' on the secret agent comedy series *Get Smart,* for the season five, episode five entitled, *"The Treasure of C. Errol Madre"* that was telecast on October 24, 1969. The script, written by Bob De Vinney and Chris Hayward, was a clever and funny tribute to the Hollywood adventure film classic *The Treasure of Sierra Madre* (1948) which starred Humphrey Bogart and Walter Huston. Don Adams, who also directed, played Agent Maxwell Smart imitating Bogart and Brod Crawford played enemy K.A.O.S. Agent C. Errol Madre imitating Walter Huston's old prospector character. In one scene C. Errol Madre contacts K.A.O.S. headquarters via a phone embedded in the horseshoe of his pack mule, and he signs-off with his trademark *Highway Patrol* "Ten-4!"

Canada Dry TV Commercial (1976)

In 1976, the Canada Dry beverage company used movie tough guys from Hollywood's Golden Era for their *"Not Too Sweet"* ginger ale advertising campaign. The screen legends sang the Canada Dry jingle to the tune of *"Ain't She Sweet"*. A hatch opens on a U.S. Army tank and Sergeant Aldo Ray holds a bottle of Canada Dry while belting out the jingle over the tank's radio! Attila The Hun (Jack Palance reprising his role from 1954's *Sign of the Pagan*) holds a Canada Dry bottle and croons the jingle! The color commercial closes with Chief Dan Mathews (Broderick Crawford in white shirt, tie and fedora hat) of *Highway Patrol* standing next to a squad car. Holding the car's radio microphone in his right hand and a bottle of Canada Dry in his left, he sings this jingle to all units: "Not too sweet, I repeat it's not too sweet, Canada Dry Ginger Ale, it's a taste that can't be beat, TEN-4!" Television audiences were delighted to see Broderick Crawford and his fellow movie legends kid their own images in both commercials. The commercial is available on You Tube.

Look What's Happened to Rosemary's Baby (1976)

Look What's Happened to Rosemary's Baby (1976) is a made-for-TV movie produced by Paramount Pictures that was telecast in color on the ABC network on October 29, 1976 with a running time of 92 minutes. It is a miserable, made-for-TV movie sequel to the horror classic *Rosemary's Baby* (1968) that was directed by Roman Polanski. Incredibly in *Look What's Happened to Rosemary's Baby,* Broderick Crawford has second 'Guest Star' billing after Patty Duke in a fleeting cameo! Taking place twenty years after the first film, Broderick Crawford again appears (this time in uniform) as the chief of the Highway Patrol who warns the Devil's offspring to stop drag-racing or face arrest! With less than a minute of screen time and only two lines of dialogue, Broderick Crawford doesn't appear until twenty-nine minutes into the film for a cameo inserted to successfully lure adults to the expected teenage/adolescent audience. Anyone who expected to see the relentless lawman battling the Devil himself and his diabolical son was sadly disappointed. *Look What's Happened to Rosemary's Baby* scored high in the ratings and was popular in syndication so Broderick Crawford received hefty residual checks. He would finally get his chance to beat the Devil a few years later in a far better film, *Harlequin* (1980).

Saturday Night Live (1977)
The 157th episode of *Highway Patrol!*

Broderick Crawford hosted the 90-minute, NBC comedy series *Saturday Night Live* on March 19, 1977. Musical guests were Linda Ronstadt, with Dr. John, Levon Helm and Paul Butterfield appearing as the *RCO All-Stars*. It was broadcast *'In Living Color'*. It was directed by Dave Wilson with a filmed segment by Gary Weis. Producer Lorne Michaels created an American version of the BBC-TV comedy series *Monty Python's Flying Circus.* He hand-picked his *'The Not Ready for Primetime Players'* and had rotating celebrity hosts for his comics to bounce off of every week. He insisted the show be telecast live from Studio 3B at NBC's Rockefeller Center. As host Broderick Crawford has the time of his life making millions of people laugh in two great comedy skits in one of the genuine highlights of his forty-year career.

After the opening credits, announcer Don Pardo says to thunderous audience applause, "Ladies and gentlemen, Broderick Crawford!" Brod Crawford struts onstage to sit down in a living room chair at the footlights and forgoes the opening monologue. He says "Oh thank you very much! As an old and dear, and rather rotund friend like myself used to say, how sweet it is!" He spellbinds the audience by recalling being a young, starving New York actor thirty-seven years earlier and being fired by NBC radio. He closes, "I'm very happy after 40 years NBC is giving me another chance! [audience roaring with laughter] and please cross your fingers and hope I don't blow it this time!" Kelly Crawford related to the author (Goltz) that his father Broderick told Lorne Michaels that there was no way he would stand at the end of a runway right after St. Patrick's Day! So, Michaels offered him a comfortable living room chair and this was the only episode in the history of the series to open in this manner! Broderick Crawford is the subject of a poignant short film by Gary Weis. The cameras are never intrusive as they follow Broderick Crawford wandering the sidewalks of his old New York neighborhood. Normally cynical New Yorkers welcome the Oscar-winning star back home with open arms. One elderly woman says she last saw him in the neighborhood when she was an infant. Broderick Crawford protests,

"That makes me ninety-five!" While signing autographs and posing for photos, crowds of fans tell him how good he looks but Broderick Crawford laughs "Boy, I'm nothing but a blown up Dead End Kid! I love New York!" Gary Weis's cameras reveal a gentle man with a heart of gold under Broderick Crawford's tough guy veneer. The best sketch is a parody of *Highway Patrol* (telecast in black and white using the series' actual opening credits). Dan Aykroyd mimics Art Gilmore's narration and also plays Dan Mathews' Sergeant (wearing an authentic uniform from the series). During the live broadcast Aykroyd accidentally dropped his police revolver. Broderick Crawford barks "Pick it up!" and the audience erupts into cheers! For the series' trademark epilog, Broderick Crawford says, "Be sure and see *Highway Patrol* in action next week. Until then remember when you drive, use a car! 10-Four!"

The final sketch is a funny parody of Broderick Crawford's new film *The Private Files of J. Edgar Hoover.* President Richard Nixon (Dan Aykroyd) and his daughter Julie Nixon (Laraine Newman) break-in to Hoover's bedroom for blackmail. With his deadpan delivery he gets big laughs as J. Edgar Hoover tells the President "Oh, you're really an idiot Nixon, blackmailing me is like trying to bribe Howard Hughes!" The skit ends with Hoover telling his 'boys' to meet him later in the steam room! He goes to bed cuddling his teddy bear and the audience response is wild cheers and applause. The audience is astonished that Broderick Crawford's rapid, booming voice has lost none of its timber over the decades. Onstage for the end of show, this time Broderick Crawford (still wearing his J. Edgar Hoover pajamas and robe) actually walks to the end of the stage and stands to thank the audience and the cast. John Belushi runs over to shake his hand, and the ladies Gilda Radner, Jane Curtin, and Laraine Newman shower the Oscar-winner with hugs and kisses. As the credits roll, Broderick Crawford shakes hands with Dan Aykroyd and Bill Murray, who kneel down front. Linda Ronstadt stands next to Broderick Crawford as the audience applauds wildly.

This often hysterically funny episode of *Saturday Night Live* is a magnificent tribute from a splendid young cast to Hollywood movie great Broderick Crawford. To appear on a live television, show in front of a studio audience with millions of people watching coast-to-coast was like walking a tightrope without a safety net. Unlike before in the 1930's on an NBC radio broadcast, Broderick Crawford sailed through with flying colors. This episode is available on DVD from Universal.

Below Left: Broderick Crawford as Chief Dan Mathews in the Highway patrol skit on Saturday Night Live March 19, 1977 (Photo Goltz Collection).

Below Right: Photo of author Gary Goltz (with his HP squad car) enjoys a laugh with Dan Ackroyd while imitating Broderick Crawford at the Hollywood Christmas Parade (Photo Goltz Collection).

CHiPs (1977)
His Last Bow

"Hustle" (1977) is a 60-minute color episode of the NBC series *CHiPS* originally telecast November 24, 1977. It was produced by Rick Rossner for MGM Television. It was directed by Georg Fenady and written by John Groves.

Officers Jon Baker (Larry Wilcox) and Francis Llewellyn Poncherello 'Ponch' (Erik Estrada) patrol the Los Angeles freeway. Jon and Ponch pull over a sedan for running a stop sign. Jon asks the driver for identification, but Ponch recognizes that it's Broderick Crawford (himself). Jon insists they don't make shows like *Highway Patrol* anymore as Ponch begs him to bark "2150 to headquarters! Ten-4!" Officer Baker hands Broderick Crawford a written warning promising Ponch a copy after he signs it.

"Hustle" is an exciting episode of this hit series. Audiences tuned-in to watch charismatic stars Larry Wilcox and Erik Estrada as the dedicated but human heroes of the California Highway Patrol, who enforce the law on beautiful, sleek, Kawasaki police motorcycles. The breezy theme music of *CHiPs* was composed by John Carl Parker. Georg Fenady, who previously directed Broderick Crawford in *Terror in The Wax Museum* (1973), keeps the action and comedy moving fast.

Larry Wilcox plays the confident, easy-going Officer Jon Baker. Co-star Erik Estrada plays Officer 'Ponch' Poncherello with great wit and a genuine flair for light comedy. In an interview with the authors (Goltz and Schiller) Erik Estrada said, "That show with Broderick Crawford was great and so was he! I wasn't acting there. I always watched *Highway Patrol* because that was my favorite show. In fact, that was my favorite episode of *CHiPs* working with Brod Crawford"

Broderick Crawford enjoyed kidding himself and his *Highway Patrol* image. The *CHiPs* cast, crew, and producers went out of their way to honor him with this episode. Officer Jon Baker was wrong when he said they don't make shows like *Highway Patrol* any more. They made *CHiPs!* This episode is available on DVD, *CHiPs: The First Complete Season* from Turner Entertainment.

Note the autograph "To Frank – me and my God-damned 502's, Brod" (502 is CHP code for DUI Photo Goltz Collection).

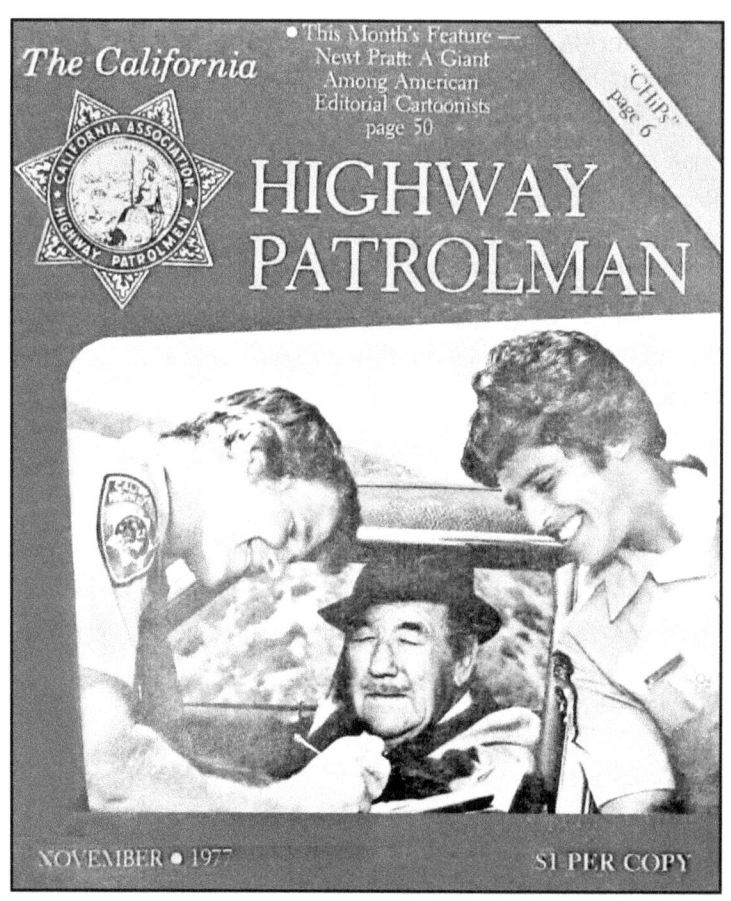

Chapter Four: After *Highway Patrol*
The Second Television Series: *King of Diamonds* (1961-1962)

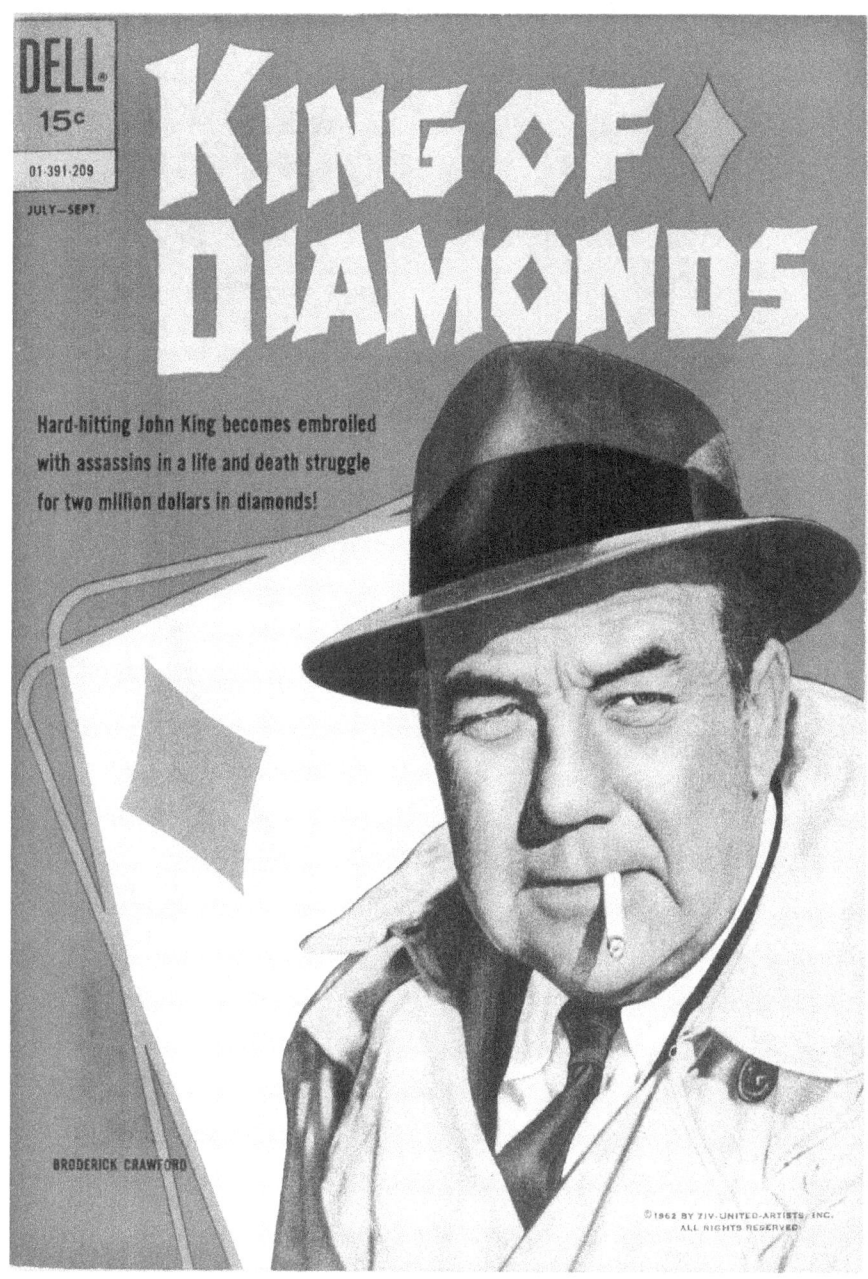

Dell Comics tie-in of Broderick Crawford as private detective John King for *King of Diamonds* (Photo Goltz Collection).

Portrait of Broderick Crawford as Private Detective John King (Photo R. Schiller).

King of Diamonds (1961) was a syndicated weekly series. It was produced by ZIV-United Artists in black and white with a thirty-minute running time. The Executive Producer was Babe Unger with Broderick Crawford as Associate Producer. The score was composed by Warren Barker. Art Gilmore was narrator. *King of Diamonds* was launched with great fanfare as Broderick Crawford's comeback series but audiences were ultimately disappointed. It was cancelled after thirty-eight episodes. John King (Broderick Crawford) is a private investigator for Continental Diamond Company. His assistant is college-educated Casey (Ray Hamilton). They battle an international syndicate of diamond thieves, Illicit Diamond Buyers Inc. (IDB). King is based on Mickey Spillane's Mike Hammer. He wears a fedora hat, a white trench coat, and carries a .38 caliber police special. He's quick on the draw, fast with his fists, and loves beautiful dames and fine liquor. Warren Barker's jazzy musical score is worthy of a *Mike Hammer* movie. The pilot episode, *"The Wizard of Ice"* is a good mystery, with a good screenplay by producer John Robinson, and fine direction by Irving Lernert.

In New York City, a Continental Diamond Company courier is murdered and robbed of two million dollars in diamonds by masked armed men, Jerry Larch (Telly Savalas with mustache and thinning hair!), and partners Phil McNally (John Marley) and Bert (Bert Freed). The mastermind is Jerry's bombshell girlfriend Margie Howard (Lola Albright), who romances all three pitting them against each other. Margie sends Bert to murder King, but Casey saves his life. Jerry dies in a car crash. Margie goes to jail, with the diamonds returned to Continental. King celebrates at the *Four Winds* lounge with glamorous piano player/singer Jo (Joan Tabor). Guest stars Lola Albright, Telly Savalas, John Marley, and Bert Freed are excellent. Unfortunately, the rest of the series falls short of the high standards set by the pilot.

"Commando Tactics" is a mediocre episode written by Steve Fisher with colorless direction by John Rich. In World War Two, U.S. Army commandos snatched a diamond treasure from the Third Reich's ill-gotten wealth. In 1962, ex-commandos John King and Cliff Hale (Gerald Mohr) have dinner. Hale goes to London where a diamond exchange in London is cleaned-out of millions in diamonds by robbers using commando tactics. Continental sends King and Casey to London. Cliff sells the stones to the IDB for a half-million, but steals them back. The IDB sends gunmen who shoot Cliff. King and Casey kill the IDB hit men. A dying Cliff gives the diamonds to King.

"Alias Willie Hogan" was badly written by Steve Fisher with routine direction by Robert Gordon. After a diamond theft in Johannesburg, South Africa, Casey impersonates diamond thief Willie Hogan (also Ray Hamilton), to fence gems back to Continental. He falls in love with Hogan's girlfriend, Nancy (Kathie Browne) but Willie breaks jail. Casey's life is saved by John King, who shoots Willie.

King of Diamonds was syndicated in major television markets, including some network affiliates, and had the polished look of a network series. The pilot episode drew a large audience, and for a moment it looked like ZIV-UA and Broderick Crawford had another hit. The producers counted on Broderick Crawford's star power to carry the series but they should have demanded better scripts. A frantic ZIV-UA hired Frankie Ortega to compose a new theme song for the series. It was a ridiculous 'Cha-Cha' that would embarrass Mike Hammer with dopey lyrics like, "When Johnny King breaks a door down he's not saying Ten-4 now."

Ray Hamilton is colorless as Casey, King's partner but he is fine in *"Alias Willie Hogan"*. Hamilton was dropped from the series mid-season and little else is known about him. Richard Kiel appears in the pilot of *King of Diamonds* as a tall uniformed doorman/bouncer who tips off John King. Ironically the towering seven-foot, two-inch actor really was a nightclub bouncer. In an interview with the author (Schiller) the late Richard Kiel said, "Oh yeah I remember making the pilot [*"The Wizard of Ice"*] with Broderick Crawford. He was a sweet guy with a good sense of humor. That show was fun to make!" Richard Kiel died in 2014.

Broderick Crawford is easy-going, and witty as the jet-setting, private investigator John King who pursues diamonds and beautiful blondes at the same time. In the first episode King is at La Guardia Airport to catch an international flight when he spots a gorgeous-looking blonde in a fur coat. Casey wonders if she is on the same flight and King cynically says, "That kind of luck I don't have!" Joan Tabor decorates *King of Diamonds* as the gorgeous, piano-playing, torch singer Jo. In real life Tabor and Broderick Crawford were married. When John King romances Jo, Crawford isn't acting, and he even looks hopelessly smitten. At the end of the first episode Jo brings a lovely brunette along for a double-date with King and Casey. King grabs Jo and tells Casey, "She's yours!" Both their series and marriage were short-lived. Broderick Crawford was part-owner of *King of Diamonds,* and a hit series would have made him more money than he ever did as a film star. (In fact, ZIV-UA held up his 10% share of *Highway Patrol's* gross, over two million dollars until Crawford agreed to sign for the new series *King of Diamonds*). His hopes were crushed by this expensive failure. Television audiences wanted to see Broderick Crawford battle crime while carrying a police badge. ZIV-UA missed the boat in not bringing back *Highway Patrol* in color.

A 16MM can of film of an episode of Broderick Crawford's *King Of Diamonds* series (Photo Goltz Collection).

A pensive, older Broderick Crawford as private detective John King on the set of his short-lived TV series *King of Diamonds* (Photo Goltz Collection).

Cover of 1962 *Baltimore Sunday Times* TV program guide with Broderick Crawford with Ray Hamilton in his less successful TV series *King of Diamonds* (Photo Goltz Collection).

This Page and Next: Newspaper ads for King Of Diamonds (photos Goltz Collection).

Kingfish of Tough Guys

Broderick Crawford likes to act tough.

The gruff actor developed his muscles in his Academy Award winning portrayal of the late Louisiana Senator Huey Long in "All The King's Men."

COVER STORY

As the flinty-voiced chief of TV's "Highway Patrol," Crawford slugged it out with many a mobster at highway roadblocks.

And age doesn't seem to soften him any.

Crawford, once down for the count as an actor, has bounced back in great form for a third thrust as an indefatigable muscleman.

In "King of Diamonds," which began on WBAL two weeks ago, he plays John King, chief of the diamond industry's security forces.

His job, obviously, is to protect the precious gems from theft during shipment and to recover any that have been stolen.

In his new role, with Ray Hamilton as assistant Al Casey, he will get plenty of opportunities to display his expansive brawn in the risky business of international intrigue.

Crawford was born Dec. 9, 1911, in Philadelphia, Pa. He was in the Merchant Marine before turning to radio and later TV. He is divorced from his first wife and has two sons.

He appeared as "Lennie" in the 1939 Broadway production, "Of Mice and Men." He won his Oscar in 1949 for his role as Sen. Long.

Hamilton

Crawford

Rare Press release for Broderick Crawford's *King of Diamonds* (Photo Goltz Collection).

Cover of *King of Diamonds* script of episode *Kato the Clown* (Photo Goltz Collection).

The Last Television Series
The Interns **(1970-1971)**

The Interns was a one-hour CBS network series that ran for one season (1970-1971) of twenty-four episodes. It was produced by Columbia Pictures in Technicolor. The producer was Charles Larson. The theme music and score was written by Shorty Rogers. The series was based on Richard Frede's salacious, best-selling 1960 novel of the same name. Columbia Pictures purchased the movie rights, and slickly produced a modest black and white film *The Interns* (1962) starring Cliff Robertson, Stefanie Powers, Nick Adams, Michael Callan, Suzy Parker, James MacArthur, and Telly Savalas. Overloaded with sex and drugs, it closely followed the novel's shocking, sensational look at the medical profession. It was a hit and Columbia produced an even sleazier sequel *The New Interns* (1964) in black and white. Based on an original script, Telly Savalas, Stefanie Powers, and Michael Callan repeated their roles in this flop. In 1969, medical dramas made a big comeback on television with the MGM produced *Medical Center* with Chad Everett for CBS, and Universal's *Marcus Welby, M.D.* with Robert Young for ABC with both running for seven years. Columbia dusted off *The Interns* for television. The studio discarded most of Frede's original novel as unacceptable for primetime television, and built a new series starring young, appealing, unknown actors around polished, veteran star Broderick Crawford. In the original 1962 film Telly Savalas played a crabby chief surgeon with a proverbial heart of gold. Crawford played the same character renamed Dr. Peter Goldstone. CBS picked-up the series, which premiered on September 18, 1970.

The Interns is set at fictional New North Hospital of Los Angeles with stories revolving around the hospital's senior staff surgeon, Dr. Goldstone (Broderick Crawford) and his five interns, Dr. Cal Barrin (Hal Frederick), Dr. Lydia Thorpe (Sandra Smith), Dr. Sam Marsh (Mike Farrell), and two bachelors, Dr. Pooch Hardin (Christopher Stone) and Dr. Greg Pettit (Stephen Brooks). Dr. Marsh is newly-wed to beautiful, caring Bobbe Marsh (Elaine Giftos). *The Interns* is currently unavailable but the author (Schiller) tracked down ten of the twenty-four episodes. The series was a fine medical drama distinguished by good acting and intelligently-written screenplays without maudlin tear-jerking. The cast routinely shied away from the theatrical over-acting on other medical shows in favor of sincerity.

Broderick Crawford's Dr. Goldstone is identical to his Dr. Aaron in *Not As A Stranger* (1955). Like Aaron, Goldstone is a martinet who demands perfection from his interns while hiding his kind heart behind an abrasive exterior. Although he'll jump down their throats in his office, Goldstone ferociously defends and protects his interns from incompetent, interfering outsiders. He admires his interns' dedication while putting them through rigorous training. Goldstone knows they're the best and that after he's gone they'll be running New North Hospital. Although the interns tremble in Goldstone's wake, they respect his brilliant surgical skills and knowledge. They will become better doctors because they interned under him. Broderick Crawford never overshadows his young co-stars and underplays Goldstone with a steeled look in his ever-narrowing eyes.

Unlike the racy novel and two racier motion pictures, *The Interns* aimed high with good writing, directing, and acting. It was a failure that had a noble death in 1971 when CBS cancelled the series after one season. It was one medical show too many. It disappeared except for sporadic repeats. Ironically, in a 1970 interview for now defunct *Movie Digest* magazine, Joan Crawford was asked which television shows she enjoys. Her first choice was *The Interns* saying, "I always watch Broderick Crawford. He can say and do more with one little twitch of his eyebrow than all these young method actors put together!" The producers of *The Interns* should have handed Joan Crawford a plum, guest-starring role.

The premiere episode, *"The Quality of Mercy"* had guest shots by film star Diane Baker and television star Sherry Jackson. In an interview with the author (Schiller) Diane Baker's eyes lit up when asked about *The Interns,* "Oh! I remember that was a great show. I enjoyed working with Broderick Crawford very much. He was so kind and professional, and oh! He won an Oscar!" In an interview with the author (Schiller) Sherry Jackson said, "At first I was intimidated by Broderick Crawford because he was such a powerful actor, but he was really a very sweet man!" One of the best episodes is *"Miss Knock-A-Bout"* with ravishing, raven-haired Bridget Hanley as a professional clown. Miss Knock-A-Bout hides her loneliness behind an endless barrage of jokes and one-liners. Only Dr. Hardin sees through the greasepaint and gags to touch the heart of the beautiful woman inside the clown. In an interview with the author (Schiller) Bridget Hanley said, "You know, when you work with someone of Broderick Crawford's caliber, it's really a gift, I had a wonderful time doing *The Interns* and it's one of my favorites. I was blessed; I got to work with him again on *Simon & Simon*." Pamela Susan Shoop made her acting debut in a frightening 1970 episode entitled *"Mondays Can Be Fatal"*. In a letter to the author (Schiller) Ms. Shoop recalled, "That was my first time in front of the cameras. Everyone on the set was so nice to me, especially Broderick Crawford but then he always was. I don't remember much about that show except that I was strapped to a hospital bed doing a lot of screaming [on a bad trip]!"

Upcoming actor Pete Duel, who later died tragically, is brilliant as a dying patient in a 1970 episode *"The Price of Life"*. Pete Duel and Broderick Crawford worked together again in a funny, season 2 episode 17 of Duel's hit western comedy series *Alias Smith And Jones*. By the time the episode *"The Man Who Broke The Bank At Red Gap"* was telecast on January 20, 1972, Broderick Crawford was stunned that Pete Duel was already dead. The handsome and gifted actor took his own life on New Year's Eve, December 31, 1971. In an intriguing 1971 episode, *"Metamorphosis"*, Broderick Crawford's pal and co-star Skip Homeier was psychoanalyst Dr. Hugh Jacoby and Lois Nettleton was a disturbed nurse with a split personality. In an interview with the author (Schiller) Skip Homeier said, "Brod asked me to do that show and I always enjoyed working with him. To me he was one of the family."

David Lowell Rich, who previously directed Broderick Crawford in a 1958 episode of *Highway Patrol*, directed two episodes of *The Interns*, including the series finale. Shorty Rogers' jazzed-up theme music for *The Interns* symbolizes dynamic young doctors. Although the theme was trendy, the rest of the score is traditional and more effective.

Mike Farrell is splendid as Dr. Sam Marsh, the married intern. The handsome six-foot, three-inch actor has expressive eyes perfect for emoting the caring physician's empathy. Marsh adores his lovely, kind-hearted wife Bobbe like a lovesick school boy. Farrell married actress Shelley Fabares, whom he first met on *The Interns* in 1971 when she was guest star! Elaine Giftos was ideally cast as Dr. Marsh's leggy, gorgeous wife, Bobbe. She is devoted to him and is the 'den mother' for the other interns when they need a shoulder to cry on. Giftos adds badly needed humor to this intense series and has great chemistry with Broderick Crawford in their scenes together. Only Bobbe gets a smile out of Goldstone! Giftos did excellent dramatic work in a suspenseful episode *"The Oath"* (1971).

For Broderick Crawford starring on a major network, primetime television series in color was a dream come true. After thirty-three years in front of the cameras he knew that *The Interns* was his last chance for a comeback. He couldn't possibly have guessed that he'd get his comeback in a great movie role six years after the series was cancelled. In the epilog of the episode *"The Casualty",* the interns enjoy dinner and drinks with Dr. Goldstone at the restaurant near the hospital. Bobbe, noting that a writer's book on New North Hospital will be published soon, asks "Dr. Goldstone if they make a movie out of the book, which actor do you want to play you in the film?" Goldstone narrows his eyes to mere slits and says while walking-out the door, "Well, I don't know the actor's name, but he looks like a cop!"

Below: Rare CBS publicity release ballyhooing their new medical series *The Interns* (1970-1971) starring Broderick Crawford and his young cast. (Photo Goltz Collection).

Chapter Five
Broderick Crawford's Later Career and Life

The high-water mark of Broderick Crawford's film career was his magnificent performance in the 1949 motion picture *All The King's Men*. He was nominated for an Academy Award for 'Best Actor in a Starring Role' but his ferocious competition was Gregory Peck in *Twelve O'Clock High*, Kirk Douglas in *Champion*, Richard Todd in *The Hasty Heart*, and John Wayne for *The Sands of Iwo Jima*! These were great performances in great films but Broderick Crawford topped them all to win the coveted Oscar! During the 1950's he was a bona fide film star whom movie audiences paid money at the box office to see.

When he wasn't cranking out one film after another, Broderick Crawford avidly pursued several hobbies to relax including sailing, fly-fishing, and collecting antique shaving mugs!

Broderick Crawford polishes his beloved shaving mugs in 1952 (Photo Goltz Collection).

Broderick Crawford, an avid angler, with his fishing rods and tackle in 1952 (Photo Goltz Collection).

Broderick Crawford (with unidentified man in center) and his co-star James Cagney from the film *Time Of Their Lives* enjoy a day at the races in 1948 (Photo Goltz Collection).

Broderick Crawford also dabbled in oil painting which he found relaxing. He even studied art at Ted De Grazia's *Gallery of the Sun* near Tucson, Arizona.

Ted De Grazia's Gallery In The Sun near Tucson, Arizona—Note the posted hours sign! (Photo Goltz Collection).

Broderick Crawford's watercolor of a matador at the moment of truth (Photo Goltz Collection)

Broderick Crawford's life and career went through turbulent changes. Like many other famous Hollywood movie stars Broderick Crawford's personal life was sometimes stormy. In 1940 he married elegant, socialite Kay Griffith. The couple had two boys, Kelly Crawford and Kim Crawford. For many years the marriage was a happy one. In 1958 at the height of his national popularity for *Highway Patrol*, Kay divorced Crawford, who was shattered by the split. Later he became romantically involved with a young, gorgeous, blonde actress, Joan Tabor, who co-starred with him on his new *King of Diamonds* television series. They married in 1962 and divorced in 1967. Joan Tabor, who later remarried, died at age thirty-six from an accidental overdose in 1968. In 1973 Broderick Crawford married lovely actress Mary Alice Moore in a happy union that lasted for the rest of his life. The couple acted together on the dinner-theatre circuit in the 1970's and 1980's.

At their 1962 wedding, Broderick Crawford kisses his flinching bride Joan Tabor (Photo Goltz Collection)

When *Highway Patrol* ceased production, Broderick Crawford immediately traveled overseas to make two foreign film productions (one a silly 1960 *Hercules* epic, but the other a brilliant 1961 World War Two drama, *Square of Violence*). He spent the next 22 years making thirty-eight films in increasingly smaller roles in mostly minor films along with several hundred television appearances. Just to keep working he accepted film assignments in Italy, Germany, Spain, Austria, Mexico, Canada, Japan, Australia, the Philippine Islands, and France. Crawford also starred in two well-produced television pilots *"Shadow of A Man"* (1963) and *"Le Hot Spot"* (1981) that sank without a trace. Occasionally a great role fell in his lap (playing the title role in the superb *Private Files of J. Edgar Hoover* in 1977) and Broderick Crawford would still hit one right out of the park! For his last film, the little-seen but under-rated drama *Liar's Moon* (1982), Broderick Crawford bowed out with one last powerhouse performance. Just like his own parents, loving father Broderick Crawford warned his son Kelly Crawford about a career in show business, "The film industry is one hell of an industry so long as you're not an actor!" In an interview with the author (Goltz), Kelly Crawford said that director Michael Richie and Robert Redford were enormous fans of Broderick Crawford's Oscar-winning performance in the political film *All The King's Men*. Kelly proudly went on to say they insisted on giving a role to Broderick Crawford in their political film *The Candidate* (1972). Sadly all they gave him was a completely thankless, humiliating, not-on-camera, and uncredited role of Crawford's booming voice coming out of a speaker at a political rally. For Broderick Crawford this was a sheer waste of his enormous talent as he could do so much with so little on camera. Certainly it was nothing to be proud of.

Broderick Crawford died on April 26, 1986 at the age of seventy-four after a series of crippling strokes. He was laid to rest next to his parents in Ferndale Cemetery, in Johnstown, New York. His sons, Kelly Crawford and Kim Crawford, are both deceased with no children. All that remains of Broderick Crawford's legacy are his ninety-five films and several hundred television appearances. He was an extraordinary actor and film star with an incredible body of work. He enjoyed a durable career in show business spanning forty-five years that hit Hollywood's lofty heights and bottom-scraping depths more than once. According to IMDb.com when asked about his fame as an actor Broderick Crawford answered with great humility, "My trademarks are a hoarse, grating voice and the face of a retired pugilist with small narrow eyes set in puffy features which look as though they might, years ago, have lost on points."

Below: Broderick Crawford's final resting place at Ferndale cemetery, Jamestown, New York next to his beloved parents (Photo Goltz Collection).

Note of Mystery:

While traveling cross-country in author Gary Goltz's Buick *Highway Patrol* Enforcement Unit (squad car) following the original Route 66, the late Kelly Crawford revealed to Goltz a strange tale. He said that Broderick Crawford's Oscar statuette for *All The Kings Men* is actually a replacement for the original that was provided by the Motion Picture Academy. Goltz asked what had happened to the original Oscar. However before permanently closing the subject Kelly Crawford said it was hidden in a collector's safe deposit box in a Las Vegas bank vault! He never spoke of it again for the rest of his life.

Kelly Crawford and Gary Goltz pose with Broderick Crawford's Academy Award Oscar (the original or replacement?) for *All The King's Men*. (Photo Goltz Collection).

1970 AP wire photo and press release of Broderick Crawford proudly watching his son Kelly Crawford scrub his star on Hollywood's Walk Of Fame in front of Grauman's Chinese Theater (Photo and article Goltz Collection).

Character actor George Tobias sits on Santa Claus' lap under the watchful eyes of Broderick Crawford and three, unidentified, photogenic reindeer lovelies at the Hollywood Chamber of Commerce Christmas Parade on November 25, 1975 (Photo Goltz Collection).

Above Left: Broderick Crawford's mother Helen Broderick on NBC Radio during her Hollywood heyday circa 1936. Above Right: like mother, like son Broderick Crawford also on NBC radio in 1947 (Photos R. Schiller).

Below: Always happiest with his own family, Broderick Crawford is picture here with his wife Kay, his son Kelly, his mother Helen Broderick, and his father Lester Crawford, circa 1955 (Photo Goltz Collection).

Appendix A
Plot summary with original script pages for the pilot episode of *Highway Patrol* that successfully launched the series, "*Prison Break*".

Convicted murderer Ralph Neal (Robert Stevenson) makes a daring escape from prison. He is pursued by the Highway Patrol under Chief Dan Mathews (Broderick Crawford), with roadblocks surrounding the area. Neal injures a Highway Patrol Officer, and impersonates him to get past the roadblocks. He meets partner Vince (Gil Rankin) at a roadhouse restaurant parking lot as Mathews arrives. When Neal pulls out a gun, Mathews shoots out the tires of their car. With sirens of approaching police vehicles heard, Neal aims his gun, but Mathews gets off three shots. Neal goes down, as squad cars and motorcycle cops arrive in force. In the epilog before the closing credits, Broderick Crawford, sitting at his desk in headquarters, says with a smile "How do you do ladies and gentlemen, I'm Broderick Crawford. I hope you enjoyed the program we brought to you and you'll be with us next week at this time."

SERIES NO. 11
1B

by

Stuart Jerome

Copyright: 1955

ZIV TELEVISION PROGRAMS, INC.　　　FINAL MASTER SCRIPT
7324 Santa Monica Boulevard
Hollywood 46, California　　　April 6　1955

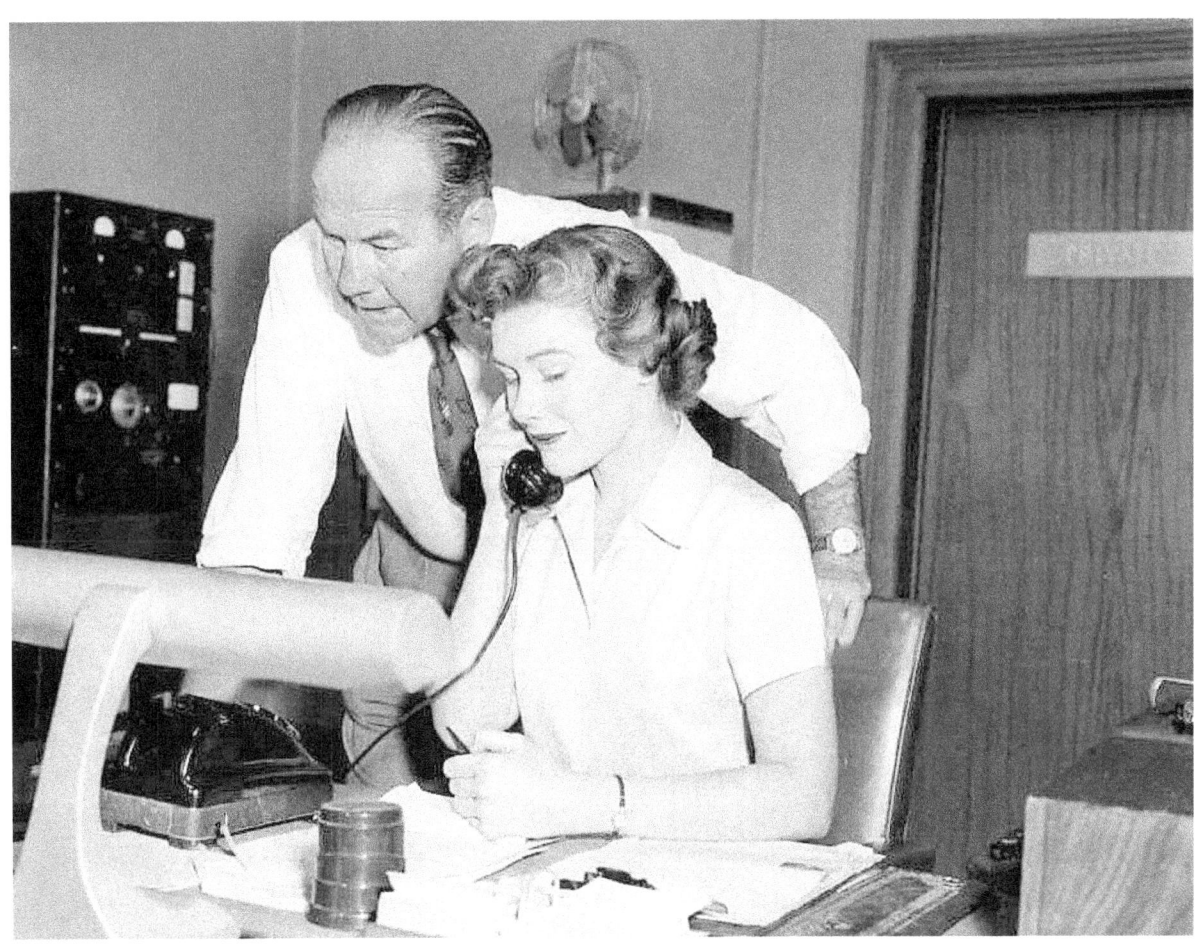

Dan Mathews learns of the attack on Officer Peterson from the dispatcher (beautiful actress Diane Brewster) in *'Prison Break'* (Photo Goltz Collection).

Paul Burke as Officer Halsey and Broderick Crawford as Dan Mathews plan a roadblock in *'Prison Break'* (Photo Goltz Collection).

Dan Mathews meets back-up units in *'Prison Break'* (Photo Goltz Collection).

SERIES NUMBER ELEVEN #1B

by

Stuart Jerome

Final 4/5/55

1-4   TENTATIVE OPENING FORMAT   1-4

FADE IN:

5   TRAVEL SHOT - ALONG OPEN HIGHWAY   5

SHOOTING THRU A WINDSHIELD or from the front of a CAMERA
CAR (showing no part of the car). MUSIC: STACCATO PORTION
OF THEME. Speed of the car to be consistent with the
tempo of the THEME.

CAMERA sees a straight run down this highway gradually
approaching a curve. We see a curve and just a little
around the curve, and as far as we can see, the highway
is entirely open. At this spot, SUPERIMPOSE TITLE
anticipated for 'Sponsor presents'. As this FADES OUT,
a second SUPERIMPOSURE : "BRODERICK CRAWFORD".

As the car goes into the curve, we have our third SUPER-
IMPOSURE reading: "Starring In", at which point the car
is now around the curve and about fifty yards away we see
an impressive roadblock. Probably two parked patrol cars
with some sort of a barricade, perhaps a motorcycle.
Three uniformed men are in front of the barricade. The
man in the middle has one hand outstretched to halt the
approaching CAMERA CAR. The other two men are each off
to one side of them standing ready with sub-machineguns
pointed at the CAMERA CAR.

As we MOVE IN on this scene, we have the next SUPERIM-
POSURE: "Officer of the State". At this point, the
THEME reaches a CLIMAX and then goes into MELODY. As it
is blended down, the NARRATOR'S VOICE COMES IN and covers
the next group of scenes with:

                    VOICE OVER
          Whenever the laws of any state are
          broken, or when the welfare of its
          citizens is endangered, each state
          has a duly authorized organization
          that swings into action. It may be
          called the State Militia or the State
          Police or the Highway Patrol. It is
          to these organizations, by whatever
          name they may be called, and wherever
          they may be found, that this program
          pays tribute.
                                        (CONTINUED)

5   CONTINUED: 5

                    VOICE OVER
                     (continuing)
               These are the stories of the men
               whose training, skill and courage
               have enforced and preserved our
               State laws. These are the men whose
               highest ranking officers often came
               up through the ranks and continued
               to receive outstanding respect and
               loyalty from their men because they
               do their commanding from the scene
               of action.

                                                       CUT TO:

INT. LARGE OPERATIONS ROOM

6   SHOT - ROOM   6

    complete with all equipment, communications, maps, tele-
    type, etc. CAMERA PANS room, picks up teletype operator
    and MOVES IN on operating teletype machine. CAMERA MOVES
    IN on an ANGLE so as to indicate simply that the machine
    is in operation and not to attempt to read the message.
    Machine stops, girl tears off message in duplicate, and
    gives both copies to a Clerk. Clerk is in motion almost
    at the time the message is in his hands. He takes one
    copy direct to a microphone operator who immediately and
    silently starts broadcasting.

7   ANOTHER ANGLE   7

    The Clerk continues on toward map area. On the way to
    the maps he is intercepted in motion by what is appar-
    ently an Officer -- his back to CAMERA. Clerk hands
    him the message as they continue to walk toward the map.
    Officer moves one indicator on the map to a given point
    and then indicates in pantomime with his hand to the
    Clerk how to move other indicators to converge toward a
    given area and makes a hurried exit thru the exterior
    door. Perhaps as we see the exterior door open, we dan
    also see a Patrol Car parked at the curb.

                                                       CUT TO:

8   SHOT - PATROL CAR   8

    speeding away from this area.

                                                       RAPID CUT TO:

3.

9 SHOT - PATROL CAR 9

 speeding down the highway.

            CUT TO:

10 SHOT - PATROL CAR 10

 speeding around curve and making a clean CAMERA exit. Over the b.g. thru which the patrol car has just passed, we place the ZIV SUPERIMPOSURE. At this point, the VOICE OVER should be completed. However, the THEME is not quite finished.

 We now come in with a CREDIT CARD stating:

> "WE GRATEFULLY ACKNOWLEDGE THE
> TECHNICAL ASSISTANCE OF THE
> CALIFORNIA STATE HIGHWAY PATROL,
> THRU WHOSE COOPERATION THE
> AUTHENTIC PRODUCTION OF THIS
> PROGRAM WAS MADE POSSIBLE."

 (The above copy is tentative and has yet to be decided upon and checked.)

 The THEME is now UP and OUT and we

            FADE OUT:

     (OPENING COMMERCIAL)

FADE IN:

11 SHOT - HIGHWAY   11

CAMERA is mounted in a ditch alongside the highway and
is pointed at right angle to the highway. Close to
CAMERA is some fairly heavy foliage. CAMERA studies the
highway thru the foliage. The o.s. SOUND of an automobile motor approaching is heard. A pair of hands come
from behind CAMERA into the foliage, followed by a
shoulder and the back of a man'w head. The hands part
the foliage and we SEE the car go by as we look thru the
opening provided by the hands. Almost immediately, a
second car goes by. The SOUNDS of both cars rapidly
fade into the distance. The man releases the foliage and
turns around into a

12 FULL HEAD CLOSEUP - MAN   12

He is looking just OFF CAMERA. This is RALPH NEAL.

(As the above scene FADED IN, the MUSIC also FADED IN
with the opening of the THEME. THEME continues, but is
blended down and goes UNDER and OUT when Neal begins to
speak.)

His VOICE is flat and shows the effect of being slightly
winded.

                  NEAL
        Lots of traffic for six o'clock
        in the morning.

Neal continues talking, as the CAMERA PANS SLOWLY DOWN
to REVEAL the upper part of his wardrobe and a convict's
number above his left shirt pocket. Under the number,
there is another line reading "State Penitentiary."

                  NEAL
              (continuing)
        And the bushes acoss the street
        aren't too close. We're gonna
        have to keep running all the way.

He turns, takes another look at the highway thru the
bushes. This time when he turns back, he's not quite
as close to CAMERA. (The above speech and this action
is all continuous and simultaneous.) As he turns back
from the bushes, he moves toward the person to whom he's
been talking. CAMERA PANS with him and picks up a LOOSE
HEAD CLOSEUP of JEFF PARKER. Neal's profile is slightly
in the SHOT.

                  NEAL
              (continuing)
        Can you make it?

                                                      (CONTINUED)

Below: Dan Matthews receives an update on Officer Peterson's condition in *'Prison Break'* (Photo Goltz Collection).

Above: The actual *Golden Pheasant* restaurant location used in the pilot episode *'Prison Break'* (Photo Goltz Collection).

Below: The same location today (Photo Goltz Collection).

Broderick Crawford as Dan Mathews praying for hostage children in *'Prison Break'* (Photo Goltz Collection).

162 CONTINUED:

Dan motions down to Neal's motionless Body. One of the men bends down and grabs Neal by the shoulder and starts to turn him over. As soon as we see what his gesture is going to be, we CUT AWAY.

163 SHOT - SERGEANT

SERGEANT
Dead?

VOICE (o.s.)
Yes, sir.

MATHEWS
(motioning at Vince)
Here's his running mate. Take him in. We'll book him back at Headquarters.

Dan pauses for a moment, then continues.

164 C.U. - DAN

MATHEWS
(continuing)
Sergeant, will you clean up the details here? This man's car is over there with a flat tire... the body, and so forth. I'm going on ahead. I want to see if I can get back to town in time to take Pete's kids to the circus tonight.

HOLD momentarily on Dan as we start the THEME. Dan turns, walks toward his car, gets in and drives off, as the THEME plays to conclusion.

FADE OUT.

Below: Broderick Crawford as Dan Mathews and his fellow officers at the grim finale to the pilot episode *'Prison Break'* (Photo Goltz Collection).

Release No. 1001A

Production No. 1B

HIGHWAY PATROL - Pilot #1 - "Prison Break" by Stuart Jerome

CAST:

Dan Mathews	Broderick Crawford		
Ralph Neal	Bob Forrest		
Peterson	Fritz Ford	Patrolman Halsey	Paul Burke
Jeff Parker	Harry Cody	Radio Operator	Diana Lee Brewster
Matt	Paul Bryar		
Garage Man	William Challee		
Dorsey	Jay Douglas		
Les Wilkins	Charles Seel		
Billy	Bobby Mittelstaedt		
Margie	Isa Ashdown		
Policeman Brown	Paul Hahn		
Patrolman Stevens	Jim O'Neill		
Patrolman Harris	Bill Slack		
Sergeant	Frank Hanley		

CREW:

Cameraman	Curt Fetters	Set Dec.	Bruce MacDonald
Production Supervisor	Maurice Unger	Property	Robert Benton, Sr.
Director	Herbert L. Strock	Wardrobe	Alfred Berke
Assistant Director	Eddie Bernoudy	Make-up	George Gray
Film Editor	Ace Clark	Script	Larry Lund
Sound Mixer	Jay Ashworth		
Sound Editor	Gus Galvin		

SYNOPSIS:

RALPH NEAL is a hardened criminal. He's smart, ruthless, and brutal. His outward personality belies his vicious character. He escapes from a state penitentiary. During the escape, he kills a guard. The convict who escapes with him is wounded during the escape. When this man's wounded leg slows the pair down, Neal immediately appraises this as an obstacle to his getaway and slugs the man into unconsciousness. The State Patrol is notified and as soon as the convicts have gone over the wall. DAN MATHEWS, head of the State Patrol, immediately swings his organization into action. Mathews is a real pro. He works from the field and this operation is urgent enough that he handle it personally. Mathews and Neal do not know each other, but little by little, as Mathews bottles up every avenue of escape, and closes in on Neal, and as Neal commits one ruthless act after another to break through a trap that is closing in on him, it becomes apparent that there is almost a personal conflict between these two men -- a conflict that ends only when they meet face to face in the final scene.

Appendix B
Official ZIV Television Writer's Guide for the *Highway Patrol* series from the Goltz Collection.

```
CABLE ADDRESS                                              NEW YORK
 "ZIVTEEVEE"                                               CHICAGO
                                                           CINCINNATI
                        ZIV                                HOLLYWOOD
                   Television Programs
                   7324 SANTA MONICA BLVD.
                   HOLLYWOOD 46, CALIFORNIA
```

PERSONAL & CONFIDENTIAL

GENERAL INFORMATION FOR WRITERS ON HIGHWAY PATROL

1. This is basically an action documentary series. We take great care not to imitate any of the other well-known police, detective, sheriff, or district attorney type shows that are on the air.

2. We <u>show</u> the <u>crime quickly</u> or let it have happened. Our crooks are clever or the problem insurmountable and Mathews solves it. We do not like to have criminals caught or the crime solved because thieves fall out. It must be solved by Mathews thinking and using good police work.

3. <u>The tag</u> must wrap up the crime and all the criminals leaving no loose ends. Another very important element in our tag is that after Mathews has apparently solved the crime, some other last minute thing must happen so that our audience will not know the picture is over. An example would be -- two minutes before the end, Mathews solves the crime and holds the criminals at bay -- but a minute and a half from the end they do something which makes it look as though they are going to get away and Mathews' quick thinking and courage stops them. We like to have a last line to the criminal and final going away shot.

Dan Mathews, played by Broderick Crawford, is the head of the Highway Patrol and as such, travels from town to town and office to office. There should always be a crisp clean introduction of Broderick Crawford as Dan Mathews as though the dialog and camera or voice over are saying, "This is Dan Mathews, Head of the Highway Patrol." Dan has no personal life so we don't talk about wives, children, girlfriends nor does he, at any time have any personal relationship with any of the characters. This does not mean, however, that he cannot know his officers and their families. It is very important that he is not written tough. He can fight and enter gun play. He walks very well and we prefer not to have him run unless absolutely necessary. He should never be brought into anything that would be out of his jurisdiction, such as -- investigating a pick pocket, etc.

4. The scripts are written in two acts with the end of the first act having a menace. We use voice over which opens our act and is always in the third person. The opening voice over in act one is in two parts:

   The first paragraph is a statement of law enforcement in general; the Highway Patrol in particular.

   The second paragraph talks about the crime we are about so see.

   The voice over opening act two is usually one paragraph and is generally a statement of the problem of the crime we are watching.

   We like out voice overs to use picture words such as "highly charged imagination," etc. The voice over can be, and is used as, a bridge throughout the script but we prefer to think, at this time, of only two pieces of voice over; one at each act opening.

5. We do not use any opitcals with the exception of a dissolve indicating a long time lapse, which necessitates bridge scenes. Do not indicate dissolves, fades or other opticals. Because we do not use dissolves in our format it is necessary that the writer keep this in mind and use cut away scenes to get out people from one place to another, but every scene must move the story.

6. We hold our cast units at ten or less. This means one man working two days is two units. Broderick Crawford is not counted in this ten unit group.

7. It is important that your stories are ones that we can do production-wise. We like the scripts set up so that they shoot one day on location and one day on the stage. We prefer to have two days on location rather than a day and a half, which presents

certain production problems.

Our scripts should run from 38-41 pages. We work from a premise to a step outline to a screen play Our scripts have certain policy restrictions:

- a. <u>No food or drink</u>. People can eat and can drink but they cannot order food by name such as -- a sandwich. Their ordering must be general such as -- blue Plate Special.

    Their drink can be something served in a cup, but not named -- can presume to be coffee or tea but not milk or beer or hard liquor of any kind. A soft drink can be ordered, but not named, as in case of children, but this presents a problem in bottle recognition.

- b. <u>Smoking.</u> Our people can smoke but we cannot identify the cigarette either by package or length of the cigarette. If a cigarette is offered, it must be taken, A cigarette cannot be stamped out as a dramatic piece of business.

- c. <u>Kidnapping.</u> We cannot do kidnapping stories unless the person kidnapped is obviously an adult.

- d. <u>Cursing</u>. This of course is prohibited.

- e. <u>Words</u> like <u>idiot</u>, <u>crazy</u>, etc. Extreme care must be taken in the use of these common place words or other words or phrases that mean the same, such as "off your rocker.

- f. <u>Juvenile Delinquents</u> are forbidden. Any delinquent must be an obvious adult.

8. In the <u>opening of act one</u> be sure to have an <u>exterior scene</u> that <u>allows footage</u> to be shot for title, music, etc. The same applies to the closing of act two. The closing can be an interior scene if absolutely necessary but we definitely prefer an exterior.

9. We have <u>theme music</u> in the series but for purposes of story, do not plan on using it in the body of the picture.

10. We prefer one <u>day action stories</u> with each scene progressing the story and dialog leading into cutaways.

11. <u>Violence</u>. We want violence and impact but we try to stay away from unnecessary violence and wanton killing unless this is a story point.

12. While Dan Mathews is the head man and makes the final solution, we like our other patrolmen to do something other than be a guy that Mathews talks to.

13. Authenticity. We try at all times for complete authenticity. You should be cautioned that the technical advisor's word is law, Don't count on a dramatic license, which he may not understand

    In our authenticity we use code numbers when talking over the radio between cars and headquarters. When one officer calls another he uses his badge number. Dan Mathews is 2150 so his call would be 2150 to headquarters or 2150 to 3310 and the answer would be headquarters bye, or from 3310 bye.

    At the end of the radio conversation the numbers 10-4 are used first as a question meaning, "do you understand?"; and second as a an answer, "I understand." "I am going to catch the heavy, 10-4." The answer coming back would be "10-4." One often used number is 10-20, which means "your location." So that a message would be "what is your 10-20?" The answer would be, "My 10-20 is 5th and Main." Another use would be, "I will be at your 10-20 in ten minutes." Various officers are not generally referred to by name over the radio. All Patrol cars have radios, which are used between cars and between, headquarters, rather than telephones. It is all right for officers in a house to call headquarters by telephone and give instructions, but generally speaking they use the car radio. All officers keep headquarters informed at all times such as:- an officer that pulls a suspect car to the side of the road would tell headquarters that he has stopped a suspect car and is now going to investigate. If headquarters does not hear again from the officer they will investigate immediately.

    Another commonly used term is AFB which means - "All Points bulletin." AFB's are put out on every suspect and on every new piece of information.

    MO means Modus Operandi, or method of operation. This is used in reference to a criminal pattern. The voice at headquarters can be male or female but bear in mind that the voice becomes a cast unit as do radio voices, etc.

    The following is a general police term: --
    DMV - Department of Motor Vehicles. This is used whenever they are checking license plates and numbers.

14. In the matter of portraying the patrol, our men are all very smart and efficient. We try not to use patrolmen's names nor have the patrolmen, when speaking to Dan Mathews, use his name. So dialog should be designed in such a way that names are not necessary. However; a patrolman introducing a civilian to Mathews would say, "Mr. Jones, this is Mr. Mathews."

    They are polite at all times and do not push people around unless the situation calls for it.

15. <u>Technical advisors</u> are Officer Frank Runyon and Sgt. Mark Benson. They are available for questions but please call us first so that we can either answer your question or tell you which man to call.

Appendix C
The Complete *Highway Patrol* Episode Guide.

Each episode is rated between one to five stars * but even the 1-star shows have some 'camp value'! The guide lists the writer, director, notable recurring actors, and a plot synopsis.

Abbreviations: PN = Production Number, RN = Release Number.

Season #1 1955-1956

Prison Break/ Road Block *****

PN 1B, RN 1001

Writer: Stuart Jerome, Director: Herbert L. Strock, Recurring Actors: Jay Douglas, Paul Burke is Officer Halsey

A hardened criminal, whose personality belies his viciousness, escapes from prison and kills a guard. Dan Mathews swings into action. The man commits one ruthless act after another to break through the trap closing in on him. It is apparent there is a personal conflict between the two men that ends when they meet face to face in the final scene.

Machine Story Copter/ Machine Napping Copter ****

PN 2B, RN 1002

Writer: Gene Levitt, Director: Herbert L. Strock, Recurring Actors: Ray Bourgois

An expensive, giant computer, a twentieth century wonder which does tremendous administrative work in just a few hours, is ingeniously 'kidnapped' from an electronics company by two men. The company's owner is told to get $100,000 from his bank at two o'clock the next day and wait for instructions. A helicopter chase helps Dan Mathews stop the men from collecting the ransom and getting away.

Reckless Driving ***

PN 3B, RN 1003

Writer: Donald A. Brinkley, Director: Leon Benson, Recurring Actors: William Boyett

Systematic traffic checks and increased patrols begin on a high accident freeway. Hoping to determine causes and cures, Dan questions drivers who get citations there. One man refuses to obey Dan's safety philosophy and his license is suspended. His wife drives him to an important business meeting but her glasses break. He takes over behind the wheel but panics at a routine traffic check and flees. This results in a severe accident and his wife is critically injured. He learns the hard way (too late) what Dan warned him about.

Lookout ***

PN 5B, RN 1004

Writer: Jack Laird, Director: Herbert I. Strock

An innocent bystander sees two brothers hold up a diner and kill its owner. He flees and is terrified of being killed by the criminals. As Dan searches for him, one man is killed, two are critically wounded, and the man who just a few short hours earlier was an average law-biding citizen, is chased to the point where he is willing to shoot it out with police. Dan shows him the errors of his ways.

Gambling *

PN 6B, RN 1005

Writer: Don Mullally, Director: Les Goodwins

A sheriff asks Dan's help with an illegal gambling house that has defied his efforts to shut it down. Dan's conducts a surprise raid but the efficient club yields no evidence. There are two doors that stall the raid long enough for the gambling equipment to be hidden. Dan and his sergeant take control of those doors in the next raid and the place is closed.

Hitchhiker ****

PN 7B, RN 1006

Writer: Michael Cramoy, Director: Lew Landers, Recurring Actors: Jon Locke

A man picks up a hitchhiking migrant worker, hits him with a tire iron, plants false ID on his body, and wrecks the car to make his death appear accidental. The doctor's report indicates murder and Dan finds five similar 'accidents' for insurance fraud. After following several blind leads, he traces the insurance payoffs to the same address – a rural store that is the unofficial post office for migrant workers. The evidence points the guilt at an ex-con but Dan exposes and apprehends the real culprit before he can kill a sixth time.

Desert Town *****

PN 4B, RN 1007

Writer: Stuart Jerome, Director: Eddie Davis

In this mystery, Dan inspects outlying patrol stations and stops for breakfast in a tiny, isolated town. However, the restaurant's stove just conked out and the second diner closes as he walks in. The general store is also closed with nobody around. His curiosity turns to suspicion when he finds an out-of-state car that checks out as stolen. The entire town is covering up a crime but finally a townsperson cracks. He leads Dan to a deserted mine where a corpse is about to be buried and the terrible secret that turned the village into a ghost town.

Radioactive *****
PN 9B, RN 1008

Writer: Gene Levitt, Director: Paul Guilfoyle

One man poses as a narcotics agent, and a woman poses as a dope dealer. Together they dupe people into believing close relatives are members of a dope ring.

Reformed Criminal ****

PN 10B, RN 1009

Writer: Robert Wesley (Gene Roddenberry), Director: Lambert Hillyer, Recurring actors: Terry Frost

A farmer's cooperative agent is reported missing while carrying a large sum of the firm's money. Learning he has a criminal record, Dan assumes he is still a thief and sets up roadblocks. His efforts to prove his innocence are blocked by Dan's search for what appears to be a dangerous criminal. Finally, Dan takes a heavy professional risk to let the men prove he is straight.

Father Thief *****

PN 11B, RN 1010

Writer: Robert M. Fresco, Donald Brinkley, Director: Herbert L. Strock, Recurring actors: Jack Douglas, Frank Gerstle as Sgt. Tom Betts

A young man stopped for speeding and accidentally runs down the patrolman who had gotten suspicious over the auto parts in the back of the pick-up truck. He drives the officer to the hospital which saves his life and earns Dan's sympathy. Dan is shocked when the pick-up is linked to recent thefts of auto parts. Dan suspects the boy is shielding his father. His thorough investigation clears the boy and convicts his cowardly parent.

Retired Gangster ****

PN 12B, RN 1011

Writer: Rik Vollaerts, Director: Alvin Ganzer

Dan must protect ex-crime boss McCall, a rancher who will testify at a grand jury probe in five days. Since McCall refuses to go to a hotel for safety, Dan joins him at the ranch. They survive a sniper's attack, explosives hidden in a truckload of alfalfa, and a bomb sent by mail. A car smashes through but the mobsters are captured in a gunfight. McCall is impressed that a cop risked his own life to save and vows to be a willing witness.

Phony Insurance *****

PN 13B, RN 1012

Writer: Jack Rock, Director: Les Goodwins

A protection man is running what appears to be a legitimate maintenance service. His men cause trucks to break down on the highways. He then offers his service which guarantees no 'accidents'. The truckers have no idea that he is behind the 'accidents'. One trucker refuses the service and Dan is called in to investigate. One of the leader's henchmen-mechanics is murdered and Dan breaks-up the operation.

Escort ****

PN 8B, RN 1013

Writer: Norman Jolley, Director: Alvin Ganzer, Recurring Actors: Emil Sitka, veteran Three Stooges supporting player

An anonymous caller tells Dan that mobster Johnny Barr is planning to kill an important man. Deducing that the caller is an accountant making investments with Barr's money, Dan bugs his office. He learns that the intended victim is a senator who is setting up a crime commission to go after Barr. The senator insists on going through with his planned trip and his safety is in Dan's hands. Using a series of decoys Dan gets him through the roadblock attack and to his destination. Dan arrests Barr for attempted murder and assures him the crime commission is now in session.

Resort ****

PN 15B, RN 1014

Writer: Donald A. Brinkley, Director: Paul Guilfoyle

Dan learns that heroin is being smuggled into the area under the hubcaps of innocent people's cars. After they reach their destination the narcotics are collected by local drug pushers. The heroin is traced back to its source, a fashionable resort hotel. Dan goes undercover and eventually with the help of a can opener gets the evidence that incriminates and smashes the dope ring.

Girl Bandit *****

PN 16B, RN 1015

Writer: Michael Cramoy, Director: Lambert Hillyer, Recurring Actors: Jeanne Cooper

At his wife's insistence, a bank messenger steals a large sum of money. Arriving home early, he overhears his wife planning to double-cross him and run off with another man. Confronting them, he is beaten and flees. Driving erratically, he is stopped by the Highway Patrol and sent to hospital in coma. Dan discovers he was planning to leave the country but finds his wife has left with the loot. Dan is always a step behind her until he finally catches up to her with her cohort and the money.

Below: Broderick Crawford as Dan Mathews checks with a nurse on the victim of a 'Girl Bandit' (Photo Goltz Collection).

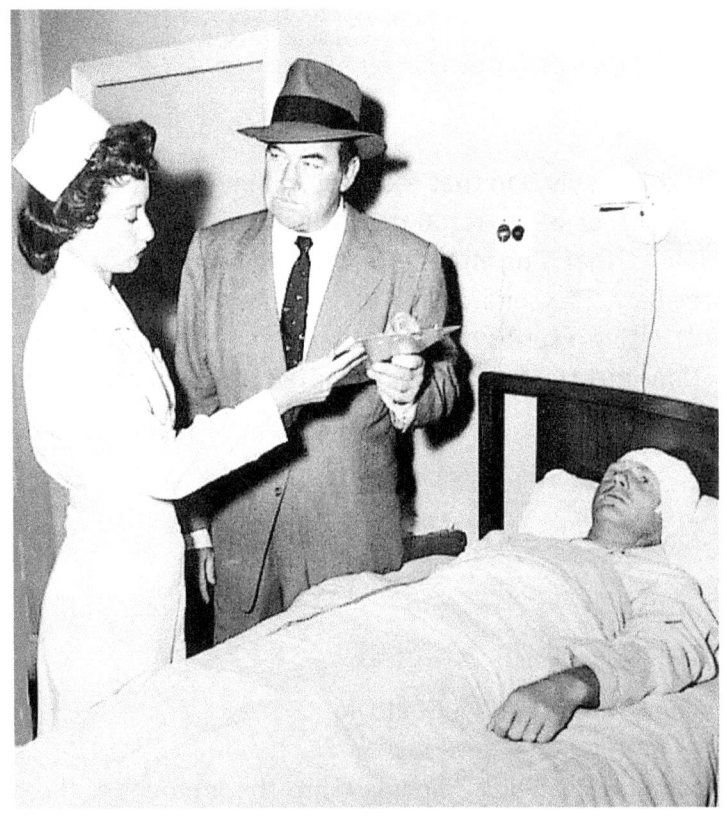

Mountain Copter *****

PN 17B, RN 1016

Writer: Donald A. Brinkley, Director: Herbert Strock, Recurring Actors: Roy Bourgois

A couple finds an injured, feverish, hungry and armed man in their remote mountain cabin. The woman nurses him while her husband notifies the ranger, who radios the Highway Patrol. The frightened young hoodlum is running away from a murder he did not commit. Dan helicopters to the area and finds the man in a panic has overpowered the woman, wounded the husband, and fled. Dan's deductive powers, the ranger's knowledge of the terrain, the chopper's ability is too much for the hood. With the boy cornered, Dan gambles his own insight of human nature against the young man's desperation.

Lie Detector ****

PN 19B, RN 1017

Writer: Norman Jolley, Director: Eddie Davis

Dan is called to arrest Taylor for trying to force an elderly motel owner to reveal where her money is hidden. Both undergo lie detector tests that show them as truthful. Taylor is booked but while he is out on bail, the woman is convinced by her nephew Henry to put her money in the bank. Faking care trouble on the highway, he stops and his accomplice robs the old woman, knocks her out, and slugs Henry for cover. When he recovers Henry names Taylor as the culprit. Taylor passes another polygraph and Dan suspects Henry framed him. He arrests Henry and his accomplice and says his lie detector has never let him down yet.

Scared Cop *****

PN 20B, RN 1018

Writer: Bill George, Director: Lambert Hillyer, Recurring Actors: Terry Frost

    Officer Mark Reynolds comes face-to-face on the highway with his escaped criminal brother Bill who overpowers him and flees. Mark has an opportunity to shoot his brother but can't. Mark doesn't report the incident and suddenly resigns. Dan doesn't wish to lose one of his best officers and talks to his wife who knows nothing. He also meets at the house Mark's ailing father who thinks that Bill is a dead war hero. Mark has lied because he thinks the truth will kill his father. Bill is caught and escapes again. Dan suspect's that Bill is Mark's brother. This time Bill tries to murder his brother but is captured by Dan and Mark. Dan protects their father, and keeps Mark on the force.

Harbor Story *****

PN 18B, RN 1019

Writer: Lou Huston, Director: Paul Guilfoyle, Recurring Actors: Stuart Whitman, Terry Frost

    Three bandits rob a bank in a small coastal town and shoot a bystander. Dan orders roadblocks to cut off all escape routes and an abandoned car is found. In a well-organized plan, the bandits anticipate roadblocks and head for the beach dressed as fishermen. A launch comes to take them down the coast and they assault a skin-diver leaving him for dead. He is found alive in time and Dan finds a clue that links the robbery to the beach assault. The next time they strike again, Dan has his units close-in on the beach. However, he must remove two small children from danger without exciting them or tipping off the bandits. An old ruse works but Dan nearly loses his life stopping them three men single-handedly to prevent them from reaching the beach.

Hit and Run ****

PN 21B, RN 1020

Writer: Arthur Weiss, Director: Eddie Davis, Recurring Actors: Jack Douglas

After an emotional argument with her husband over her mother ruining their lives, the emotional, weak-willed wife drives to her mother's farm. On the way, she hits a pedestrian and flees. Her husband gives her an alibi to prevent her mental breakdown. Dan investigates but the mother falsely confesses to the accident. A shoeprint at the scene of the accident convinces Dan that her daughter is the guilty one. She returns to the accident scene expecting to see the man's body. She decides to jump off the nearby bridge but Dan persuades her back to safety by telling her the man will recover.

Car Theft ****

PN 22B, RN 1021

Writer: Jack Laird, Director: Herbert L. Strock

A junkyard employee calls Dan to say that a man paid $800 for a '55 Ford Thunderbird as salvage but never called for it. Dan uncovers an elaborate stolen car racket. The criminals buy late model wrecks for their license registrations, steal identical vehicles which are repainted with the plates switched. Dan apprehends the ringleader but one man is dead and another injured.

Human Bomb *****

PN 23B, RN 1022

Writer: Robert Wesley (Gene Roddenberry), Director: Leon Benson

A disgruntled electrical engineer has lost his job at a chemical company and vows revenge. He uses stolen explosives to convert his car into a giant bomb and drives to the city to blow up the building. Dan learns about the suicide mission and sets up roadblocks which the man bypasses. Dan is the last unit between the four-wheeled bomb and the city.

Plane Crash ****

PN 24B, RN 1023

Writer: Stuart Jerome, Donald Brinkley, Director: Leon Benson, Recurring Actors: Guy Williams

Patrolling a desolate section of forest, a ranger calls the Highway Patrol to report a small plane making a forced landing. Dan arrives to find an empty plane and no ranger. Later they find his murdered body. The plane's registration shows the owner as a racketeer who left the city that morning with his wife and a private pilot. Dan catches up with them in a deserted resort settlement deep in the mountains and uncovers another crime that leads back to the ranger's murder.

Desert Copter *****

PN 25B, RN 1024

Writer: Lou Huston, Don Mullaly, Director: Herbert L. Strock, Recurring Actors: Roy Bourgois

Warren, a smooth con man wanted for murder, speeds to the desert. Dan gives out his description to radio stations and a gas station attendant calls with a tip. Dan knows that Warren will leave the state on one of the desert roads. After hearing the radio flash, Warren changes clothes and joins two college professors searching for fossils. A café manager identifies Warren to Dan from a photo and says he is in a jeep with the professors. Dan pursues with a helicopter but Warren ties up one of the men in the desert and takes the other hostage in the jeep. Dan rescues the tied-up man and sets up a blockade with an officer in a truck. The trap works but the officer is wounded. With the helicopter, Dan is able to capture Warren.

Plant Robbery ***

PN 6B, RN 1025

Writer: Ed Adamson, Director: Henry S. Kesler, Recurring Actors: Jack Douglas, Terry Frost

When a duplicate armored truck is used to stage a daring robbery, Dan uses all his resources to track it down. The lab analysis shows it was built by auto expert Walt Burns, who has vanished. While the Highway Patrol searches for him, he is murdered by his partner Denson. Footprints at the crime scene help the lab use art and science to get an accurate description of Burns who is arrested.

Released Convict ***

PN 27B, RN 1026

Writer: Arthur Weiss, Director: Paul Guilfoyle, Recurring Actors: William Boyett, Gary Roark

Dan's officers follow a tail-wise ex-convict just released after serving time for a half-million armored car robbery. He heads to Smokey Hills to get the loot from its hiding place. Dan's units follow his progress from concealed positions, and a transmitter planted on his car is successfully triangulated by the Highway Patrol radio stations.

Motorcycle A *****

PN 28B, RN 1027

Writer: Donald A. Brinkley, Director: Lambert Hillyer, Recurring Actors: Jack Douglas, Jack Edwards, and Clint Eastwood

Eight months after a tiny town was raided and ransacked by a renegade motorcycle gang. The wife of the diner's owner Bernie Sills (Jack Edwards) was crippled in the attack. When two members of an accredited motorcycle club stop at his diner for breakfast, Bernie chases them out at gunpoint and a fight ensues. A pursuing patrolman is killed in an accident caused by a truck driver failing to stop at an intersection. Sills and his wife tell Dan the two bikers caused the trouble and are responsible for the officer's death. The bikers claim they are innocent. Dan sends two motorcycle officers to town dressed as regular bikers. Sills runs them out of his diner at gunpoint and Dan moves in for an arrest.

Mental Patient ****

PN 29B, RN 1028

Writer: Robert Wesley (Gene Roddenberry), Director: Leon Benson

A farmer is found beaten to death. Dan learns that a mental patient has escaped from the state hospital and is in the area. The Highway Patrol knows it has an insane killer on the loose but the man evades all the roadblocks. Local hysteria grows as more evidence builds against the mental patient. Dan protects the suspected killer from a lynch mob and his policy of not jumping to conclusions pays off!

License Plates ***

PN 30B, RN 1029

Writer: Bill George, Director: Paul Guilfoyle

A very unpredictable bank robber has been very successful. He operates without pattern, and his nondescript looks make it tough for anyone to identify him. His polite robberies hit a snag when an alert little boy memorizes his getaway car's license plate number. Dan follows his hunch and the clever, smooth-talking robber talks his way to prison.

Hitchhiker Dies ****

PN 31B, RN 1030

Writer: Jack Laird, Director: Herbert L. Strock, Recurring Actors: William Boyett

With inside help a bandit robs a plastics plant payroll office of $28,000. He is wounded in a shoot-out with a guard and flees in a gray convertible. Engine trouble forces him to abandon the car and he hitch-hikes a ride from an identical make gray convertible. The driver fights for his life and in a struggle over a gun, the bandit is shot dead. At the police roadblock, the driver is taken into custody and suspected of the plant robbery. The bandit's insider accomplice at the plant also helps to frame him. Dan is suspicious of the evidence piling up against the driver and sets a trap that catches the real culprit.

Blast Area Copter *****

PN 34B, RN 1031

Writer: Donald A. Brinkley, Director: Lew Landers, Recurring Actors: Roy Bourgois

A fugitive gunman has hijacked a woman (Helene Stanton, real-life mother of Dr. Drew Pinsky) and her car. They run out of gas and wander into an area not knowing that the Highway Patrol has cleared for blasting to build a flood basin. Dan flies over the area in a helicopter after the signal for the blast was given. The gunman fires at the helicopter taking out its radio leaving Dan no way to stop the explosion. Dan remains with the captured prisoner and lets the woman take his seat in the small helicopter as it flies to safety. Dan sweats it out with seconds to the blast time until the helicopter transmits the 'hold' signal to the control base.

Anti-toxin ****

PN 32B, RN 1032

Writer: Tony Barrett, Director: Leon Benson

While inspecting patrol stations, Dan is thrown into a terrifying situation and race for time. A youngster has gas gangrene (an infected closed wound of festering bacteria causing deadly gases). The doctor is strapped for time in a remote location. Dan has his men race the anti-toxin to the dying boy. When the serum is lost a greedy extortionist nearly causes the boy's death until Dan saves the day.

Dead Patrolman ***

PN 33B, RN 1033

Writer: Arthur Weiss, Director: Jack Herzberg, Recurring Actors: William Boyett, Jack Douglas

An officer's patrol car is found abandoned on a country road. Dan discovers he was killed by two men in a stolen car racket. They rode in a car that was repainted. It belongs to a woman who at first says she doesn't own it but later says she borrowed it to a friend. Dan convinces her to act as bait to trap the killer. The plan goes awry when she loses her cool and the killer get wise and leaves. Dan brings him to justice.

Art Robbery ***

PN 36B, RN 1034

Writer: Michael Cramoy, Director: Donald A. Brinkley, Recurring Actors: William Boyett, Jack Douglas

An art collector's business manager plans to steal valuable paintings and hold them for ransom. His plans go awry and he and his men commit murder to escape the *Highway Patrol*. Dan casts a web of evidence against the criminals and withholds the fact that the priceless paintings were already recovered. The thieves turn against each other and get caught in their own net.

Runaway Boy ***

PN 35B, RN 1035

Writer: Lou Huston, Director: Harry Gerstad, Recurring Actors: Guy Williams

Fearing an eye operation, 12-year old Jimmy runs away. Dan is informed the boy needs immediate surgery to prevent blindness or injury from his impaired sight. A friend tells Dan that Jimmy is running away to a town 75 miles away. A trucker accidentally damages Jimmy's bike, and suspecting he is a runaway notifies the Highway Patrol. Jimmy continues to flee a step ahead of Dan until he joins a tramp on the road. The tramp does not want to be involved with a runaway and police so he sends Jimmy to a remote, dangerous area. Dan locates the boy in time and gets him to willingly return home for the surgery.

Taxi ***

PN 37B, RN 1036

Writer: William N. Robson, Director: Paul Guilfoyle, Recurring Actors: Terry Frost

Joe Flynn in his most famous role of Captain Binghampton on *McHale's Navy* (Photo R. Schiller).

A gunman (Joe Flynn, not wearing his trademark horn-rim glasses as ruthless Captain Binghamton from the popular *McHale's Navy* (1962-1966 series) holds up a gas station and while fleeing in a taxi and kills a Highway Patrolman. He later steals a Jaguar and drives it until the tank is empty. He hides at a farmhouse and takes the farmer and wife captive. Dan's roadblocks turn up empty so he sends his men to search the minor roads for the stolen car. They find it near the farmhouse. One officer bangs on the front door while Dan enters through the back, disarms the man and rescue the couple

Below: Joe Flynn's contract with ZIV Television
(Photo Goltz Collection)

Missing Witness ***

PN 39B, RN 1037

Writer: Donald A. Brinkley, Director: Lew Landers

On the day, a man is sentenced to death for the Sunrise Park murders, a woman comes to Highway Patrol headquarters and says the man is innocent and that she can identify the real murderer. Dan's intensive questioning of the woman disproves her story as a desperate attempt to save the life of her ex-boyfriend. The story had already hit the newspapers and an attempt on her life leads Dan to suspect she may be telling the truth. A carefully planted news story traps the real killer and freedom for the wrongly convicted man.

Prospector ***

PN 38B, RN 1038

Writer: Robert Wesley (Gene Roddenberry), Director: Lew Landers

Old prospector Asa McQueen discovers a large sum of money that was hidden on his mining claim. He goes on a spending spree that attracts the attention of the robber who hid the loot and the police. Dan tries to reach Asa before the robber kills him but the prospector is already pinned down by the robber's high-powered rifle. Dan uses a clever but dangerous ruse to capture the gunman.

Christmas Story ****

PN 14B, RN 1039

Writer: Donald A. Brinkley, Director: Herbert L. Strock

A neglected wife takes her daughter on Christmas Eve and leaves her workaholic architect husband. On their way to the wife's sister's home, mother and daughter spend the night at a motel. The next morning the little girl is missing and a frantic mother calls the *Highway Patrol*. Dan investigates and uses psychology to determine the little girl left on her own to find Santa Claus. The father joins his wife searching for the daughter. Finally Dan finds a Salvation Army Santa Claus who located the little girl with a stray puppy. The parents reconcile after this near-tragedy and go home for Christmas. Dan does a double-take when Santa Claus turns down an offer of a ride with "I've got my own transportation!"

Season #2 1956-1957

The Search ***

PN 40B, RN 1040

Writer: William L. Driskell, Director: Jack Herzberg, Recurring Actors: William Boyett, Terry Frost

    Slick-talking killer Irv Desmond is a failure at bank robberies but a genius at getaways, fleeing with innocent people who refuse to believe he is a criminal. An elderly couple helps him past a roadblock but he is spotted by a café manager. The couple wind-up in the line-of-fire when Dan catches up with him.

Kidnap Copter **

PN 42B, RN 1041

Writer: Donald A. Brinkley, Director: Lew Landers, Recurring Actors: Terry Frost, Jon Locke, Jack Douglas, Roy Bourgois

    A millionaire's son Jerry Watts is kidnapped and held in an isolated mountain shack. A game warden calls the *Highway Patrol*. Jerry runs to the police but injures himself falling down a canyon. Dan realizes that a helicopter to the rescue from any angle would be in the direct line-of-fire of the kidnappers so it approaches straight down! The boy is rescued.

Trailer Story **

PN 44B, RN 1042

Writer: Joel Malcomb Rapp, Director: Jack Herzberg, Recurring Actors: Jack Douglas

    Jewel thief Steve Talbot dodging the Highway Patrol that knows he likes fancy cars, flees in a battered old sedan. His car breaks down after passing a roadblock so Steve hijacks a newlywed couple and their trailer. Dan lets Talbot through the next roadblock because he fears for the couple's safety. They have a new passenger on the roof, Dan who saves the couple and apprehends Steve.

Fisherman's Luck ***

PN 43B, RN 1043

Writer: Jerry Sackheim, Director: Harry Gerstad, Recurring Actors: Jack Douglas, William Boyett, Stuart Whitman

Dan dismisses as a coincidence an accident report of a car matching one used in a bank robbery until the wrecked vehicle is stolen. It is found abandoned in a junkyard with proof it was the getaway car. Dan suspects that the car was stolen to recover the loot and that the robbers went to a nearby resort to join their leader. Dan surrounds the resort with his force and rounds up the robbers.

Magazine Writer ***

PN 46B, RN 1044

Writer: Lou Huston, Director: Herbert L. Strock, Recurring Actors: Stuart Whitman

Dan identifies the body of petty criminal Vince Garrow who received a traffic ticket in a car owned by reporter Sam Dahlquist who is now missing. Dan thinks that racketeer Jake Mallek had Garrow murdered and kidnapped the reporter to stop his expose. The trail leads to Mallek's mountain lodge where Mallek is holding Dahlquist at gunpoint. With seconds to spare, Dan launches a daring plan that saves the reporter's life.

Typhoid Carrier **

PN 48B, RN 1045

Writer: Donald A. Brinkley, Director: Eddie Davis

Farmer Hank Dooley's daughter dies of typhoid fever and the carrier is the farmer's hired hand Len Frazier. Dooley carries a hunting rifle and wants to find him before the Highway Patrol can. Frazier in terror of Dooley, is now on the run and a threat to the entire community. Dan finds him in time and stops a murder.

Hot Rod ***

PN 45B, RN 1046

Writer: Leonard Heideman, Director: Jack Herzberg, Recurring Actors: William Boyett, Jack Douglas

    Ex-con Harry Burke and his brother Tom commit two robberies and outrun the law with a souped-up hot rod. After they wantonly run down a woman, Dan gets the head of the local hot rod club to help trace the car's owner.

Hot Cargo ***

PN 47B, RN 1047

Writer: Robert Ryf, Director: Herbert L. Strock

    Racketeers feign road accidents to lure drivers from their trucks before slugging them and stealing their cargo. Truckers will no longer stop to help innocent accident victims but Dan rounds up the ring.

Oil Lease ***

PN 49B, RN 1048

Writer: Eugene Roddenberry, Director: Lambert Hillyer

    Two men steal a bazooka from the army and use it to hold-up an oil field payroll. With no way to fight back or save the fields from ruin, Dan successfully carries out a desperate plan.

Ex Con ****

PN 50B, RN 1049

Writer: Stuart Jerome, Director: Lambert Hillyer

Reformed ex-con Al Baldwin is forced to hide his former cellmates in his home while they plot to rob a farm combine courier. The police find the truck with the courier's body in it and the robbers hold Al's wife hostage to silence him. Dan senses trouble and rescues Al's wife from danger.

Motel Robbery ****

PN 51B, RN 1050

Writer: Leonard Heideman, Director: Gilbert Kay, Recurring Actors: William Boyett, Vance Skarstedt

Two motels are robbed on the same day and a man was almost murdered. Dan works out their pattern to catch them when they strike again. He winds up looking down a gun barrel at a desperate killer who 'works' with his wife and her sister. *Note:* This episode was actually highlighted in the film *Dragnet* (1987) for a scene in Captain Gannon's (Harry Morgan) home with the television on!

Stolen Car Ring ****

PN 41B, RN 1051

Writer: Arthur Weiss, Director: Lew Landers

A tough-looking man is found in an expensive stolen car. He claims he is the owner but the police are dubious. Dan discovers that he's the victim of a car theft ring and using a newspaper ad, sets up a trap for the criminals posing as a prospective buyer.

Escaped Mental Patient ***

PN 53B, RN 1052

Writer: Arthur Weiss, Director: Paul Guilfoyle

A deranged old man who thinks he's a famous violinist escapes from a mental hospital. Dan picks up his trail with bloodhounds but the man kidnaps a woman. Dan rescues the woman.

Armored Car ****

PN 56B, RN 1053

Writer: Ellis Marcus, Director: Gilbert Kay

Thugs steal an armored car outside a country market with the guard locked inside. Dan learns the bandits have abducted the guard's wife to force him to open the truck. Dan rescues the wife and rounds up the bandits.

Migrant Workers ****

PN 57B, RN 1054

Writer: Donald A. Brinkley, Director: Paul Guilfoyle, Recurring Actors: Stuart Whitman

Itinerant fruit pickers move to a new camp where they are robbed of their pay and one murdered. Dan deduces the killer had inside help and uses his skill and tact to unmask the men who would rob the poorest of the poor.

Ranch Copter ****

PN 52B, RN 1055

Writer: Bill George, William Driskell, Director: Jack Herzberg, Recurring Actors: Roy Bourgois

George Wilson (Douglas Henderson) who settled on his bride's ranch, doesn't get along with her two brothers. When his wife Iris is accidentally shot, they blame him. Iris regains consciousness and reveals his innocence. Dan uses a helicopter to find her hot-headed brother who has gone after George in the brush with a rifle.

Amnesia ***

PN 60B, RN 1056

Writer: Jack Rock, Director: Herbert L. Strock, Recurring Actors: Stuart Whitman

Mimi Karney falls off a cliff and has amnesia. The *Highway Patrol* finds her and search for her husband somewhere in the forest, also injured. Dan turns Mimi loose where she was found, and subconsciously leads them to her husband.

Statute of Limitations ***

PN 59B, RN 1057

Writer: Jack Laird, William Driskell, Director: Eddie Davis, Recurring Actors: Jon Locke

Reckless driver Eddie Beekman injures a little girl but pays off her father not to press charges. Dan, suspicious because Eddie is not a wealthy man, learns he was a suspect in an old bank heist where the loot was never found. Dan gets Eddie to tip his hand before midnight when the statute of limitations run out and arrests him.

Resident Officer ****

PN 58B, RN 1058

Writer: William Driskell, Director: Eddie Davis, Recurring Actors: Terry Frost

Highway Patrol officer Joe Kline is found dead in what appears to be a hunting accident but Dan finds a marijuana leaf in his pocket and realizes that Kline was trailing drug dealers. Dan tracks down the cold-blooded murderers.

Psycho *

PN 55B, RN 1059

Writer: Teddy Sherman, Director: Jack Herzberg

After finding an abandoned car, Dan is shot at as he starts up a nearby hill. The car belongs to writer Guy Pemberton. His psychiatrist claims he is temporarily deranged from pain medication and acting out his latest mystery story. He thinks he is the killer but Dan saves the man from himself.

Counterfeit **

PN 61B, RN 1060

Writer: Lambert Hillyer, Director: Eddie Davis, Recurring Actors: William Boyett

Forgers are passing checks in towns and then vanishing without a trace. Dan figures out their pattern and pinpoints their next strike. The crooks escape in traffic but Dan apprehends them before they flee to the next state.

Suspected Cop ***

PN 63B, RN 1061

Writer: Donald A. Brinkley, Director: Eddie Davis

A gem collector has a heart attack on the highway and his car is impounded. Valuable, uncut diamonds are missing, and a *Highway Patrol* officer is the only person who had access to the car's truck. With an hour before the story breaks in the evening newspapers, Dan saves the officer's reputation.

Trojan Horse ***

PN 64B, RN 1062

Writer: Bob Mitchell, Director: Jack Herzberg, Recurring Actors: Vance Skarstedt

Two safecrackers hide in a truck to rob a manufacturer's safe overnight. The driver their cohort drives away next morning. Dan sees through the scheme and heads off the truck before it can disappear in a maze of country.

Female Hitchhiker ***

PN 66B, RN 1063

Writer: Jack Rock, Director: Eddie Davis

Posing as a salesman, Warren Childs lines-up wealthy prospects in motels. His two female accomplices pas as hitchhikers and rob the victims of their money. When a victim is murdered Dan swoops in. At the finale, the smell of perfume leads him into a desperation situation before bringing the criminals to justice.

Nitro **

PN 65B, RN 1064

Writer: Arthur Weiss, Director: Jack Herzberg, Recurring Actors: Terry Frost, Wayne Heffley

In a tungsten min, counterfeiters hide their plates in nitroglycerin, packed in suitcases. Gun crazy Richard Gulf grabs the suitcases and flees not knowing about the nitro inside them. Dan finds the wounded counterfeiters who describe Gulf and his car. Dan speeds after Gulf down a rough road. Gulf leaps out and faces Dan with his gun drawn. Dan shoots it out of his hand and finds the nitro which is still intact. Dan buries it in the ground and walks away but is followed by a blinding flash! Actor John Vivyan who later starred on the CBS series *Mr. Lucky* (1959-1960) also appeared on this episode.

Motorcycle B **

PN 68B, RN 1065

Writer: Lambert Hillyer, Director: Eddie Davis

Three bandits elude all police roadblocks by riding off on motorcycles and hiding them in a waiting truck. Dan catches on and orders that all vehicles be stopped. Seeing the roadblock, the bandits unload their cycles and get away. One hijacks a fire truck, donning its lone occupant's uniform. At the roadblock, Dan catches him when he doesn't answer a radio call.

Officer's Wife ****

PN 69B, RN 1066

Writer: William L. Driskell, Director: Jack Herzberg, Recurring Actors: William Boyett, Guy Williams

When an officer is killed in the line of duty, Linda Wylie hysterically demands that her husband Ed quit the *Highway Patrol*. Dan gives Ed a leave of absence and then using psychology invites Linda to his office. She sees the officer's widow working as a dispatcher and changes her mind.

Stripped Cars *****

PN 70B, RN 1067

Writer: Donald A. Brinkley, Director: Eddie Davis, Recurring Actors: Terry Frost

The Hogan brothers hijack a truck delivering new cars. They hide the cars in a barn and ditch the truck on a side road. When the truck is found, Dan reads the odometer and calculates the distance to where the cars are hidden.

Convict's Wife ***

PN 67B, RN 1068

Writer: Bob Mitchell, Director: Jack Herzberg

Escaped convict Niles Brandon orders his estranged wife Betty to meet him at a restaurant. She notifies the *Highway Patrol* and Dan sets a trap. Niles smells a trap, goes to her house, attacks the officer on guard, and kidnaps her. Dan throws down a roadblock but Dan leaps out aiming his gun. Betty steps on the gas and saves Dan's life.

Reformation **

PN 71B, RN 1069

Writer: Jack Rock, Director: George Blair, Recurring Actors: William Boyett

Ginny Summers convinces her husband Ray to return some stolen money. He tells the money's owner Oliver that he is returning it. Oliver calls the *Highway Patrol* in case of trouble. The couple travel to a cabin to get the loot, unaware that they are being watched by an armed thug. Dan finds the cabin but is jumped by the thug who runs. Dan downs him with lethal accuracy. Ginny and ray return the money with a police escort.

Stolen Plane Copter ****

PN 62B, RN 1070

Writer: Teddy Sherman, Director: Eddie Davis, Recurring Actors: Roy Bourgois

Two convicts hijack a plane and escape from prison. They run out of gas and crash in the mountains. Unhurt, they meet an old prospector who offers help. They hear Dan's Highway Patrol helicopter and take the old man hostage in a cave. Dan smokes them out and saves the old-timer.

Gem Robbery ***

PN 73B, RN 1071

Writer: Donald A. Brinkley, Director: Felix Feist, Recurring Actors: Stuart Whitman

Gem cutter Dr. Corbett masterminds a jewel robbery. Dan arrests him but his cohort, George Haley, heads for the train station with the jewels hidden in his dog's collar. Cornered he sends his ferocious dog to attack Dan while he flees. He is shot by a patrolman and lies on the tracks. With a train coming around the bend, Dan frees himself from the dog and makes a daring rescue.

Wounded ****

PN 74B, RN 1072
Writer: Bob Mitchell, Director: Paul Guilfoyle

Eight-year old Tommy Evans plays in a deserted woods and stumbles upon two criminals. He notifies the *Highway Patrol* but is captured by the desperate men. Dan poses as Tommy's uncle and gets him released. The fugitives flee but Dan sets up roadblocks and opens fire. One is wounded and fires back while the other slips unnoticed behind Dan. Tommy uses his slingshot to sting the man's face and save Dan's life!

Fake Cop **

PN 75B, RN 1073

Writer: Lambert Hillyer, Director: Eddie Davis, Recurring Actors: William Boyett

As a young woman stands inside a store window, an armed man bursts in, robs the register and flees. The woman runs out screaming for help. A man in a Highway Patrol uniform appears and chases the thief. The clerk doesn't notify the police thinking an officer has already done so. Dan finds out about the phony cop and alerts the businesses to report all robberies immediately. When a gas station is hit, Dan sets up roadblocks and uses a clever ruse to catch the gang. Note: Former 'Dead End Kid/Bowery Boy' Bobby Jordan plays a market manager (billed as Robert Jordan).

Double Cross ****

PN 77B, RN 1074

Writer: Arthur Weiss, Director: Jack Herzberg, Recurring Actors: Stuart Whitman, Vance Skarstedt

Bonded messenger Henry Wigram and John Grolier plot a payroll holdup. However, Grolier double-crosses and murders Wigram. The Highway Patrol finds his body and Dan is astonished at the widow's (Jean Ruth) calm reaction to her husband's murder. Under police surveillance the widow rushes to the arms of Wigram. Dan moves in to arrest the murdering accomplices.

Narcotics *****

PN 78B, RN 1075

Writer: Bob Mitchell, Director: Eddie Davis, Recurring Actors: Stuart Whitman

Sid and Ginny Rawlings kill the elderly owner of a restaurant and then use the place as a front for their narcotics racket. The place is staked-out and when a notorious drug pusher leaves with a carton of coffee, Dan chases and catches him. The coffee carton contains pure heroin and Dan doubles-back to the restaurant. The couple has taken an old man hostage until Dan bravely rescues him and smashes the dope ring.

Hired Killer ***

PN 76B, RN 1076

Writer: William L. Driskell, Director: Jack Herzberg, Recurring Actors: Terry Frost

Set to testify against a big-time racketeer, the Santell brothers flee town. The mobster sends a hit man who kills one of the Santell's while his brother is enjoying a picnic in the park with a girl. After the Highway Patrol finds the murdered man, Dan screeches through traffic to save his brother. The killer is already there but Dan thinks fast and prevents another murder.

Hostage Copter *****

PN 72B, RN 1077

Writer: William L. Driskell, Director: Jack Herzberg, Recurring Actors: Stuart Whitman, Roy Bourgois

Two bandits wound a restaurant owner and kidnap his daughter Kathy (Barbara Eden in her first role) as hostage. Dan spots them from the air but fearing for Kathy's safety hesitates to shoot. Hidden by clouds he follows them until they ditch their truck and hijack a convertible leaving the driver and Kathy behind. Dan moves in and accurately fires a snub-nose .38 revolver from the chopper!

Barbara Eden in her most famous role from
***I Dream Of Genie* (1965-1970)**
(Photo R. Schiller).

Rabies ****

PN 54B, RN 1078

Writer: Bob Mitchell, Director: Eddie Davis

When a little girl, on vacation with her mother, is bitten by a dog at a gas station, no one is worried until the attendant discovers the dog has rabies. Dan searches for the mother in daughter in time for treatment that will save the girl's life.

Season #3 1957-1958

Hypo Bandit ***

PN 83B, RN 1079

Writer: Lee Berg, Director: Jack Herzberg

A bandit robs a jewelry store, drugs the owner, and makes a clean getaway. After learning the drug he uses is deadly, Dan jumps into action and sets up roadblocks everywhere. Dan and the robber wind up in a pitched battle.

Efficiency Secretary ****

PN 85B, RN 1080

Writer: Vince Skarstedt, Director: Herbert L. Strock

A rancher's group praises the efficiency of their secretary Doris Malden who uses a duster pilot to steal $50,000 from her bosses. None of the three ranchers suspect the truth until Dan uses a slim clue to expose her in an unusual finale.

Temptation ***

PN 80B, RN 1081

Writer: Jack Rock, Director: Henry (Hank) S. Kesler

Construction foreman Preston refuses rightful payment to a young employee who in a rage punches the firm's owner and flees. Finding his boss unconscious, Preston robs the safe, and accuses the employee of the robbery. Dan clears the employee and traps Preston on top of a huge cement mixer.

Safecracker **

PN 81B, RN 1082

Writer: William L. Driskell, Director: Eddie Davis, Recurring Actors: Vance Skarstedt, William Boyett

Knowing the police are watching him, safecracker Stanley Wright goes to church. He sneaks out the back, pulls a job and sneaks back in before the mass ends. After he hits a jewelry store, Dan uses a high school chemistry trick to catch him.

Mistaken Identity ***

PN 84B, RN 1083

Writer: Arthur Weiss, Director: Sutton Roley

A timid carpenter is mistaken for a diamond merchant and abducted by a hood who demands a fortune in diamonds. Dan quickly realizes the kidnaper's mistake and uses an attractive, young policewoman as decoy to lure him into a clever trap.

Hostage Family Copter ****

PN 82B, RN 1084

Writer: Rik Vollearts, Director: Herbert L. Strock, Recurring Actors: Wayne Heffley

A fugitive kidnaps a family of three as they change a tire on the road. He keeps them in their backwoods cabin. Dan locates them but realizes that the slightest sound may get the family killed. Instead he risks his own life with a million-to-one gamble and saves them.

The Sniper ***

PN 79B, RN 1085

Writer: Bob Mitchell, Director: Jack Herzberg

A driver is killed as cars passing over certain sections of a highway are hit by a sniper's bullets. Dan suspects the shootings are a deliberate attempt to frame an innocent man, and he unearths one of the most unusual crimes he has ever encountered.

Hot Dust ****

PN 91B, RN 1086

Writer: Richard Landall, Director: Lee Berg

A young lab worker (a baby-faced Leonard Nimoy) accidentally exposes himself to radioactive isotopes. He panics and flees town. News of this freak accident creates mounting public hysteria. Dan hunts down the terror-stricken and now homicidal man.

Witness Wife ****

PN 87B, RN 1087

Writer: David Boehm, Director: Lee Berg

Martin Jensen sees two men bury a body near his farm. Alarmed he calls the Highway Patrol just before the men burst into his farmhouse. Dan careens across town to save Jensen and his wife.

Dead Hunter ****

PN 86B, RN 1088

Writer: Lou Huston, Director: Herbert L. Strock

On a hunting trip, William Foster kills his partner to gain control of their business. Dan is suspicious of the 'accident' and the crime lab backs him up. Dan and his officers corner the murderer at the crime scene.

Convicted Innocent ***

PN 88B, RN 1089

Writer: Jack Rock, Director: Jack Herzberg

Dan discovers a convicted murderer is innocent and gets him released. However, the bitter exonerated man hunts down the witness whose mistaken testimony got him convicted and plans to kill him. Dan fights wildly to avert a murder.

Chain Store **

PN 89B, RN 1090

Writer: Don Clark, Director: Herbert L. Strock, Recurring Actors: William Boyett

When a masked gunman holds up three supermarkets in broad daylight, Dan ferrets out his mysterious method of operation. He sets a trap that catches him red-handed.

Double Death **

PN 92B, RN 1091

Writer: Lee Berg, Director: Jack Herzberg, Recurring Actors: Terry Frost, Ron Foster

Tom Thorton served 13 years for a murder he did not commit.   Released for good behavior, Thorton fids the man he was supposed to have killed. Dan prevents Thorton for committing a cold-blooded murder and then walking away scot-free since under the law he can't be convicted twice for the same crime.

Hideout *****

PN 94B, RN 1092

Writer: Richard Adam, Director: Jack Herzberg, Recurring Actors: William Boyett

A woman calls Dan and is hysterical saying that she shot a man in her diner. Dan discovers her victim was a known killer, thief and that she killed in self-defense. Then he unearths the victim's loot and a flaw in the woman's alibi!

Mother's March ***

PN 90B, RN 1093

Writer: Ellis Marcus, Director: Herbert L. Strock

A hospital committee chairman is robbed on his way to the bank of $10,000 collected for charity. Only his wife and a local businesswoman knew his route. Dan recovers the money and brings the robber to justice.

Slain Cabby ***

PN 93B, RN 1094

Writer: Bob Mitchell, Director: Jack Herzberg

Two armed men hijack a taxi and stage a series of whirlwind robberies. They ditch the cab and vanish in their own car. Dan rigs an ingenious radio code with cab drivers in the area which traps the bandits when they strike again.

Insulin ****

PN 98B, RN 1095

Writer: Lee Berg, Director: Leon Benson

A diabetic ex-con is kidnapped to keep from testifying at a government investigation. Dan uses a 'grain of sand' to build a mount of trouble for the hoods and rescue the man.

The Seventh Green ****

PN 96B, RN 1096

Writer: Jack Rock, Director: Otto Lang, Jr.

The groundskeeper at an elite country club, Bruno Keeley, shelters notorious criminals for a price. After one of his 'tenants' runs out of money, Keeley shoots him dead. Dan is playing golf with a judge when he discovers that someone has been killed at the club.

Foster Child ****

PN 99B, RN 1097

Writer: Bob Mitchell, Director: Jack Herzberg, Recurring Actors: Ron Foster

Young Danny Sears triggers an 'empty' rifle and accidentally wounds his pal Chet Bates, whose father accuses Danny of deliberately shooting his boy. In a panic, Danny grabs his gun and flees with Bates in angry pursuit. Dan risks his life to stop another needless shooting.

Lady Bandits ****

PN 97B, RN 1098

Writer: Rik Vollaerts, Director: Jack Herzberg

Two girls disguised as men stage a series of armed robberies. Afterward they quickly change to female clothing and slip through the police roadblocks undetected. Dan uses the bandit's own femininity to snare them into his trap.

Revenge ***

PN 95B, RN 1099

Writer: William L. Driskell, Director: David Lowell Rich, Recurring Actors: William Boyett

Ex-con Gerald Grey vows to kill Dan for sending him to prison. He challenges an innocent farmer to a gunfight to lure Dan.

Tear Gas Copter ****

PN 102B, RN 1100

Writer: William L. Driskell, Director: Monroe Askins, Recurring Actors: Frank Miller

Three gunmen flee to a sparsely populated farm area, attack the Highway Patrol officer on duty, and take a terrified housewife hostage. Dan swoops out of the sky to attack the hoods with tear gas. Note: Bob Gilbreath is the helicopter pilot.

Deaf Mute **

PN 100B, RN 1101

Writer: Lawrence Menkin, Director: Leon Benson

A twelve-year old deaf-mute Susie Haskell is taken hostage after witnessing a couple shoot her father and rob his general store. The girl, petrified with fear, can't cry for help.

Hit and Run **

PN 104B, RN 1102

Writer: Lee Berg, Director: Jack Herzberg, Recurring Actors: William Boyett, Wayne Heffley

Lois Emory runs a man down and in a panic flees. Conscience-stricken she calls the Highway Patrol and returns to the scene, but the body has vanished! Only the skid marks confirm her story to Dan and the lab men who solve the mystery. The victim was Lou Parker who with his brother Mike had just burgled a safe in a plastics factory.

Fear **

PN 101B, RN 1103

Writer: Jack Rock, Director: Eddie Davis, Recurring Actors: Wayne Heffley

Respected family man Keith Tobin is actually the 'Polka Dot Bandit' and panics when he is discovered. He flees with Dan in hot pursuit, and neither is aware that Tobin's tiny daughter is hidden in the trunk of the car!

Careless Cop ***

PN 103B, RN 1104

Writer: Vince Skarstedt, Director: Leon Benson, Recurring Actors: Vince Skarstedt

After five flawless years of service, Officer Wilkie makes a fatal error. Stopping a speeding car, he finds a gun in it but forgets to frisk the driver, who draws a hidden gun. He kills officer Wilkie and flees. Dan is enraged and pursues the murderer to justice.

Policewoman ****

PN 105B, RN 1105

Writer: Richard Adam, Director: Leon Benson, Recurring Actors: Terry Frost, Ron Foster

Martha Cole poses as a member of a gambling syndicate until a freak accident tips off the mob to her identity. She calls Dan but is captured before she can give her location. Dan makes a life-or-death struggle to save her. Note: Famed Judo expert, physical trainer, and close friend of George Reeves and author (Goltz), Gene LeBell stunts for Broderick Crawford in the fight scene.

The Truckers **

PN 106B, RN 1106

Writer: Rik Vollaerts, Director: Monroe Askins, Recurring Actors: William Boyett, Ron Foster

Bill and Julie Gibson stage a series of ingenious truck robberies. They follow a pharmacy delivery truck and when the driver stops to eat, they drug is coffee. After he gets drowsy and pulls off the road, they plunder the truck and flee.

Credit Card **

PN 109B, RN 1107

Writer: Jack Rock, Director: Eddie Davis, Recurring Actors: Wayne Heffley, Ron Foster

Two men kidnap Janice Carlyle, hijack her car, and use her credit card to purchase auto parts. Dan cordons off the area with the patrol cars and head for a showdown with the criminals.

Psycho Killer ***

PN 110B, RN 1108

Writer: Lee Berg, Director: Jack Herzberg, Recurring Actors: Vance Skarstedt, Frank Miller

A madman uses 'Lonely Hearts' newspaper ads to meet and murder women. Dan deduces his method of operation and uses a policewoman as bait to catch him!

Suicide **

PN 113B, RN 1109

Writer: Rik Vollaerts, Director: Barry Sullivan, Recurring Actors: Ron Foster

Brothers Joe and Pete Curran get out of prison. After Joe goes straight, Pete is ordered by the mob to take out his own brother for deserting the syndicate.

Phony Cop **

PN 111B, RN 1110

Writer: Jack Rock, Director: Monroe Askins, Recurring Actors: Vance Skarstedt, Frank Miller

Pretending to be a hysterical robbery victim, Mae Loman drive the Highway Patrol away from the area where he husband's robberies occur. Dressed like an officer, Bert Loman gets away before the police realize they were sent on a wild goose chase. Dan studies the thieves' method of operation to figure where thy will strike next and sets a trap.

The Judge **

PN 114B, RN 1111

Writer: Ellis Marcus, Director: Jack Herzberg, Recurring Actors: Ron Foster, Wayne Heffley

Red Baker escapes from prison and is compelled to kill the judge who sent him there. Judge Crosson is unperturbed and refuses police protection or change his routine. He never dreams that death awaits him at the barber shop.

Dan's Vacation ***

PN 115B, RN 1112

Writer: Bob Mitchell, Director: William Hole, Jr., Recurring Actors: William Boyett

Taking a needed vacation at his favorite fishing lodge, Dan discovers it under new management and with some very strange guests. A wounded stranger arrives and Dan links him to a narcotics ring and suspects that the lodge is now a dope distribution center.

Explosives ***

PN 116B, RN 1113

Writer: Richard Adam, Director: Jack Herzberg, Recurring Actors: William Boyett, Ron Foster

After being fired from a chemical firm, Larry Bolton steals a truck loaded with volatile potassium. He takes his wife hostage and intends to blow the city sky-high. Dan uses an attractive policewoman as bait to stop the human bomb!

Hostage Officer ***

PN 117B, RN 1114

Writer: Jack Rock, Director: Derwin Abbe, Recurring Actors: Ron Foster, Vince Skarstedt

In hot pursuit of two thieves, Officer Hoffman's motorcycle skids and he is taken hostage. They stash his cycle in the back of their truck but not before Hoffman depresses his motorcycle key to send out a continuous signal. Dan uses his expert radio electronic skills to locate the fugitives and save the officer.

Double Copter *****

PN 112B, RN 1115

Writer: Rik Vollaerts, Director: Eddie Davis

A state penitentiary lifer convict, (former 'Dead End Kid and Bowery Boy' Bobby Jordan billed as Robert Jordan) escapes prison in a stolen helicopter thanks to some friends. Dan chases them in his own copter and battles the fugitives in mid-air.
Note: Bob Gilbreath plays the stolen helicopter pilot.

Dan Sick **

PN 108B, RN 1116

Writer: Marnie Sloan, Director: Barry Sullivan

Dan arrives at his office in great pain. The cause of his illness is a mystery until he remembers that he touched a boy's toy gun painted with lead paint.

Reward ****

PN 107B, RN 1117

Writer: Richard Adam, Director: Jack Herzberg, Recurring Actors: Wayne Heffley

A dangerous armed robber with a $10,000 reward on his head hides in a farmer's barn. The farmer and two neighbors recklessly try to capture him without police help in order to collect the big reward. After a farmer is wounded, Dan and the *Highway Patrol* take command and capture the robber. Police officers are never entitled to a reward because that is their job.

Season #4 1958-1959

Frightened Witness **

PN 119B, RN 1118

Writer: Lee Berg, Director: Eddie Davis, Recurring Actors: William Boyett

Joe Norton holds up a roadside café and kills the owner. In a weak moment he lets two witnesses, newlyweds, leave but his brother sets out to silence them.

Hostage ***

PN 127B, RN 1119

Writer: George and Gertrude Fass, Rik Vollaerts, Director: Leon Chooluck, Recurring Actors: William Boyett, Wayne Heffley

A convicted murderer (Peter Breck, who later co-starred with Barbara Stanwyck on *The Big Valley*) is wounded in the leg by police. He hides in a stationary store and takes the woman owner and her invalid mother as hostages.

Family Affair **

PN 118B, RN 1120

Writer: Rik Vollaerts, Director: Jack Herzberg, Recurring Actors: William Boyett, Ron Foster, Vance Skarstedt

Myra Davis and her son spring her husband from a courthouse and kill a police officer. Myra hides her husband in a culvert and coolly returns home to head off the Highway patrol. Dan sees through her phony innocence and gets her to expose her husband.

Transmitting Danger ***

PN 123B, RN 1121

Writer: Charles B. Smith, Director: John Florea, Recurring Actors: William Boyett, Frank Miller

Only Dan knows that a safe has been rigged by two men who TNT to blow it up. The trigger is a radio signal and the thieves will be blown to smithereens if a transmitter is turned on within a two-mile radius of the safe.

Gambling Story **

PN 137B, RN 1122

Writer: L. Wells, Director: Jack Herzberg, Recurring Actors: William Boyett

A gambling czar decides to eliminate his rival's illegal gambling casino by staging a murder there. Dan solves the murder and prevents another killing with just seconds to spare.

Train Copter *****

PN 122B, RN 1123

Writer: Bob Mitchell, Director: Lew Landers, Recurring Actors: William Boyett, Ron Foster, Roy Bourgois

Charlie Holman and Vince Crater rob a bank of $35,000 in new bills. Unknown to Vince, Charlie ships the loot as baggage to another town. In a rage, Vince kills him and holds up the baggage train to regain the spoils. Dan uses a helicopter to catch him.

Portrait of Death ****

PN 131B, RN 1124

Writer: M. Braus, Rik Vollaerts, Director: John Florea, Recurring Actors: William Boyett

An artist who mysteriously withdrew from society years earlier is found murdered near a mountain resort. Dan exposes the killer's strange motive.

Train Robbery ***

PN 120B, RN 1125

Writer: Robert Shaw, Director: Jack Herzberg, Recurring Actors: William Boyett

Two gunmen take over an isolated railroad station and plan to murder the crew of an arriving train and escape with a fortune in loot. Dan discovers the plot and races against time to save the lives of everyone on the train.

Deadly Diamonds **

PN 124B, RN 1126

Writer: Lee Berg, Director: Jack Herzberg, Recurring Actors: William Boyett

The disappearance of a diamond firm employee who just received a consignment of precious gems puts her under suspicion. Dan discovers another co-worker gave insider information to kidnapers but is able to trick him to taking him to their hideout.

Blood Money ***

PN 130B, RN 1127

Writer: Lee Berg, Rik Vollaerts, Director: Joe Tinney, Recurring Actors: William Boyett

After racketeers kill his brother, a freight yard worker who wouldn't pay protection money, Joe Mason hunts the killers (including Leonard Nimoy) down. Dan springs into action to save the foolish amateur detective.

False Confession *

PN 128B, RN 1128

Writer: Joel Malcolm Rapp, Rik Vollaerts, Director: Lew Landers, Recurring Actors: William Boyett

Jim Rogers sees two men rob a warehouse and kill the watchman. He confesses to the crime so his family collects the reward. However, it is not payable before the conviction and he escapes. Dan realizes that the true killers will try to murder Rogers and does everything he can to find him before it is too late.

Confidence Game **

PN 132B, RN 1129

Writer: Stuart Jerome, Rik Vallaerts, Director: Walter Doniger, Recurring Actors: William Boyett

Con man Paul Gayle swindles kindly Gus Fields out of his lifetime savings. Gus dies of a heart attack and Dan sends his officers to capture Gayle. Note: This episode contains a violent beating of a nice old man.

Split Robbery ***

PN 138B, RN 1130

Writer: Bob Mitchell, Director: Jack Herzberg, Recurring Actors: William Boyett

Two armed criminals hold a supermarket manager's wife hostage until he hands over the store's receipts. Dan deduces where they will strike next.

The Trap **

PN 121B, RN 1131

Writer: Richard Adam, Director: William Conrad, Recurring Actors: William Boyett, Ron Foster

Dan takes convicted felon Ted Wilson to prison but is ambushed by members of his gang. Dan detects the ambush in advance and takes a well-calculated risk to counter the attack.

Expose ***
PN 144B, RN 1132

Writer: Nathan McGinnis, Director: Jack Herzberg, Recurring Actors: William Boyett, Frank Miller

Crusading reporter Merrill Hartman (future gifted comic actor Ted Knight who played anchorman Ted Baxter on the beloved *Mary Tyler Moore Show* in the 1970's) exposes a protection racket whose victims are afraid to give evidence to the law. Racketeers bait a trap for the nosey reporter, but Dan detects it, saves him, and wipes out the mob!

Breath of a Child ***

PN 136B, RN 1133

Writer: Robert Shaw, Director: Henry (Hank) S. Kesler, Recurring Actors: William Boyett

A sailor, unaware that he was exposed to deadly contagious spinal meningitis when he saves a baby's life, elopes with his girlfriend. They run away from police trying to help them assuming the bride's father sent them because he was against the marriage.

Narcotics Racket *

PN 135B, RN 1134

Writer: Stuart Jerome, Director: Jack Herzberg, Recurring Actors: William Boyett

Two men pose as a narcotics agent and a dope dealer, and dupe people into believing their close relatives are members of a drug ring. They get their victims to offer bribes to protect their family members. Dan uses their greed to get them to make a bad move in this unbelievable episode. Note: The lovely daughter of Loretta Young and Clark Gable (Broderick Crawford's former co-stars) Judy Lewis has a good role in this otherwise weak episode.

Copter Cave-In ****

PN 142B, RN 1135

Writer: Jack Rock, Director: Jack Herzberg, Recurring Actors: William Boyett, Frank Miller

Escaped convict Nolan Wilbur forces a prospector to hide him in an abandoned gold mine. A cave-in traps the prospector while the *Highway Patrol* helicopter spots Wilbur ready to shoot it out. Dan uses the copter to free the prospector and outmaneuver the convict.
Note: Bob Gilbreath plays the HP helicopter pilot.

Gem Robbery **

PN 134B, RN 1136

Writer: T. Maples, Rik Vollaerts, Director: Joe Tinney, Recurring Actors: William Boyett

Pete Madison, an elevator operator in in New York's wholesale diamond center, steals the itineraries of three traveling salesmen and tips off his confederates to rob them. Dan figures out where and when they will strike, and stops them.

Mexican Chase ***

PN 125B, RN 1137

Writer: Jack Rock, Director: Lew Landers, Recurring Actors: William Boyett

A dashboard cigarette lighter becomes the key when the Mexican Highway Patrol helps Dan track a gang that alters stolen cars before smuggling them across the border.

Framed Cop ***

PN 147B, RN 1138

Writer: Nathan McGinnis, Director: Jack Herzberg, Recurring Actors: William Boyett

Paul Carson wants revenge on *Highway Patrol* Sgt. Ken Williams who sent his brother to prison. He steals William's car, dons an officer's cap, and deliberately runs down a pedestrian. Dan makes a shrewd deduction and clears Williams of the false hit-and-run charge.

The Collector **

PN 129B, RN 1139

Writer: Rik Vollaerts, Director: Otto Lang, Jr., Recurring Actors: William Boyett

Nathan Colley blackmails ex-cons who have gone straight but their past is unknown to their bosses and family. Colley pulls a gun on Jerry Singleton when he refuses to pay. In a struggle for the gun, Colley is accidentally killed and Singleton flees. With the help of Singleton's wife, Dan finds the victimized runaway and convinces him that self-defense is no crime.

Revenge *

PN 146B, RN 1140

Writer: Richard Benedict, Jack Rock, Director: Monroe Askins, Recurring Actors: William Boyett, Frank Miller

Tommy Chugg (Robert Conrad) plans to get even with Robert Hoffman who was acquitted for a car accident that killed Tommy's father. He murders Hoffman's son and then heads for Hoffman's mountain retreat. Dan races against time to stop a second murder. Note: Future glamorous film star Dyan Cannon (billed Diane Cannon and here a brunette beauty) also appears in this bad episode.

Brave Boy *

PN 133B, RN 1141

Writer: Ellis Marcus, Director: Jack Herzberg, Recurring Actors: William Boyett

Young Billy Redmond's father is killed by a burglar who thought the family was out of town. With an eyewitness account of the murder, Dan corners the killer.

Diversion Robbery ***

PN 139B, RN 1142

Writer: Lambert Hillyer, Director: Derwin Abbe, Recurring Actors: William Boyett

Two robbers use a time bomb that explodes harmlessly but with a terrifying noise to divert attention from their getaways. Dan traces a lone fingerprint to one of them and roars in pursuit along a trail marked by further robberies.

Cargo Hijack **

PN 141B, RN 1143

Writer: Stuart Jerome, Director: Lew Landers, Recurring Actors: William Boyett

Vance and Sheila Nolan elude capture by pulling their hijacking jobs over a large area. However, when they murder a trucker, they change their method of operation and hand Dan his first lead.

Hitchhiker **

PN 140B, RN 1144

Writer: Lee Berg, Director: Jack Herzberg, Recurring Actors: William Boyett

To pay their way from New York to California, Joe Parker thumbs rides and robs the drivers. Afterward he meets his wife Dolly at a pre-arranged location. When one driver fights back, Joe kills him. Dan uses the latest scientific equipment to catch-up with the couple.

Illegal Entry ***

PN 126B, RN 1145

Writer: Ellis Marcus, Director: Joe Tinney, Recurring Actors: William Boyett

Ben Douglas smuggles field workers from Mexico and gets them farm jobs. Then he extorts money from the migrants by threatening to report their illegal status. One migrant attacks him which draws suspicion from the *Highway Patrol*. Dan sets an ingenious trap and identifies Douglas as the culprit.

Killer on the Run ***

PN 149B, RN 1146

Writer: Lambert Hillyer, Director: John Parker, Recurring Actors: William Boyett, Frank Miller

Les Curtis double-crosses a counterfeiting gang and flees with $20,000. With one hood in pursuit, Curtis hitches a ride with two middle-aged women. Dan realizes the women's unknown peril and commences an intensive search to save them in time.

Prisoner Exchange Copter ****

PN 152B, RN 1147

Writer: Nathan McGinnis, Director: Jack Herzberg, Recurring Actors: William Boyett

A small-town sheriff captures racketeer Jack Avery and notifies the *Highway Patrol*. Avery contacts his henchman Rick Herron who abducts the sheriff's wife and demands a prisoner exchange. Dan takes to the air and finds the kidnapper. Note: Bob Gilbreath plays the police helicopter pilot.

Dan Hostage ***

PN 145B, RN 1148

Writer: Robert Shaw, Director: Leon Chooluck, Recurring Actors: William Boyett, Wayne Heffley, Ron Foster

   Amateur gunman Ed Leggett bungles a restaurant hold-up. He wounds the owner and takes his wife hostage when Dan arrives on the scene. Dan persuades Legett to accept himself as a substitute hostage and let the woman go. With Dan as his shield, Leggett attempts a getaway.

Woman Escapees ****

PN 148B, RN 1149

Writer: Jack Rock, Director: Jack Herzberg, Recurring Actors: William Boyett, Vance Skarstedt

   Lita Morgan and Caroline Craig are serving life in prison for murder. They escape and stop and kill a driver on the highway. Dan cuts off all escape routes, but they hijack a bus at gunpoint and blast through a roadblock. Dan, in hot pursuit, bring the female convicts to justice.

Auto Press ****

PN 143B, RN 1150

Writer: Bob Mitchell, Director: Leon Benson, Recurring Actors: William Boyett

   A married holdup team bungles a gas station robbery and kills the owner. Hemmed in by roadblocks, they desperately have their identified car demolished in a junkyard. This brings them out into the open for Dan and the *Highway Patrol*.

Express Delivery **

PN 151B, RN 1151

Writer: Jack Rock, Director: Eddie Davis, Recurring Actors: William Boyett, Frank Miller

Two men abduct a European courier, thinking he is carrying $200,000 in gems. They learn that the jewels are due at the airport later that day, and one poses as the courier to receive the shipment. Dan is alerted and races to the airport to set a daring trap.

Desperate Men **

PN 154B, RN 1152

Writer: Bob Mitchell, Director: Eddie Davis, Recurring Actors: William Boyett

Two criminals (one played by former 'Dead End Kid' Billy Halop) flee a after a robbery/murder and hide in a hospital boiler room. Cornered by the *Highway Patrol*, they offer a grisly bargain. Unless they are allowed to grow free they build the boiler's pressure until it explodes and destroys the hospital.

Confession **

PN 153B, RN 1153

Writer: Rik Vollearts, Director: Jack Herzberg, Recurring Actors: William Boyett

Three bank robbers gun down a fourth who had stolen their loot. Dan stakes out the dead man's house because the robbers didn't find the money on him. The hoods close in to wrest the money from their victim's wife.

Detour to Death ***

PN 150B, RN 1154

Writer: Joel Riordan, Director: Monroe Askins, Recurring Actors: William Boyett

   Two men and a girl use a fake detour sign to lure drivers to a lonely road. With a fake police car and uniforms, they stop the drivers and rob them.   Dan gets his first clue after one robbery ends in murder.

Fire **

PN 156B, RN 1155

Writer: Jack Rock, Director: Eddie Davis, Recurring Actors: William Boyett, Ron Foster

   Fire-bug Joe Patterson (Robert Fuller) sets a warehouse ablaze and later an unwitting farmer hires him as a laborer. Overcome with the desire to set another arson fire, Joe pours gasoline around the barn. Dan races to the scene to prevent a tragedy in this bad episode.

Bank Messenger **

PN 155B, RN 1156

Writer: G. Callahan, Jack Rock, Director: Jack Herzberg, Recurring Actors: William Boyett

   Sue and Red Hammond pull two robberies in one day. Sue lures bank messengers to a secluded spot where Red shoots and robs them. Their greed drives them to a third robbery attempt but this time Dan picks up the trail.

Appendix D
Highway Patrol - *Star Trek* connections

Gene Roddenberry, the future producer of the *Star Trek* (1966-1969) television series and blockbuster movie franchise spinoffs, began his long Hollywood career working at ZIV-TV as a staff screenwriter. In World War Two, Roddenberry served as an officer with the U.S. Army Air Corps and was awarded the Distinguished Flying Cross. After the war, Gene Roddenberry was a civilian pilot for Pan American World Airways and became one of Bernard Caldwell's sergeants at the California Highway Patrol before pursuing his dream of becoming a writer. Frank Runyon told the author (Goltz) "Gene Roddenberry was a nice guy and a former LAPD sergeant." He began at ZIV Studios writing scripts for the televisions series *Mr. District Attorney* under the pseudonym of Robert Wesley. He also wrote for other ZIV-TV shows, including *Harbor Command*, *I Led 3 Lives*, and *Dr. Christian*. Soon he was the head writer for the *West Point* series. He also wrote the scripts for five episodes of *Highway Patrol* including *"Oil Lease"* that is credited under his actual name Eugene Roddenberry. His excellent and thrilling episode *"Human Bomb"* brought a science-fiction theme to *Highway Patrol*! Prophetically Rodenberry met Leonard Nimoy, who later became a major part of the success of *Star Trek*, on the ZIV Studios lot when he was making the *Highway Patrol* episode *"Hot Dust"*. Roddenberry thought at the time that this young actor Nimoy (who appeared in two episodes of *Highway Patrol*) had a unique face. He made a note to cast him as an Alien being in some future science-fiction series. Gene Roddenberry stated that he was irritated with Frederick Ziv's changing his storylines to the point that he decided right then and there to make his own productions!

Appendix E

'55 Highway Patrol Buick

Recreating The Most Famous Cop Car In Television History

Originally printed in the June 1997 issue of *Motor Trend* magazine (copyright 1997)

by John Pearley Huffman

Interior dashboard of Gary Goltz's Highway Patrol Car replica.

Gary Goltz is a health-care entrepreneur and a fifth-degree black belt in judo, but when he's driving his '55 Buick, his most consuming passion is obvious: This guy's nuts for that '50s TV series, "Highway Patrol."

"Every day after school back in 1961," writes Goltz, "I could hardly wait until 5:30. Glued to the my family's old black-and-white portable TV, I waited to hear that familiar refrain, 'da, da-da-daaa.' Across the screen were the words 'Broderick Crawford starring in "Highway Patrol." ' He was a real hero, enforcing law and order, while serving as judge and jury too. There were no lawyers, bondsmen, or even Miranda rights. The good guys always won and the bad guys got just what they deserved." And Crawford, as no-nonsense Chief Dan Mathews, drove a '55 Buick.

Actually, during the series' production from 1955 to 1959 (it's been in reruns around the world ever since), Mathews drove everything from a '54 Olds 88 through a '59 Dodge Coronet; but that '55 Buick personified the character as much as his crisp fedora and snub-nosed .38. "The first cars were actual California Highway Patrol units, borrowed from the CHP," explains Goltz. "They had the Special 48 coupe body, Century engine, and Roadmaster brakes. These were among the first cars built specifically for police use." Buick built 270 of these "Century 68" two-doors, half with three-speed column-shift manual transmissions and half with slushy Dynaflow automatics. All served with the CHP and just two are known to survive.

Like all '55 Buicks, the Century 68 featured updated styling with "tower" taillights and a large "widescreen" front grille. The Century series was Buick's performer, combining the Special's (relatively) lightweight bodies with the Roadmaster's 322-cubic-inch OHV V-8. The 9.0:1-compression-ratio engine inhaled through a Carter four-barrel carburetor and produced a gross-rated 236 horsepower at 4600 rpm. According to the April 1955 issue of Highway Patrolman Magazine, "During dynamometer tests, the car developed 148 horsepower at the rear wheels and reached a wheel speed of 108 mph against the 4-horsepower drag of the machine. At this point, the test was terminated abruptly when the rubber tread spun off the tires of one of the rear wheels that was being tested."

Century models carried, like the top-of-the-line Roadmaster, four portholes alongside their front fenders to denote the high-output of their V-8s. Count the portholes alongside Goltz's Buick and it comes up one short. The Goltz car is a Special 46R: a pillarless hardtop as opposed to the two-door "post" sedan the CHP actually had. "It wasn't such a big compromise," says Goltz. After he bought his Special, he took it to Les Randolph's Brockton Automotive in Riverside, California, near Goltz's own home in Upland. "Les was into restoring cars and owned several Buicks. His favorite was his genuine '55 Buick Century model 68 CHP car. When I saw that car I was in awe! At first Les and I discussed some form of trade, but we decided to redo my car instead. Les felt my Buick could be made to look like a rather realistic highway patrol car. We decided against adding extra portholes or changing the Special nameplate to a Century. I wanted to protect my Buick's integrity as a

Special. Besides as a boy, I always thought the '55 Buicks used on "Highway Patrol" were Specials." Under the hood of Goltz's car lies a 264-cubic-inch version of the Buick V-8 topped by a two-barrel carb and rated at just 188 gross horsepower at 4800 rpm.

To create the ambience of a "Highway Patrol" cruiser, Goltz's Special was painted in proper skunk colors, the interior was finished in the same material as genuine CHP units, and spotlights were ordered from the original supplier, the Unity Manufacturing Company of Chicago. With an old-time siren under the hood, the TV show's no-particular-state logo was added to the doors, and Chief Mathews' 21-50 call sign was painted on the hood and trunk. Finally, the words "Broderick Crawford Special" were stenciled on the glovebox door.

The reaction that Goltz's black-and-white Buick elicits from pedestrians and other drivers proves he isn't the only one who remembers "Highway Patrol." "Almost every one of the episodes had a chase in them," asserts Guy Daniels, now 72, who created the show. "The kids weren't there for the dialog anyhow."

Episodes were filmed by Frederick W. Ziv World Television in glorious black and white over two-day shoots on a microscopic budget. "Each show had to be done on time, and it had to be there under $25,000. If it wasn't, you were gone," explains Daniels. Ziv was a television factory turning out other shows like "Sea Hunt" throughout the '50s. While writers like "Star Trek" creator Gene Roddenberry got their starts on Ziv shows, the frugality of the company was so deep that the "Highway Patrol" theme had actually been previously used as the theme music for the "Mr. District Attorney" radio show in the '40s. [Extensive research by Gary Goltz has not uncovered any evidence for this oft-repeated claim.]

Motor Trend shoots Gary Goltz and his famous car.

To keep costs down, "Highway Patrol" was filmed almost entirely outdoors in Southern California's then-rural San Fernando Valley. What sustained the show were straightforward stories that ads claimed were "based on the experiences of highway patrol officers in all 48 states" and the undeniable presence of Crawford barking "Ten-four, ten-four," into his squad car's radio. Born into a show business family in 1911, Crawford earned an engineering degree from Harvard and won the 1949 Best Actor Oscar for his portrayal of corrupt political demagogue Willie Stark in "All the King's Men." But he wasn't a conventional leading man; he was big and jowly. CHP technical adviser, Officer Frank Runyon, "sure liked working with Brod and felt "he was straight-shooting guy that was all man." Crawford's drinking was legendary during production of "Highway Patrol." "We got all the dialog in by noon, or else we wouldn't get it done at all," recalls Daniels. "He'd bribe people to bring him booze on the set." For a while, it was Officer Runyon's job to keep the actor sober. "What six-foot-four Irishman didn't like to drink? I was told to keep that son of a bitch away from a bottle. I think his license was suspended. Some scenes had to be shot on private roads so that Brod could drive." Eventually the drinking strained the show's relationship with the CHP and Crawford's relationship with Ziv. While Runyon continued as technical advisor, the series bought its own cars and the emblems on uniforms were modified to not so closely resemble those of the CHP. And Ziv brought in William Boyett (later to appear as Sergeant McDonald on "Adam-12") in the role of Sergeant Ken Williams as a regular to support Crawford. Crawford died in 1986, and Frank Runyon remembers attending the funeral and finding no one from the CHP there except himself. "So I called up Ed Gomez, the district supervisor and a good friend of mine, and 15 motorcycle cops showed up. Boy, they were spit and polished. The man put the Highway Patrol on the map. He did nothing but good for us."

Gary Goltz emulates his boyhood hero Broderick Crawford.

While Gary Goltz's "Highway Patrol" Buick may not be strictly authentic, his practiced Crawford voice, mannerisms, and pure enthusiasm make it better than authentic. There's true affection in his voice when he shouts into his vintage two-way radio, "Twenty-one-fifty bye."

Gary Goltz with Guy Daniels, the former PR for the CHP and Motor Trend Editor Van Tune

Appendix F
The complete article on the California Highway Patrol in *Zenith* magazine of September 2001.

Art Gilmore (right), narrator of the television series (right), is pictured with Gary Goltz.

This is the 1955 Buick that was used in the Highway Patrol television program.

The Fictional CHP and the Real CHP

Mark 75th on Patrol Force

By Gary Goltz

Officer Rebecca Estrada (16368), Commissioner Mike Brown and Sgt. Troy Lukkes (13798) took time out for a picture while holding a picture of Broderick Crawford.

A proclamation was received from the City of Los Angeles recognizing the 75th anniversary of the department. From left: Erik Estrada, Commissioner Mike Brown, Los Angeles City Councilmembers Tom LaBonge and Eric Garcetti and Johnny Grant.

It was "10-4" on 10/4. Los Angeles City Councilmember Tom LaBonge was joined by several cast and crew members of the original Highway Patrol television series, Erik Estrada, star of CHiPs, Johnny Grant, honorary mayor of Hollywood, and CHP Commissioner Mike Brown (8800) to commemorate the 75th anniversary of the CHP at a special parade and ceremony on Hollywood Boulevard.

The event began at the Los Angeles Fire Museum with a parade of classic CHP cars, including a '55 Buick, '59 Harley and a '63 Dodge. The parade ended at the star of Broderick Crawford who was the lead actor in the original television series (it ran from 1955-59). The ceremony was emceed by Johnny Grant, who remarked, "This ceremony celebrates both the real and the fictional CHP-both of which reflect the outstanding virtues of the officers who patrol California's vast network of roadways." Other remarks were made by Commissioner Brown, Kelly Crawford, son of Broderick Crawford, Erik Estrada, Councilmember LaBonge, and Gary Goltz, H-99 life member.

Appendix G:
A Mystery from World War Two

(Buck) Private Broderick Crawford, Corporal Ray McKinley (drummer) and Captain Glenn Miller of the U.S. Army Air Corps broadcast a USO show on CBS Radio in 1943 (Photo Goltz Collection)

The incredible book *The Glenn Miller Conspiracy* by Hunton Downs reads like a lost episode of *The Twilight Zone*. Author Downs interviewed the three, still-living people who knew the secret behind the death of the famous bandleader. They were film star David Niven (an active duty Major with the British Army), Col. Otto Skorenzy (SS Commando in the Third Reich), and Broderick Crawford (on active duty as a U.S Army Military Police Sergeant). Only Brod Crawford admitted that Miller was on a mission for General Dwight D. Eisenhower (the Supreme Allied Commander) that went wrong.

Staff Sergeant William Broderick Crawford, serial number 39267223, called Glenn Miller 'Mill' since they hit it off when they were both assigned by the army to Yale University to make overseas broadcasts. Later they, along with Major Niven, spent the rest of the war in London. U.S. Army Air Corps Major Glenn Miller, who was born Mueller of German immigrants, made orchestra broadcasts to the Third Reich. Miller spoke fluent German and urged German troops to surrender and then be well-treated. A secret pact was made between Ike and German General von Rundstedt that was kept from Hitler, Stalin and the Russians. A gap would be left in the Allied front so three SS Panzer divisions would be led into a trap and destroyed. Von Rundstedt and his other generals would capture Hitler and negotiate a surrender to end the war in 1944 before the Russians could invade Berlin.

Miller was flown from Versailles (Ike's Supreme Allied HQ) in an Army plane to a German airfield. He was supposed to broadcast on the Berlin radio network and speak to the German troops to stop the fighting. Instead he flew into a trap and was captured by Col. Otto Skorenzy, the daring swashbuckling German Commando. Miller was tortured to reveal Ike's whereabouts because Hitler had ordered Skorenzy to assassinate Eisenhower. Miller never talked and was flown back to the American airbase in a captured/repaired B-24 bomber with an all-German SS crew that spoke fluent English and wore American uniforms. The injured Glenn Miller was taken off the plane on a stretcher and then transported via Army ambulance to a Bordello in Paris owned by the SS. Miller was tortured until he died. The famous bandleader's body was dumped outside the doorstep of the bordello to stain his reputation. The author Hunton Downs, a WWII veteran, had every door slammed in his face by several governments and the Estate of Glenn Miller. David Niven never mentioned Miller in his two autobiographies. Downs was having a charming, friendly conversation with Niven on the set of the big-budget adventure film *Escape To Athena* (1979) until he mentioned Glenn Miller. Niven coldly and abruptly ended the discussion. Thirty-five years later Brod, on the set of *A Little Romance* (1979) was still sad about it since he watched his friend board that plane to oblivion. It would make for a great movie. One final note Major Glenn Miller was officially awarded the Bronze Star by the U.S. Army, which by Federal law is only given out for valor in combat. A routine plane crash would only rate a Purple Heart.

Ralph Schiller, 3-14-2016

Postscript1:
MeTV **Article 10-03-2017**

THIS 'HIGHWAY PATROL' SUPER-FAN PERFECTLY RECREATED THE SHOW'S FLASHY 1955 BUICK

WARNING: THIS POST WILL INDUCE CAR ENVY. AS DAN MATHEWS SAID: "IT ISN'T WHAT YOU DRIVE, BUT HOW YOU DRIVE THAT COUNTS!"

BY: METV STAFF POSTED: OCTOBER 3, 2017, 10:42AM

Photo by Patrick Ecclesine

Between 1955 and 1959, TV audiences tuned in for 30-minute episodes of *Highway Patrol.* Filmed in striking locations and artfully shot, the show was a stunner, and it featured Oscar-winning actor Broderick Crawford singlehandedly delivering justice, speaking gruff orders into his police radio while he leaned against his trusty 1955 Buick.

It was the kind of car that doctors drove at that time, and not typically associated with cops. It was a flashy show that got attention. That's probably why, for a lot of young kids glued to TVs back then, Crawford's role as the head of Highway Patrol Dan Mathews was not just a barking authority. Dan Mathews was as invincible as a superhero. *Highway Patrol* super-fan Gary Goltz was one of those young kids, and police chief Dan Mathews was his idol. He especially loved the early episodes produced by Herb Strock, which had plots driven more by mystery and suspense, like "Father Zee" and "Desert Town.""In one half hour, he cracked the case, he got the bad guys, he usually shot them, and he made restitution to the victims," Goltz tells MeTV. "If that's not a superhero, you tell me what is."Today, Goltz has grown to become a different kind of authority — an expert on all things *Highway Patrol*. He's run the top *Highway Patrol* fan site since 1996, and to fit the part, he's also built a replica of Crawford's signature vehicle. Goltz has gone to great lengths to match his modified 1955 Buick so that it looks as close as possible to Crawford's original. Goltz bought his Buick in 1995 after stumbling upon the exact model he wanted in an old car trader magazine. This was before eBay and other internet tools simplified how people search for collectibles. It so happened that he was going on a business trip where the car was stored, and it took just one good look at the vehicle for him to agree to buy it for $6,500. At the time, Goltz did not consider himself a "car guy." The Buick was missing a gas cap, and he knew he could start by fixing that. As it turns out, that gas cap was the key to the door that led Goltz to recreate the car of his dreams.

"When I got the car, it was just a regular Buick, three-tone, and the first thing I noticed, the gas cap was missing," Goltz says. "I looked up in the Yellow Pages and there was a place called Classic Buick not too far from me, so I drove down there to buy a gas cap." "While I'm buying the gas cap, I see a picture of a *Highway Patrol* Buick up on the wall, and I'm looking at it and I'm telling the guy, 'That's why I bought the car, because I love that show and Broderick Crawford.'" "And he says, 'Well, I always tell my customers if they get a classic car like this, they should follow their dream and do what you want with it.'" He added, 'You know, I don't usually do this, but here's a guy's phone number, I think you should give him a call.'" Goltz called the number and met Les Randolph a classic car restorer who has helped him chase every detail ever since, to exactly modify his Buick to mimic the features of the *Highway Patrol* Buick. He's since spent close to $200,000 to become the proud owner of his Buick replica, based on the ones he first fell in love with watching episodes of *Highway Patrol*. "As a kid, I'm watching this show with these Buicks and this guy in a suit instead of a uniform, and unlike like the rest of [cop shows], helicopters," Goltz says. "And Broderick Crawford is there, being a big-time Academy Award-winning film actor, and doing this show with his eyes closed. He owns the character. He just mesmerized everyone. I remember seeing my grandmother watch that show in the '50s. I looked at that guy and said to myself, 'I want to be like him when I grow up!'"

Gary Goltz with 'Highway Patrol' producer Herb Strock, actor Bill Boyett, and CHP officer Frank Runyon who served as the program's technical advisor.

Although Goltz didn't grow up to become a police chief as you might suspect, he does help lead initiatives that benefit and raise awareness for police today. Not only is he a Lifetime Member of the California Highway Patrol (CHP) 11-99 Foundation — which provides emergency benefits to CHP employees and families in times of crisis — he is also the brains behind 10-4 Day, an event that takes place every year on October 4 and recognizes the service and sacrifice of highway patrol officers and public safety officials.If you remember the little messages at the end of each *Highway Patrol* episode that urged viewers to practice safety first, you'll be pleased to know the Annual 10-4 Day Parade keeps that spirit alive each year. Goltz's involvement with 10-4 Day came about the way many things do for Goltz: because of the car. After participating in parades for years, Goltz was named as then–Los Angeles City Councilman Tom LaBonge's "Dollar a Year Man" in charge of parades. In 2004, LaBonge asked Goltz how they could commemorate the 75th anniversary of CHP, and Goltz immediately came up with 10-4 Day. "I said, 'Let's gather all the cars like mine and drive down Hollywood Boulevard,'" Goltz explains. And that's just what they do, as replicas of famous TV and movie cars drive alongside police vehicles. The parade visiting both of Crawford's stars on the

Hollywood Walk of Fame. Yes, the acclaimed actor has *two*. Of course, there aren't many cars quite like Goltz's Buick, which is souped up even beyond the car that fans will remember from *Highway Patrol*. He rigged a complete light arrangement and added a loud siren. He's also got a sound system that allows him to blast the *Highway Patrol* theme song or entertain parade-goers with his impressions of Crawford and *Highway Patrol* narrator Art Gilmore. "I can change the narration, talk about 10-4 Day, and that's what I do when I take it into parades," Goltz says. "Between the sirens going and the music blaring and the lights all flashing, it's a homerun. It's been in tons of parades. I've done a lot of stuff with the car and taken a lot of celebrities in the car."

Gary Goltz with Jay Leno (left) and Laurence Fishburne (right).

The list of celebrities Goltz has met through the car is long, including huge car aficionados like Jay Leno, Adam Carolla, Laurence Fishburne, Neil Young and many more. It also includes *Highway Patrol* fans like Dan Aykroyd, with whom Goltz once performed, when he was unexpectedly called onstage at a fundraiser for the LAPD. "I get up there and I do my best Broderick impersonation, and I went, 'Oh, I'm on highway patrol and we have Sergeant Friday from the LAPD come out here in a minute, come out here!' and Aykroyd comes out, and we're trading barbs!" Goltz fondly recalls. "He's doing Jack Webb (impressions from *Dragnet*), and I'm doing Broderick Crawford. I'm telling you, it was all impromptu, and I'm thinking to myself, 'How many people get themselves in a situation like this?'" Goltz adds with a laugh, "And you wanna know something? Between me and you, I did Broderick Crawford better than he did Jack Webb." His fandom has also introduced him to people involved with the show like Herb Strock, Bill Boyett, Frank Runyon and more. Of all the places the car has taken Goltz, though, perhaps the most memorable was when he and Crawford's son, Kelly, went on a trip down Route 66 that lasted two weeks. It cemented a real friendship between the *Highway Patrol* superfan Gary Goltz and the son of the show's star, who even invited Goltz to see his father's Oscar statuette. It seems that everywhere the Buick goes with Goltz, it helps connect him more meaningfully with fans and people who were connected to the show, its star and its most famous car. "It's just amazing how things happen," Goltz says. "I've been blessed that I got to know these people as real people. Most are gone now but I'll always consider them to be real friends of mine." During that time, Goltz was also driven to become a success in the healthcare business. In addition, he operates a judo school as an eighth-degree black belt. That talent brought him a different sort of fame after Goltz sent in a fan correction to *Conan*, which Conan O'Brien aired, sending half a million people to watch Goltz's video where he corrected the actor Jack Black's flawed judo tiger roll. You can watch his video, Conan's commentary and Black's response by clicking on the photo below:

Although Goltz is a fan of *Conan*, the top show in his heart remains *Highway Patrol*, which transports him to a different time, when he remembers TV was just better. "The way it's filmed, the way it's written," Goltz says. "It's great pulp fiction."

If you're in Los Angeles, California, you can check out Goltz's *Highway Patrol* car this week at the Annual 10-4 Day Parade of classic emergency vehicles on Wednesday, October 4. Participants in the parade will meet at 11AM by the Los Angeles Fire Museum, or you can watch the parade as it travels north down Cahuenga Boulevard and west on Hollywood Boulevard. The parade will also feature Shotgun Tom Kelly and actors from additional TV cop shows. **You can find <u>more details here</u>.**

Neil Young and Gary Goltz in July 1996

Postscript2:
The *Wall Street Journal* article of 07-26-2016
(Copyright 2016)

THE WALL STREET JOURNAL.

U.S. Edition ▼ | July 26, 2016 | Today's Paper

A 1955 Buick and Reruns of 'Highway Patrol'
One fan of 1950s television has kept the show running

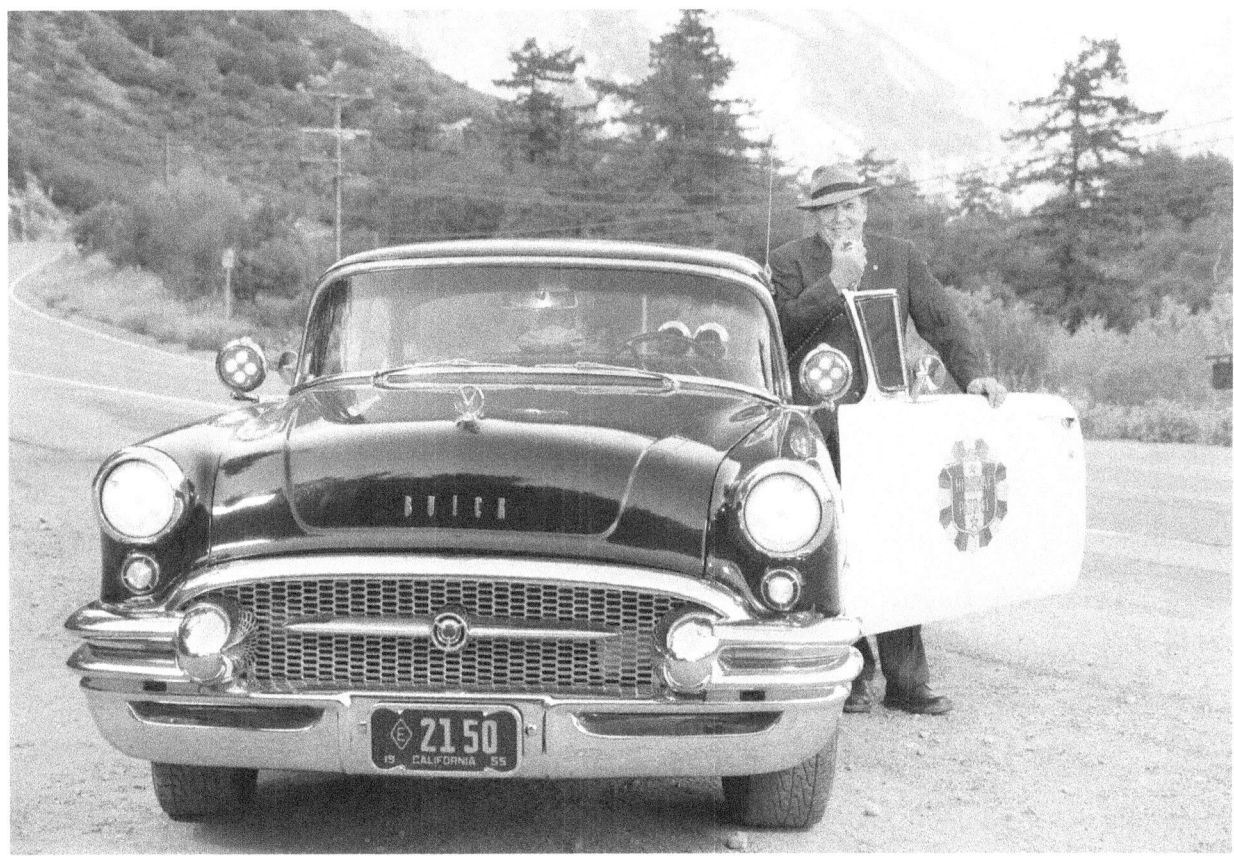

Gary Goltz, 63, a health-care industry sales strategy consultant from Upland, California with his 1955 Buick Century, which he has outfitted to look exactly like one Broderick Crawford drove in the TV show '*Highway Patrol*,' which Mr. Goltz watched avidly as a kid growing up in Pittsburgh.

By A.J. Baime
July 26, 2016

Gary Goltz, 63, a health-care industry sales consultant from Upland, Calif., on his 1955 Buick Century California Highway Patrol enforcement unit, as told to A.J. Baime.

As a kid growing up in the 1960s, I loved the TV show "Highway Patrol." Every day I'd come home from school, have a peanut butter sandwich and watch Broderick Crawford in that show, followed by "The Three Stooges" and "Popeye" cartoons. "Highway Patrol" was all about good guys winning over bad guys. Watching that heavyset cop in a fedora driving a Buick California Highway Patrol car and ordering people around—there was something mesmerizing about him. When I sold a business in 1993, I decided to indulge myself with a classic 1955 Buick, which I purchased in 1995. It cost about $25,000 to convert it into a what you see here; a Buick California Highway Patrol car like one of the cars Broderick Crawford drove in the show. Over the years, I've added power steering, power disc brakes, air-conditioning and cruise control, and a sound system that'll knock your socks off, not just internally but externally. When I want to blare the theme song from the TV show, I want it to sound like it's being played right before you. I also blare the opening narration, spoken by the famous Hollywood pitchman Art Gilmore: "Whenever the laws of any state are broken, a duly authorized organization swings into action." In 2001, I drove this car across the entire Route 66, from Chicago to the Santa Monica Pier, with Broderick Crawford's son Kelly (who died a few years ago, unfortunately). I also take the car in a parade every year on Oct. 4, to Broderick Crawford's Walk of Fame star near the Chinese Theatre. Why Oct. 4? Crawford is known for the way he barked into his mic at the end of radio messages on the show: "10-4." When we come down Hollywood Boulevard each year on that day, with about 25 classic police cars, we stop all of Hollywood in its tracks. I've owned this car now for 21 years. Every time I take it out, it still draws a crowd.

Behind the scenes of the 5-hour WSJ Photo Shoot.

Mr. Goltz with his car, photographed not far from his home. Mr. Goltz bought the car in 1995. Those holes above the front wheel aren't bullet holes; Buicks from this era are known for this styling cue. *GREGG SEGAL FOR THE WALL STREET JOURNAL*

The car's prodigious nose. There's enough chrome on this vehicle to keep its owner busy buffing for hours. *GREGG SEGAL FOR THE WALL STREET JOURNAL*

A peak into the car's interior. The Buick was not a cheap car in 1955, and the interior featured elegant art-deco styling. *GREGG SEGAL FOR THE WALL STREET JOURNAL*

Unit 2150 was Broderick Crawford's car number on 'Highway Patrol.' 'Talk to anyone over 60 about that show and they'll get a big smile on their face,' says Mr. Goltz. GREGG SEGAL FOR THE WALL STREET JOURNAL

Mr. Goltz even has an ID card for Dan Mathews, the character Broderick Crawford played on 'Highway Patrol.' GREGG SEGAL FOR THE WALL STREET JOURNAL

Some detail of the policing equipment. The TV show 'Highway Patrol' ran original episodes from 1955 to 1959, according to the Internet Movie Database, with reruns airing after that. *GREGG SEGAL FOR THE WALL STREET JOURNAL*

Mr. Goltz checking in the trunk. When he's not out driving his Buick, he is often to be found **teaching judo at his club in Claremont, CA**. He is a former President of the United States Judo Association. *GREGG SEGAL FOR THE WALL STREET JOURNAL*

More detail of the 1955 Buick. It was a slightly odd choice for a police car in the 1950s because it was expensive. 'The Buick was the car doctors drove,' say Mr. Goltz. GREGG SEGAL FOR THE WALL STREET JOURNAL

The hood ornament and the Buick logo—classic 1950s styling. *GREGG SEGAL FOR THE WALL STREET JOURNAL*

The car from behind, showing the 2150 license plate—Broderick Crawford's car number on the show 'Highway Patrol.' 'Growing up in Pittsburgh and watching that show, the cars looked so different from what police drove where we lived,' says Mr. Goltz. GREGG SEGAL FOR THE WALL STREET JOURNAL

An old highway patrol hat completes the package. GREGG SEGAL FOR THE WALL STREET JOURNAL

Everyday I'd come home from school, have a peanut butter sandwich and watch Broderick Crawford in ['Highway Patrol'], followed by 'The Three Stooges' and 'Popeye' cartoons,' says Mr. Goltz. GREGG SEGAL FOR THE WALL STREET JOURNAL

'I've had the car for 21 years,' says Mr. Goltz. 'Every time I take it out, it still draws a crowd!' GREGG SEGAL FOR THE WALL STREET JOURNAL

THE WALL STREET JOURNAL.

WEDNESDAY, JULY 27, 2016 - VOL. CCLXVIII NO. 22

Clinton Wins Historic Nomination

Hillary Clinton addressed the Democratic convention via video feed late Tuesday, topping off a string of speakers that included her husband, former President Bill Clinton.

What's News

Business & Finance

♦ Apple said its quarterly profit fell 27% as it grappled with the first prolonged slump in iPhone sales since the product was introduced in 2007. **A1**

♦ AB InBev raised its offer for SABMiller, as it sought to assuage shareholders' concerns after the British pound's plunge. **B1**

♦ Analog Devices agreed to buy fellow chip maker Linear Technology in a $14.8 billion cash-and-stock deal. **B1**

♦ Mobileye is ending a supply agreement with Tesla in the wake of a high-profile traffic fatality. **B1**

♦ Twitter's revenue rose 20%, its smallest gain and eighth-straight quarter of declining growth. **B3**

♦ Some investors aren't convinced the Fed will raise rates this year, data on bullish dollar bets indicate. **C1**

♦ KKR reported better-than-expected earnings, helped by a so-called dividend recapitalization deal. **C1**

♦ The Dow fell 19.31 points to close at 18473.75 on a busy day of earnings reports for the index. **C4**

♦ McDonald's sales lost steam in the latest quarter, and investors are looking for the firm's next big move. **B3**

♦ Caterpillar said it doesn't anticipate a rebound this year for its equipment and pared its profit forecast. **B7**

World-Wide

♦ Clinton became the first

After Tough Battle, A Landmark Moment

By PETER NICHOLAS AND BYRON TAU

PHILADELPHIA—Hillary Clinton became the first female presidential nominee of any major party on Tuesday, a historic milestone that sets the stage for a battle to prove to voters that she is someone they can trust in the White House.

The second day of the Democratic National Convention was designed to offer reassurance to an electorate that has watched her on the national stage for more than two decades as first lady, then U.S. senator and secretary of state.

The validators tapped to send that message ranged from her vanquished primary challenger, Vermont Sen. Bernie Sanders, to her husband, former President Bill Clinton.

Late in the evening, Mrs. Clinton briefly addressed the convention via a video feed, appearing after an animated pane of glass shattered. "I can't believe we just put the biggest

Please see DNC page A4

★★★ DNC ★★★
PHILADELPHIA
2016

- Messages on state of the economy reveal tensions, **A4**
- Speakers address issue of violence and police **A4**
- Democrats achieve an uneasy détente, **A5**
- Kaine runs left on social issues, **A5**
- Obama to play central role at convention, **A6**
- Clinton opposes vote on trade pact this year, **A6**

For Some Women, Gender Isn't Enough

By COLLEEN MCCAIN NELSON AND JANET ADAMY

The nomination of Hillary Clinton marked a step forward in the fight for equality in postwar America that illustrates the strides made by women since the former first lady was born in 1947.

The irony—and the problem for Mrs. Clinton—is that such progress has become so widespread that some women voters appear indifferent to another glass ceiling shattered. More women graduate from college than men. They are the main breadwinners in four of 10 U.S. households. They run General Motors Co., PepsiCo Inc. and IBM Corp.

Mrs. Clinton, who was formally picked Tuesday evening as the Democratic nominee, has struggled to lock up support from middle-aged white women. And some younger women see little urgency to crash barriers they haven't encountered.

While 52% of registered fe-

Please see WOMEN page A6

Postscript 3
The 13th Annual "10-4 Day Parade" of Classic Police Cars and Emergency Vehicles October 04, 2016

**Tom LaBonge, 'Shotgun' Tom Kelly and Gary Goltz
kick-off "10-4 Day" Parade (Photo Goltz Collection)**

On a hot and sunny Southern California Tuesday morning (October 4, 2016) in the street in front of the Los Angeles Fire Department Museum and Fire Station 27 at 1327 N. Cole Avenue, several dozen, beautifully-waxed, classic police/emergency vehicles lined-up to honor the dedicated men and women of America's law enforcement agencies, in particular the California Highway Patrol (CHP) and the Los Angeles Police Department (LAPD). Included were several vintage and great-looking CHP enforcement units from the 1940's and 1950's, along with two modern Los Angeles Police Department (LAPD) vehicles that provided security and escorted the parade during its route through the heart of Hollywood.

There were no less than three authentic replicas of Broderick Crawford's police car from his block-buster television series *Highway Patrol*. Author Gary Goltz is also the co-founder of this annual event. His HP 1955 Buick was the lead car in the procession carrying the honored guests parade Grand Marshal Tom Hatten, the beloved KTLA reporter and children's television host and screen actor, and radio legend 'Shotgun Tom' Kelly of popular Los Angeles station K-Earth 101. Movie stuntman/actor Rusty Locke, the son of *Highway Patrol* co-star Jon Locke who played Officer Garvey on the series, also drove a classic HP police car in the parade. He wore the original patrol officer uniform from the TV series and was a dead-ringer for his father!

Rusty Locke, in full *Highway Patrol* uniform, fills his father Jon Locke's shoes on "10-4 Day" (Photo Goltz Collection).

**Grand Marshal Tom Hatten in his 1960's heyday hosting Popeye cartoons on Los Angeles television
(Photo Goltz Collection)**

Other vehicles lined-up for the parade were a Detroit Police squad car, Andy Griffith's *Sheriff of Mayberry County* police car, and a rugged *Jurassic World* game warden's vehicle. A Coronet model *Highway Patrol* police car was driven by Albert Okura, the Mayor and owner of the historic *'Route 66'* town of Amboy, California. Famed automotive artist Ken Nordmann drove a vintage 1956 red Ford wagon which towed a parade float with two very lovely beauty queens riding on it, *'Ms. Route 66'* Monica J. Burrola, and *'National Ms. Route 66 Racer'* Esther C. Hollister. At 10:45AM '10-4 Day' co-founder, former Los Angeles Councilman Tom LaBonge called a driver's meeting. He introduced the parade Grand Marshal Tom Hatten, who told everyone about meeting the actual star of *Highway Patrol*, Broderick Crawford! Hatten said "I ran into Brod Crawford once and told him that I was a big fan [pause]. He thanked me and then I said, 'Of your mother, Helen Broderick!' Brod suddenly laughed out loud at the joke and then bought me a drink!" Gary Goltz took the microphone to spell out the parade route and asked everyone to donate at least $25.00 to the *Hollywood Police Activities League (PAL)* which sponsors many fun events to keep children off the streets and out of trouble. He declared that after the parade everyone would meet for lunch at the popular *Cantor's Deli* on Fairfax. Goltz, a judo master also presented Los Angeles Police Officer Taybren Lee, Jr. with his 'Certificate of Promotion to 4th Degree Black Belt'. Just before the parade commenced, Goltz asked everyone to bow their heads as he did his best impersonation of Art Gilmore by reciting the preamble to the *Highway Patrol* TV series!

'Shotgun' Tom Kelly charms a throng of well-wishers with Grand Marshal Tom Hatten on Hollywood Boulevard (Photo Goltz Collection)

The parade stops to turn-around near Madame Tussaud's Wax Museum on Hollywood Boulevard while the crowd cheers Grand Marshal Tom Hatten and 'Shotgun' Tom Kelly (Photo Goltz Collection).

Len Nordmann's famed vintage 'Route 66' pace vehicle and trailer carrying the 'Route 66' beauty Queens (Photo Goltz Collection).

Tom LaBonge, 'National Ms. Route 66 Racer' Esther C. Hollister, 'Shotgun ' Tom Kelly, Grand Marshal Tom Hatten, author Gary Goltz, Los Angeles Police Officer Taybren Lee, Jr., and 'Ms. Route 66' Monica J. Burrola (Photo Goltz Collection)

With sirens wailing the parade kicked-off with the procession heading North on Cahuenga and then turned West onto Hollywood Boulevard as Councilman LaBonge personally directed traffic to ensure that all went off without a hitch. Thousands of tourists visiting 'Tinsel Town' cheered and photographed the parade during its entire route. 'Shotgun Tom Kelly' wore his trademark Ranger hat, and leaned out of the passenger front window of the Goltz's Buick HP car to enthusiastically waive to every person he saw. The procession halted in front of the *Walk of Fame* on the East side of the Hollywood Boulevard near the famed *Chinese Theatre* next to Broderick Crawford's "Star For Motion Pictures". Ralph Schiller, riding with Tom Hatten in the back seat of Goltz's Buick, asked the Parade Grand Marshal if he wanted to pay homage to Broderick Crawford's star. Hatten said "I wouldn't miss it for the world!" Fighting through a thick crowd of applauding bystanders Tom Hatten kneeled in front the star of his old friend and said 'God Bless Brod!" At this time the Los Angeles Police Department escort, unable to block Hollywood Boulevard any further, ordered the parade to return to Cole Street. The many police vehicles took off with their wailing sirens going full blast with throngs of well-wishing onlookers waving goodbye!

A delighted spectator greets 'Shotgun' Tom Kelly. Note the other bystanders in the background covering their ears at the wailing of the sirens! (Photo Goltz Collection)

The parade ended where it began on Cole Avenue in front of Fire Station 27 before re-uniting for lunch at Hollywood's finest since 1931, *Cantor's Deli* for a well-earned, great meal with dreams of next year's parade being bigger! A complete listing of all "10-4 Days" since its 2004 inception, including photos of the cars and celebrants, videos, and news stories in both print and TV can be found on the Highway Patrol Website. www.highwaypatroltv.com We include a smattering of them here and from the 1016 event.
Note: Beloved actor Tom Hatten died in 2019 and is sorely missed by all who had the pleasure of knowing him.

Epilog
The Star & the Car Documentary

The Star and the Car is a documentary about Gary Goltz, and how his love of the 50's TV series *HIGHWAY PATROL* led to restoring a 1955 Buick to the appearance of Broderick Crawford's car used on the classic show.

Along the way, Gary used Crawford's persona combined with a judo discipline to become a successful businessman. Gary's upward mobility landed him in California, where he met the surviving *HIGHWAY PATROL* cast members and crew. When a '55 Buick came up for sale, Gary bought it and six months later was driving a fully decked out replica of Crawford's car. From there, it was non-stop charity events for the CHP's 1199 Foundation and other worthy causes...and more than a few celebrity encounters. Join us for the World Premiere of Gary's story from the 50's to the 21st century...it's a great ride!

Our premiere is at the fabulous AUTOMOBILE DRIVING MUSEUM in El Segundo (near LAX). Gary will be there with the Buick and our event begins at 1pm on Sunday, June 29th. The Master of Ceremonies for this event is Walk of Fame DJ now on SirusXM, Shotgun Tom Kelly! There's plenty of parking adjacent the museum. Tickets are free and are going fast. Seating is limited so please RSVP as soon as possible. No need to print ticket...we will have your name at the event.

10-4!
DATE
Sun, July 29, 2018
1:00 PM – 2:30 PM PDT
Add to Calendar

LOCATION
Automobile Driving Museum
610 Lairport Street
El Segundo, CA 90245

WORLD PREMIERE LIVE PRESENTATION FORMAT

09:00am Load In Buick
 Set up Audio/Video
 Set up Banners
 Set up refreshments

12noon - 1pm WELCOME GUESTS/PHOTO WITH GARY & BUICK

12:55 CALL TO AUDIENCE "TAKE YOUR SEATS"

01:00 INTRODUCTION TO SHOTGUN TOM KELLY
"Please welcome our M.C. for today's screening,
the legendary L.A. disc jockey and upcoming host
of Sirius Radio's 60's on 6….SHOTGUN TOM KELLY!"

SPEAKER - SHOTGUN TOM KELLY
Welcomes attendees
explains that short Q & A will follow movie
Introduces Museum Rep.
"Our host today is the **Automobile Driving Museum**…here to welcome you from the
museum is ERIC CARLSON (alternate: TARA HITZIG)

SPEAKER SHOTGUN -
"Turn down the lights…It's the WORLD PREMIERE of THE STAR AND THE CAR"

SCREENING - THE STAR AND THE CAR
AFTER SCREENING - SHOTGUN INTROS Q & A
"The Producer of today's video….MIKE CLARK!"
"This fellow is a former L.A. City Councilman who we hope will be
running for Mayor….please welcome TOM LaBONGE"
"And finally, the star of THE STAR and the CAR…GARY GOLTZ"

ACKNOWLEDGE ANY V.I.P. GUESTS IN AUDIENCE

Q & A

Trivia Challenge - Buick Toy prizes

Detailed Description of the entire plot:

The Star and the Car is a documentary about Gary Goltz, and how his love of the 50's TV series HIGHWAY PATROL led to restoring a 1955 Buick to the appearance of Broderick Crawford's car used on the classic show.

Along the way, Gary used Crawford's persona combined with a judo discipline to become a successful businessman. Gary's upward mobility landed him in California, where he met the surviving HIGHWAY PATROL cast members and crew. When a '55 Buick came up for sale, Gary bought it and six months later was driving a fully decked out replica of Crawford's car. From there, it was non-stop charity events for the CHP's 11-99 Foundation and other worthy causes...and more than a few celebrity encounters.

The documentary opens with Gary's childhood in Pittsburgh where he watched HIGHWAY PATROL in the late 50's with his beloved grandmother, a Russian Jewish immigrant who escaped a pogrom in the Pale. The young boy had empathy for what the refugee elder woman must have experienced prior to fleeing her homeland and settling in America. In his desire to comfort her, Gary observed the tranquilizing effect Broderick Crawford as Dan Mathews, had on her. He protected the weak who were victims of vigorous and violent criminals, much like Superman but more realistic. Gary decided to model himself after that character.

Gary went on to becoming an expert in judo, then in business and eventually settling in a suburb of Los Angeles. In the early 90's he started to collect VHS Tapes of HIGHWAY PATROL rediscovering the impact it had on his personality. This led him to purchase a 1955 Buick Century and have it converted to look like the one driven by his fictional hero.

From there the next two decades of his life have been an ongoing adventure including getting to know the cast and crew of HIGHWAY PATROL intimately. Gary became a close friend of Broderick Crawford's son and drove the classic car with him on a 2-week excursion across the entire Route 66.

Gary also formed close relationship with Tom LaBonge a prominent City Council Member whose district included Hollywood. They created 10-4 Day to celebrate the CHP and law enforcement which involves a parade down Hollywood Boulevard of classic police cars to the movie Walk of Fame Star of Broderick's.

Gary's obsession with HIGHWAY PATROL and the positive things it has resulted in is only part of this story. The other part of the film focuses on HIGHWAY PATROL the series, with an in-depth look at Ziv Studios, syndicated television, and its impact on Baby Boomers like Gary. The story is riveting and holds the viewers interest during the entire 34 minutes. Veteran filmmaker, Mike Clark has done an outstanding job writing, filming, and directing this short subject.

The production value is high, and the post premiere panel discussion video Mike Clark also created is a perfect bookend to this entertaining and educational short.

INDEX

Abbe, Derwin 278, 287
Abbott & Costello 11
Acapulco, TV series 12
Adamson, Al 86
Adam-12, TV series 89
Adam, Richard 271, 278, 279, 283
Adams, Don 132
Adams, Nick 149
Adamson, Ed 247
Ad Council 123
The Adventures Of Rin-Tin-Tin, TV series 105
The Adventures Of Superman, TV series 2, 59, 85
Akins, Claude 19
Alias Smith And Jones, TV series 150
"Alias Willie Hogan", episode King Of Diamonds 141, 142
Albright, Lola 141
All The King's Men (1949) 31, 59, 152, 158, 160
Allen, Steve 123
Allyn, Kirk 89
American-International Pictures 101
"Amnesia", episode Highway Patrol 259
Anderson, Christopher 11
Andes, Keith 13
The Andy Griffith Show, TV series 101
Annual Art Gilmore Broadcasting Award 103
"Anti-toxin", episode Highway Patrol 249
The Aquanauts, TV series 12
"Armored Car", episode Highway Patrol 85, 258
Art Gilmore Career Achievement award 102
"Art Robbery", episode Highway Patrol 250
Askins, Monroe 274, 276, 277, 287, 291
Asphalt Arabs 104
Attila The Hun 133
"Auto Press", episode Highway Patrol 290
Aykroyd, Dan 106, 134, 135
Baker, Ann 13
Baker, Diane 150
Baker, Officer Jon 137
Ball, Lucille 19
Ballantine Beer 57
"Bank Messenger", episode Highway Patrol 103, 292
Barker, Warren 141
Barrett, Tony 249
Barry, Gene 10, 12
Bat Masterson, TV series 10, 12, 95
Battle Taxi (1955) 96
Baxter, Ted 284
Belushi, John 135
Benedict, Richard 287

Benson, Leon 238, 245, 246, 248, 249, 272, 274, 275, 290
Bernsen, Corbin 86
Berg, Lee 267, 269, 271, 272, 274, 276, 279, 282, 288
Betts, Sgt. Tom 240
Between Heaven And Hell (1956) 103
The Big Valley, TV series 280
Black Dahlia murder case 2
Blanchard, Mari 13
Blackhawk, serial 89
Blair, George 263
"Blast Area Copter", episode Highway Patrol 85, 249
Blanchard, Mari 13
Blood Of Dracula (1957) 101
"Blood Money", episode Highway Patrol 282
"The Blue Moon Train", episode Cimarron Strip 89
Boehm, David 269
Bogart, Humphrey 132
Bold Venture, TV series 12
Bonanza, TV series 101
Boston Blackie, TV series 1, 12
Bourgeois, Roy 100, 243, 246, 249, 254, 259, 262, 264, 266, 274, 281
Bowman, Lee 13
Boyett, William (Bill) 58, 89, 90, 238, 247-250, 254-257, 260, 263, 265, 268, 270, 271, 273, 274, 276-292
Bradley, Truman 13
Braus, M. 281
"Brave Boy", episode Highway Patrol 287
"Breath Of A Child", episode Highway Patrol 86, 284
Breck, Peter 280
Brennan, Walter 59
Brewster, Diane 89
Brian, David 13
Bridges, Lloyd 6, 10, 13
Brinkley, Donald A. 238, 240, 241, 243, 246, 247, 249, 250, 252-255, 258, 261, 263, 264
The Broderick Crawford Benefits Program 106
Broderick, James 105
Broderick, Matthew 105, 106
Bronson Canyon, location 34
Brooks, Stephen 149
Brown, James 105
Browne, Kathie 141
Buick Century 1955 104, 106
Burke, Paul 12, 86, 89, 237
Burke's Law, TV series 85
Burrola, Monica ("MS. Route 66") 328

Butterfield, Paul 134
Cagney, James 11
California Highway Patrol (CHP) 19, 34, 58, 96, 103, 104, 105, 106, 326
California Highway Patrol 11-99 Foundation 106
Caldwell, Bernard 19, 31, 104, 105, 292, 293
Callan, Michael 149
Call Of The Wild (1935) 95
Cameron, Rod 36
Canada Dry TV commercial 133
The Candidate (1972) 158
Cannon Dyan (Diane) 287
Cantor's Deli 329, 333
Cantor, Eddie 12
Captain Binghampton 251
Carey, Macdonald 6, 12, 13
Carillo, Leo 1, 12, 33, 34
"Careless Cop", episode Highway Patrol 86, 275
"Cargo Hijack", episode Highway Patrol 288
Carlson, Richard 6, 13
"Car Theft", episode Highway Patrol 245
Case File FBI 19
Case Of The Dangerous Robin, TV series 12
"Chain Store", episode Highway Patrol 270
The Challenge (1970) 86
Champion 1949 152
Charlie Chaplin studio lot 2
"The Casualty", episode The Interns 151
Cheyenne, TV series 59, 101
The Chinese Theatre on Hollywood Boulevard 332
CHiPs, TV series 137
Chooluck, Lean 280, 289
"Christmas Story", episode Highway Patrol 253
Cimarron Strip, TV series 89
The Cisco Kid, TV series 1, 12, 34
City Of Angels, TV series 86
Clark, Don 270
Cleaver, Beaver 131
Cleaver, Wally 131
Coburn, James 12, 13
Columbia Pictures 31, 149
"The Collector", episode Highway Patrol 286
"Commando Tactics", episode King Of Diamonds 141
"Confession", episode Highway Patrol 291
Convicts 4 (1962) 89
"Confidence Game", episode Highway Patrol 283
"Convicted Innocent", episode Highway Patrol 270
"Convict's Wife", episode Highway Patrol 263
Connors, Michael "Touch" 105
Conrad, Robert 287
Conrad, William 283
Conway, Pat 13, 59, 89

Cooper, Jeanne 86, 242
"Copter Cave-in", episode Highway Patrol 285
Corey, Wendell 12, 36
"Counterfeit", episode Highway Patrol 260
Cramoy, Michael 239, 242, 250
Crawford, Broderick 13, 19, 31, 34-36, 56-59, 85, 86, 89, 95, 96, 101, 103-106, 122-125, 131-137, 141, 142, 149, 150-151, 152, 156-160, 285, 300-301, 326-333
Crawford (Griffith), Kay 31, 157
Crawford, Kelly 104, 106, 125, 134, 157-160
Crawford, Kim 125, 157, 159
Crawford, Joan 150
"Credit Card", episode Highway Patrol 276
Crittenden, Bradford 103, 105
Cugat, Xavier 132
Curtin, Jane 135
Cyril Stapleton and his Orchestra 101
Dahl, Arlene 132
Daniels, Guy 19, 31, 34, 35, 36, 58, 86, 89, 96, 101, 105
"Dan Hostage", episode Highway Patrol 289
"Dan Sick", episode Highway Patrol 279
"Dan's Vacation", episode Highway Patrol 277
The David Letterman Show, TV series 105
Davis, Eddie 239, 243, 245, 255, 259-268, 275, 276, 278, 279, 290-292
Day, Doris 131
"Dead Hunter", episode Highway Patrol 270
"Dead Patrolman", episode Highway Patrol 249
"Deadly Diamonds", episode Highway Patrol 282
"Deaf Mute", episode Highway Patrol 274
De Grazia, Ted 152
"Desert Copter", episode Highway Patrol 246
"Desert Town", episode Highway Patrol 239
"Desperate Men", episode Highway Patrol 291
"Detour To Death", episode Highway Patrol 291
Devine, Andy 59
De Vinny, Bob 132
Dial 999, TV series 6, 12
Dick Tracy 132
"Diversion Robbery", episode Highway Patrol 287
Dix, Robert 86
Doctor John 134
Dr. Aaron 149
Dr. Cal Barrin 149
Dr. Christian, TV series 12, 293
Dr. Drew Live, TV series 86
Dr. Greg Pettit 149
Dr. Lydia Thorpe 149
Dr. Peter Goldstone 149, 150, 151
Dr. Pooch Hardin 149, 150
Dr. Sam Marsh 149, 151
Doniger, Walter 283

Douglas, Jack (Jay) 13, 240, 245, 247, 249, 250, 254-256
Douglas, Kirk 152
Downs, Hunton 300-301
The Decks Ran Red (1958) 89, 103
Down Three Dark Streets (1954) 19
"Double Copter", episode Highway Patrol 278
"Double Cross", episode Highway Patrol 265
"Double Death", episode Highway Patrol 271
Dragnet, TV series 1, 19, 35, 89, 100, 102, 104, 105
Driskell, William L. 254, 259, 260, 262, 266, 268, 273, 274
Drucker, Mort 125
Dow, Tony 131
Duel, Pete 150
Duke, Patty 133
Eagle-Lion studio lot 2
Eastwood, Clint 86, 89, 247
Ebb Tide 101
Escape To Athena (1979) 301
Eddie Cantor Comedy Theatre, TV series 12
"Eddie's Double-Cross", episode Leave It To Beaver 131
Eden, Barbara 86, 266
Edwards, Jack 247
Educational Pictures studio lot 1
11-99 Foundation Banquet 106
Eisenhower, General Dwight D 300-301
Ely, Ron 12
"Efficiency Secretary", episode Highway Patrol 267
"Escaped Mental Patient", episode Highway Patrol 258
"Escort", episode Highway Patrol 241
Estrada, Eric 137
Eternally Yours (1939) 95
Everett, Chad 149
Everglades, TV series 12
"Ex Con", episode Highway Patrol 257
"Explosives", episode Highway Patrol 278
"Expose", episode Highway Patrol 284
"Express Delivery", episode Highway Patrol 290
"Fake Cop", episode Highway Patrol 265
"Family Affair", episode Highway Patrol 280
The Fastest Gun Alive (1956) 103
Faberes, Shelley 151
"False Confession", episode Highway Patrol 282
Farrell, Mike 149, 151
Fass, George & Gertrude 280
"Father Thief", episode Highway Patrol 240
"Fear", episode Highway Patrol 275
Fellini, Federico 31
"Female Hitchhiker", episode Highway Patrol 106, 261
Fenady, Georg 137

Ferndale Cemetery, Jamestown, New York 159
Feist, Felix 264
Fife, Deputy Barney 101
Film Fax magazine 95
Fisher, Steve 141
"Fire", episode Highway Patrol 292
"Fisherman's Luck", episode Highway Patrol 255
Florea, John 280, 281
Flynn, Joe 251
Formosa Café 2, 101
"Foster Child", episode Highway Patrol 273
Foster, Preston 13
Foster, Ron 271, 273, 275, 276-278, 280, 281, 283, 289, 292
"Framed Cop", episode Highway Patrol 286
Franz, Arthur 13
Frederick, Hal 149
Frederick W. Ziv Company 1
Frede, Richard 149
Freed, Bert 141
Fresco, Robert M. 240
Friday, Sgt. Joe 35, 106
"Frightened Witness", episode Highway Patrol 279
Frost, Terry 95, 240, 244, 247, 251, 254, 260, 262, 263, 266, 271, 275
The Fugitive, TV series 2, 89
Fuller, Robert 292
Gable, Clark 95, 285
Gallery Of The Sun 155
"Gambling", episode Highway Patrol 238
"Gambling Story", episode Highway Patrol 281
Ganzer, Alvin 240, 241
Gargan, William 6, 13
The Gargoyle 1
Garland, Judy 101
Garvey, Officer 327
"Gem Robbery", season 3 episode Highway Patrol 264
"Gem Robbery", season 4 episode Highway Patrol 264
George, Bill 244, 248, 259
Gerstad, Harry 250, 255
Gerstle, Frank 240
Get Smart, TV series 132
Giftos, Elaine 149
Gilbreath, Bob 278, 285, 288
Gilmore, Art 19, 35, 101, 141, 329
"Girl Bandit", episode Highway Patrol 86, 242
The Glenn Miller Conspiracy, book 300
Gog (1954) 101
Goltz, Gary 34, 58, 86, 90, 104, 105, 106, 160, 326-329
Gomez, Ed 104
Goodwins, Les 238, 241
Gordon, Gordon 19

Gordon, Mildred 19
Gordon, Robert 141
Grand National Pictures studio lot 1
Griffith, Andy 328
Griffith, D.W. 96
Griffith Park, location 34
Groves, John 137
Guilfoyle, Paul 239, 241, 244, 247, 248, 251, 258, 264
Hagen, Earl 101
Halop, Billy 291
Halsey, Brett 86
Hamilton, Ray 141, 142
Hammer, Mike 141, 142
Hanley, Bridget 150
Harbor Command, TV series 12, 36, 293
Harbor Master, TV series 12
"Harbor Story", episode Highway Patrol 244
Harlequin (1980) 133
Harvey, Steve 106
The Hasty Heart (1949) 152
Haskell, Eddie 131
Hatten, Tom 327-333
Hayden, Sterling 96
Hayes, Ron 12
Hayward, Chris 132
Heffley, Wayne 96, 262, 269, 274-277, 279, 280, 289
Heideman, Leonard 256, 257
Helm, Levon 134
Henderson, Jan Alan 95
Hersholt, Jean 12
Herzeberg, Jack 249, 254, 256, 259-263, 266, 267, 269-274, 276-292
Hell's Bloody Devils (1970) 86
"Hideout", episode Highway Patrol 271
High Chaparral, TV series 101
Highway Patrol, TV series 1, 2, 6, 19, 31, 33, 34, 35, 36, 51, 57, 58, 59, 85, 89, 95, 96, 101-106, 122, 123, 124, 125, 130-134, 137, 142, 150, 157, 158, 160, 293, 326-332
HighwayPatrolTV.com, website 104
Highway To Heaven, TV series 101
Hillyer, Lambert 240, 242, 244, 247, 256, 257, 260, 262, 265, 287, 288
"Hired Killer", episode Highway Patrol 266
"Hitchhiker", season 1 episode Highway Patrol 239
"Hitchhiker", Season 4 episode Highway Patrol 288
"Hitchhiker Dies", episode Highway Patrol 248
"Hit And Run", season 1 episode Highway Patrol 245
"Hit And Run", season 3 episode Highway Patrol 274
Hitler, Adolf 301

Hole, William Jr. 277
Holiday For Strings 101
Hollister, Esther C. ("National Ms. Route 66 Racer") 328
Hollywood Walk Of Fame 332
Hollywood Police Activities League (PAL) 329
Homeier, Skip 150
Home Run Derby, TV series 13
"Hostage", episode Highway Patrol 280
"Hostage Copter", episode Highway Patrol 86, 266
"Hostage Family Copter", episode Highway Patrol 96, 269
"Hostage Officer", episode Highway Patrol 278
Hoover, J. Edgar 134, 135
"Hot Cargo", episode Highway Patrol 256
"Hot Dust", episode Highway Patrol 269, 293
"Hot Rod", episode Highway Patrol 256
How To Make A Monster (1958) 101
Hudson, Rock 131
Huffman, John Pearley 104
Hughes, Howard 135
"Human Bomb", episode Highway Patrol 105, 245, 293
"Hustle", episode CHiPs 134
Huston, Lou 244, 246, 250, 255, 270, 274
Huston, Walter 132
Hyer, Martha 19
"Hypo", episode Highway Patrol 267
I Led Three Lives, TV series 6, 13, 95, 293
I Love Lucy, TV series 31
"Illegal Entry", episode Highway Patrol 288
"Insulin", episode Highway Patrol 272
The Interns, TV series 149-151
The Interns (1962) film 149
I've Got A Secret, TV series 124
I Was A Teenage Frankenstein (1957) 101
Jackson, Sherry 150
Janssen, David 2, 89
Jason, Rick 10, 12
Jerome, Stuart 237, 239, 246, 257, 283, 285, 288
Joe McDoakes, Comedy shorts 102
Johnson, Officer 89
Jolley, Norman 241, 243
Jordan, Robert (Bobby) 265, 278
"The Judge", episode Highway Patrol 277
Jungle Moon Men (1955) 85
Kawasaki motorcycles 137
Kay, Gilbert 257, 259
Kelly, "Shotgun Tom 327, 332
Kesler, Henry S. 247, 268, 284
Keyhole, TV series 13
"Kidnap Copter", episode Highway Patrol 254
Kiel, Richard Kiel 142

"Killer On The Run", episode Highway Patrol 289
Kimble, Dr. Richard 89
Kimble, Helen 89
King Of Diamonds, TV series 13, 139-142, 157
King, John 141, 142
Klondike, TV series 13
Knight, Ted 284
Knotts, Don 101, 123
Koza, Lou 59
LaBonge, Tom 106, 328, 332
L.A. Confidential (1997) 2
"Lady Bandits", episode Highway Patrol 273
Laird, Jack 238, 245, 248, 259
Lamarr, Hedy 11
Landall, Richard 269
Landers, Lew 239, 249, 252- 254, 257, 281, 282, 286, 288
Lang, Jr, Otto 272, 286
Larson, Charles 149
Lawrence, Marc 132
Leave It To Beaver, TV series 89, 131
Lebell, Gene 86, 275
Lee, Peggy 19
Lee, Ruta 85
Lee, Jr., Officer Taybren 329
"Le Hot Spot", 1981 TV pilot 158
Leigh, Janet 19
Lernert, Irving 141
Letterman, David 105
Levitt, Gene 237, 239
Lewis, Judy 95, 285
Liar's Moon (1982) 158
"License Plates", episode Highway Patrol 248
"Lie Detector", episode Highway Patrol 243
Little House On The Prairie, TV series 101
A Little Romance 301
Llewellyn, Ray 101
Locke, Jon 239, 254, 259, 327
Locke, Rusty 327
The Lock Up, TV series 6, 13
Lone Star (1952) 95
"Lookout", episode Highway Patrol 238
Look What's Happened to Rosemary's Baby (1976) 133
Los Angeles Fire Department Museum 326
Los Angeles Police Department (LAPD) 34, 101, 104, 131, 326, 332
Lugosi, Bela 11
Lundigan, William 13
MacArthur, James 149
Macdonald, Sgt. 89
"Machine Story Copter", episode Highway Patrol 237
Mackenzie's Raiders, TV series 13
Mad Magazine 124-125

Mad Magazine, Highway Patrol parody 126-129
"Magazine Writer", episode Highway Patrol 255
Maharlika (1970) 86
Man And The Challenge, TV series 13
Man Called X, TV series 13
The Man Who Broke The Bank At Red Gap, episode Alias Smith And Jones 150
Mannix, TV series 105
Maples, T. 285
Marcus, Ellis 258, 271, 277, 286, 288
Marcus Welby, M.D., TV series 149
Marley, John 141
Marsh, Bobbe 149, 151
Marshall, Herbert 13
The Mary Tyler Moore Show, TV series 284
Martin, Quinn 2
Marvin, Lee 19
M.A.S.H, TV series 96
Mathers, Jerry 131
Mathias, Bob 13
Mathews, Chief Dan 33, 35, 56, 103, 104, 106, 122, 125, 133
Maverick, TV series 101
McCord, Kent 90
McGinnis, Nathan 284, 286, 288
McHale's Navy, TV series 251
Medical Center, TV series 149
Meet Corliss Archer, TV series 13
Men Into Space, TV series 13
Men Of Annapolis, TV series 13
Menjou, Adolphe 6, 13
Menkin, Lawrence 274
"Mental Patient", episode Highway Patrol 248
Merlin, Jan 13
"Metamorphosis", episode The Interns 150
Metro-Goldwyn-Mayer 103, 137, 149
"Mexican Chase", episode Highway Patrol 286
MGM-UA 106
Miami Undercover, TV series 13
Michaels, Lorne 134
"Migrant Workers", episode Highway Patrol 258
Miller, Frank 95, 274, 276, 277, 280, 284, 285, 287, 289, 290
Miller, Glenn 300-301
"Miss Knock-A-Bout" 150
"Missing Witness", episode Highway Patrol 252
"Mistaken Identity", episode Highway Patrol 268
Mister District Attorney, TV series 13, 293
Mister Lucky, TV series 262
Mitchell, Bob 261, 263, 264, 265-267, 269, 272, 273, 277, 281, 283, 291
Mohr, Gerald 141
"Mondays Can Be Fatal", episode The Interns 150
Monty Python's Flying Circus, BBC TV series 134

Moore, Garry 123
Moore, Mary Alice 157
Morgan, Henry 123
Morris and Mich Highway Patrol parody 130-131
"Motel Robbery", episode Highway Patrol 257
"Mother's March", episode Highway Patrol 271
"Motorcycle A", episode Highway Patrol 86, 247
"Motorcycle B", episode Highway Patrol 26247
"Mountain Copter", episode Highway Patrol 243
Motor Trend magazine 104
Movie Digest Magazine 150
Mullally, Don 238, 246
Murray, Bill 135
Nader, George 13
Naked City, TV series 86
"Narcotics", episode Highway Patrol 265
"Narcotics Racket", episode Highway Patrol 95, 285
National helicopter 96, 100
National Transportation Safety Board films 89
Neal, Ralph 50
Nettleton, Lois 150
The New Adventures Of Martin Kane, TV series 6, 13
The New Interns (1964), film 149
New Leave It To Beaver, TV series 89
Newman, Laraine 135
Nimoy, Leonard 269, 293
"Nitro", episode Highway Patrol 262
Niven, David 300-301
Nixon, Julie 135
Nixon, President Richard 135
Nordmann, Len 328
Not As A Stranger (1955) 149
The Not Ready For Primetime Players 134
Nye, Louie 123
"The Oath", episode The Interns 151
O'Brien, Edmond 19
"Officer's Wife", episode Highway Patrol 262
O'Hanlan, George 101
"Oil Lease", episode Highway Patrol 256, 293
Okura, Albert 328
Osmond, Ken 131
Ortega, Frankie 142
Outer Limits, TV series 11
Pacific Pioneer Broadcasters (PPB) 102
Palance, Jack 133
Pardo, Don 134
Parker, John 137, 289
Parker, Suzy 149
Partridge, Joe 86
Passarella, Art 13
Patty Duke Show, TV series 11
Pavan, Marisa 19
Peck, Gregory 152
Pennell, Larry 13

Pete Kelly's Blues (1955) 19
The Phantom From 10,000 Leagues (1955) 85
"Phony Insurance", episode Highway Patrol 241
"Phony Cop", episode Highway Patrol 277
Picture Perfect 101
Pinsky, Dr. Drew 85
"Plane Crash", episode Highway Patrol 246
"Plant Robbery", episode Highway Patrol 247
Polansky, Roman 133
"Policewoman", episode Highway Patrol 275
Poncherello 'Ponch', Francis Llewellyn 137
"Portrait Of Death", episode Highway Patrol 281
Poston, Tom 123
Powers, Stefanie 149
"The Price Of Life", episode The Interns 150
"Prison Break", Pilot episode Highway Patrol 35, 86, 89, 96, 237
"Prisoner Exchange Copter", episode Highway Patrol 289
The Private Files Of J. Edgar Hoover (1977) 134, 158
Producer's Releasing Corp. studio lot 2
"Prospector", episode Highway Patrol 252
"Psycho", episode Highway Patrol 260
"Psycho Killer", episode Highway Patrol 276
"Quality Of Mercy", episode The Interns 150
Quinn Martin Productions 2
"Rabies", episode Highway Patrol 267
"Radioactive", episode Highway Patrol 89, 239
Radner, Gilda 135
"Ranch Copter", episode Highway Patrol 259
Rapp, Joel Malcomb 254, 282
Rawhide, TV series 86
Ray, Aldo 133
Raye, Martha 101
RCO All-Stars 134
The Real McCoy's, TV series 59
"Reckless Driving", episode Highway Patrol 238
"55 Highway Patrol Buick: Recreating the Most Famous Cop Car in Television History", article Motor Trend magazine 104
The Red Skelton Show, TV series 101, 102
Reeves, George 2, 59, 85
"Reformation", episode Highway Patrol 263
"Reformed Criminal", episode Highway Patrol 240
"Released Convict", episode Highway Patrol 247
Renaldo, Duncan 1, 12, 34
"Resident Officer", episode Highway Patrol 260
"Resort", episode Highway Patrol 58, 241
"Retired Gangster", episode Highway Patrol 240
"Revenge", season 3 episode Highway Patrol 273
"Revenge", season 4 episode Highway Patrol 287
"Reward", episode Highway Patrol 279

Reynolds, Officer Mark 244
Rich, David Lowell 150, 273
Rich, John 141
Riding The Range With A B-Western Bad Man, FILM FAX article 95
Riordan, Joel 291
Ripcord, TV series 13
Roadblock, 1958 TV pilot 105
Roark, Gary 247
Robertson, Cliff 149
Robinson, John 141
Robson, William N. 251
Rock, Jack 241, 259, 261, 263, 268, 270, 272, 275-278, 285-287 286, 290, 292
Roddenberry, Gene (Eugene) 240, 248, 253, 256, 293
Rogers, Shorty 149, 150
Roley, Sutton 268
Roman, Ruth 19
Rondstadt, Linda 134, 135
Rose, David 19, 33, 101
Rosemary's Baby (1968) 133
Rossner, Rick 137
"Rough Rider Rides Again", episode Simon & Simon 89
Rough Riders, TV series 13
Rouse, Morleen Getz 1, 33, 35
"Runaway Boy", episode Highway Patrol 250
Von Rundstedt, General 301
Runyon, Frank 34, 35, 90, 96, 103, 104, 105, 293
Ryf, Robert 256
Sackheim, Jerry 255
"Safecracker", episode Highway Patrol 268
Samuel Goldwyn studio lot 2
San Fernando Valley, location 34
The Sands Of Iwo Jima (1949) 152
Saturday Night Live, Highway Patrol skit (1977) 57, 134
Savalas, Telly 12, 141
"Scared Cop", episode Highway Patrol 244
Schiller, Ralph 246, 273
Science Fiction Theater, TV series 6, 13, 95
Scott, Mark 13
Screen Actors Guild (SAG) 100
Sea Hunt, TV series 6, 10, 13
"The Search", episode Highway Patrol 254
"The Seventh Green", episode Highway Patrol 272
77 Sunset Strip, TV series 101
"Shadow Of A Man", 1963 TV pilot 158
Shaffer, Paul 105
Shaw, Robert 281, 284, 288
Sherman, Teddy 260, 264
Shoop, Pamela Susan 150
Short, Elizabeth 2

Siegel, Larry 125
Sign Of The Pagan (1954) 133
Silent Trails, song 123
Silvers, Phil 132
Simi Valley, location 34
Simon & Simon, TV series 89, 150
Simpson, Officer 95
Sinn, John 1, 2, 31, 100
Sitka, Emil 241
Skarstedt, Vance 257, 261, 267, 268, 275-278, 280, 290
Skorenzy, Col. Otto 300-301
"Slain Cabby", episode Highway Patrol 272
Sloan, Marnie 279
Smart, Agent Maxwell 132
Smith, Charles B. 280
Smith, Sandra 149
Smokey the bear 123
"The Sniper", episode Highway Patrol 269
Sons Of The Pioneers 123
Spike Jones and his City Slickers Orchestra 101
Spillane, Mickey 141
"Split Robbery", episode Highway Patrol 183
Sportsman's Lodge, in North Hollywood 59
Square Of Violence (1961) 158
Stader, Paul 10
Stage 8, soundstage ZIV studios 33
Stalin, Joseph 301
Stanton, Helene 85
Stanwyck, Barbara 280
Stapleton, Cyril 132
State Trooper, TV series 36
Star Trek, TV series 293
"Statute Of Limitations", episode Highway Patrol 259
"The Search", episode Highway Patrol 254
The Steve Allen Show, TV series 123
Stone, Christopher 149
"Stolen Car Ring", episode Highway Patrol 257
"Stolen Plane Copter", episode Highway Patrol 264
"Stripped Cars", episode Highway Patrol 263
The Stripper 101
Strock, Herbert L. 1, 10, 31, 34-36, 50, 58, 95, 96, 100, 101, 237, 238, 240, 243, 245, 246, 248, 253, 255, 256, 259, 267, 269-271
Studio 3B, NBC studios Rockefeller Centre 134
Sullivan, Barry 12, 13, 276, 279
Superman, serial 89
"Suicide", episode Highway Patrol 276
"Suspected Cop", episode Highway Patrol 261
The Swindle (1955) 19
Tabor, Joan 141, 142, 157
Taeger, Ralph 11, 13
Target, TV series 13
"Taxi", episode Highway Patrol 251

Taylor, Kent 1, 12, 13
Taylor, Robert 132
"Tear Gas Copter", episode Highway Patrol 274
"Temptation", episode Highway Patrol 86, 268
Terror In The Wax Museum (1973) 137
TGG Direct, LLC. 106
This Man Dawson, TV series 13
The Three Stooges 241
Tightrope, TV series 105
Tinney, Joe 282, 285, 288
Tobey, Kenneth 19
Todd, Richard 152
Tombstone Territory, TV series 6, 13, 59, 89
Tors, Ivan 10
"Trailer Story", episode Highway Patrol 254
"Train Copter", episode Highway Patrol 281
"Train Copter", episode Highway Patrol 281
"Transmitting Robbery", episode Highway Patrol 281
"The Trap", episode Highway Patrol 283
"The Treasure of C. Errol Madre", episode Get Smart 132
The Treasure of Sierra Madre (1948) 132
Troubleshooters, TV series 13
"Trojan Horse", episode Highway Patrol 261
"Truckers", episode Highway Patrol 276
Turner Entertainment 137
Turner, Lana 2
12 O'Clock High (1949) 152
Twentieth Century Fox 89, 103
"Typhoid Carrier", episode Highway Patrol 255
Unger, Maurice 'Babe' 2, 11, 35, 36, 141
The Unexpected, TV series 13
United Artists 10, 11, 101
Universal Pictures 105, 149
U.S. Forest Service 123
U.S. Secret Service Agent, TV pilot 31
Ventura County Line, location 34
Vivyan, John 262
Voight, Jon 106
Vollearts, Rik 240, 269, 273, 276, 278-283, 285, 286, 291
Walker, Clint 59
Walters, Sgt. 89
Warner Brothers 19, 101
Warren Frank 95
Waterfront, TV series 13
Wayne, John 152
Webb, Jack 1, 19, 89, 100, 102, 106
Weiss, Arthur 245, 247, 249, 257, 258, 262, 268
Weiss, Gary 134
Weissmuller, Johnny 85
Wells, L. 281
Wesley, Robert (Gene Roddenberry) 240, 245, 248, 252, 253, 293
West Valley, location 34

West Point, TV series 13, 293
Whirleybirds, TV series 19
Whitman, Stuart 89, 244, 255, 258, 259, 264, 265, 266
Whitney, Peter 13
Wilcox, Larry 137
Wild Bill Hickok, TV series 59
Williams, Guy 246, 250, 262
Williams, Sgt. Ken 89
Wisconsin Center For Film and Theater Research at the University Of Wisconsin-Madison 11
Wilson, Dave 134
"Witness Wife", episode Highway Patrol 269
"The Wizard Of Ice", TV episode King Of Diamonds 141, 142
"Women Escapees", episode Highway Patrol 290
World Of Giants, TV series 13
The World Tomorrow, TV series 102
"Wounded", episode Highway Patrol 264
Wynn, Keenan 13
Young, Loretta 95, 285
Young, Robert 149
The Young And The Restless, CBS Daytime serial 86
You Asked For It, TV series 101
Youtube 105
Your Favorite Story, TV series 6, 13
The Zany Adventures of Xavier Cugat In Madrid (1965), CBS TV special 132
Ziv, Frederick W. 1, 3, 6, 10, 11, 19, 33, 58, 123
Ziv studio lot 1, 33, 34, 35, 58, 96, 102, 293
ZIV Television, Inc. 1, 6, 10, 19, 34, 35, 89, 95, 96, 103, 104, 105, 141
ZIV Television Programs, Inc. 1, 6, 19, 95

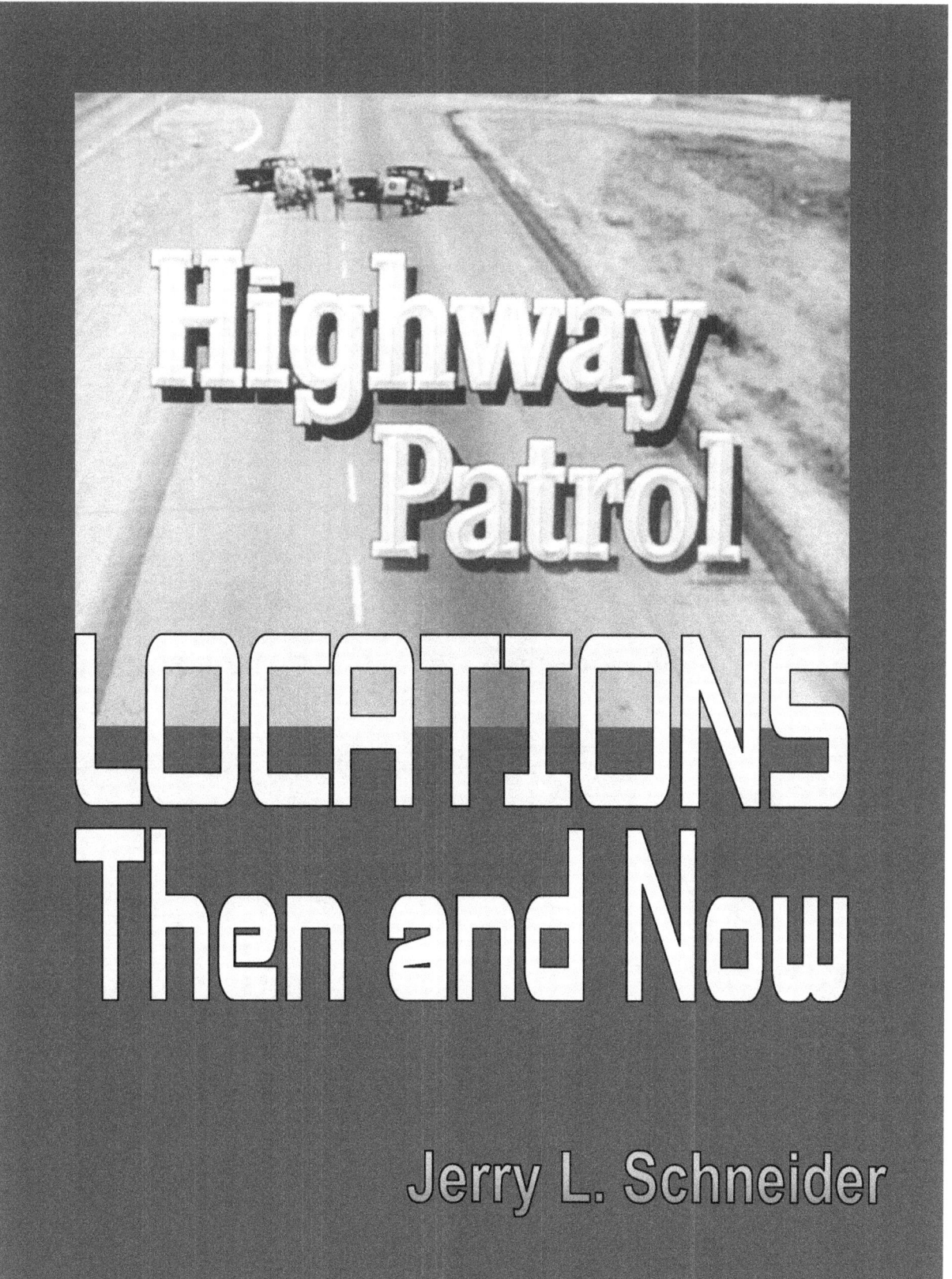

Available where you purchased this book or online at www.cpentbooks.com

The Complete Films of BRODERICK CRAWFORD

Ralph Schiller

Available where you purchased this book or online at www.cpentbooks.com